# VA VA VOOM!

# PIERS MORGAN
# VA VA VOOM!

methuen

First published in Great Britain 2004 by
Methuen Publishing Limited
215 Vauxhall Bridge Road
London SW1V 1EJ

1 3 5 7 9 10 8 6 4 2

Methuen Publishing Limited Reg. No. 3543167

A CIP catalogue record for this book is available
from the British Library.

ISBN 0 413 7745 11

Designed by **fivetwentyfive**

Printed and bound in Great Britain by the Bath Press

I dedicate this book to my sons Spencer, 11, Stanley, 7, and Bertie, 3, in the fervent hope that I live to see the day one of them runs out in the red-and-white strip and scores the winner against Tottenham.

I'd like to thank everyone at Methuen for their tireless hard work in correcting all the appalling spelling, grammar and other literal errors you'd expect from an unemployed ex tabloid editor. And, in particular, Peter Tummons for persuading me to write this book, and being such a generous, conscientious and amusing publisher. I'd also like to thank Arsène Wenger for existing, David Dein for hiring him, and Arsenal's amazing squad of players for giving fans like me such an incredible season.

## AUTHOR'S WARNING:

This diary is a personal, blindly prejudiced view of a club I have supported since I was three years old. Much of the material is therefore highly inflammatory, deeply offensive to the players and supporters of almost every other Premiership team, and on occasion quite indefensibly rude and obnoxious, even about my own team. I make no apologies for this, as this book is intended for Arsenal fans only, and they will not find any of it remotely offensive. Well, unless they particularly like Pascal Cygan, I suppose. Fans of other teams may enjoy it too, but only if they are in possession of a highly developed sense of humour. So I don't expect to sell many copies in White Hart Lane or Old Trafford.

'Even as I was kicking him
I realised I was doing
something stupid, but
by then it was too late'

JENS LEHMANN

Pre-season friendlies are fairly useless exercises. There is the chance to see who might be lurking in the recesses of reserve team obscurity to challenge for a place in the First XI. And some of the trips are quite fun for the die-hard fans who think the only holiday ever worth having is one where an Arsenal team of any description is playing football against anyone, however pitiful. This year we lost to Peterborough 1-0 (precisely why I never attend these fixtures – how do you ever deal with losing to Peterborough for God's sake?), drew 0-0 with Barnet, drew 2-2 with SK Ritzing, beat Austria Vienna 2-0, beat Besiktas 1-0, beat St Albans 3-1, drew 1-1 with Celtic, and thrashed Rangers 3-0. The most exciting revelation from these games is definitely Kolo Touré, a very lively, powerful youngster from the Ivory Coast. He deputised at centre-back in several of the games and was mightily impressive, albeit with the usual shocking positional flaws you'd expect from a raw young pup. Other than that it was all pretty dull, with most of the chatter centring on who we're signing, and more importantly who might be leaving. This is a massive season for Arsenal. We've got the squad to win things, big things. Right age, right balance, right quality, right manager. Right everything. But we have to keep the big players and we've got to replace David Seaman in goal, which is like replacing a favourite pet after years of loyal service. Very, very hard.

### 24th July 2003

Right, well, after all the rumours of Robinson, Toldo and Buffon, Arsène Wenger's done his usual trick and signed a new goalkeeper none of us has ever heard of: Jens Lehmann from Borussia Dortmund. Apparently he's big, ugly, and has been sent off FIVE times in his career. I can't think of any keeper who has been sent off more than twice, let alone five times. On one extraordinary occasion he reputedly booted an opponent's leg so hard it turned puce and there were genuine fears of amputation. Herr Lehmann, 33, admitted afterwards: 'Even as I was kicking him I realised I was doing something stupid, but by then it was too late.' He is clearly a complete nutter, which makes him an odd appointment by a manager who usually avoids problem players like the plague on the basis that, like the plague, they tend to infect the whole dressing room with their poison. But further investigation reveals that Lehmann's reputation back home is good: tall, strong, reliable and seriously pushing Oliver Kahn for the German national team. And he has the great benefit of having a name that most Arsenal fans will – incorrectly – think is pronounced the same way as Seaman, so they are likely to give him the same chant. In fact Lehmann is a LAY-mann, rather than a LEE-mann, but that trifling detail won't deter the Clock End, I'm sure. After all, many of them still call Thierry Henry 'Terry'. And quite right too; if they want to come over 'ere and play for our club then we'll pronounce their names 'owever we like mate. OK?

### 28th July 2003

Vieira, as usual, has been the subject of relentless transfer gossip all summer. It follows a familiar pattern: he says nothing in public but his agents plant all this guff about Real Madrid, Juventus and so on, with the sole intention of jacking up his Arsenal deal. I personally don't think Vieira will ever leave. He loves the club, and he loves living in London where he can have a coffee in his favourite Hampstead café and nobody bothers him. All the players who come from the Serie A, like 'Paddy', Thierry, Kanu and Bergkamp, prefer it here for the same reason: they don't get stalked from dusk till dawn. People love to bang on about the intrusive media in this country, but ask any footballer what it's like in Spain or Italy and they'll tell you it is miles worse. It would be good to see Vieira sign a new deal before the season starts though. He is the lifeblood of this team, one of the best two or three midfielders in the world right now, and we must not let him go under any circumstances.

# AUGUST

'Do you want to
win the Title this year?
Because if you do, then
this is where it starts'

ARSÈNE WENGER

# Manchester United

**COMMUNITY SHIELD, MILLENNIUM STADIUM**
**RESULT: 1-1 DRAW**

My location: at game

There is something unutterably pointless about these games. I mean, what the hell is the use of a football match that for years had the word charity in its title? Or that takes place in the middle of August? Clearly a lot of Arsenal fans agreed with me because at least 10,000 of our seats were empty. Now either we're just getting arrogantly bored with tripping up the motorway to Cardiff for these big games all the time, or there is something more sinister afoot. But it was all rather odd. Because 'charity' or 'community' or whatever you want to call it means little when Arsenal and Manchester United play football against each other. If Martin Keown played tiddlywinks against Ruud van Nistelrooy for Oxfam, it would still kick off pretty soon after the first tiddle.

I'd been invited to the match by sponsors McDonalds, along with my two older sons, Spencer and Stanley – which was a fitting reward given the gargantuan quantities of chicken nuggets and chips they had consumed in the preceding calendar year. I realised it would be a tricky afternoon when I found I had been seated next to a woman who I had literally just fired from her job as *Mirror* Education Correspondent. What made it worse was that she's a genuinely nice woman. The McDonalds PR woman was utterly mortified but I reassured her it was an occupational hazard and that there are not many people you can sit next to a tabloid editor who don't instantly recoil in horror. My sons lightened the mood by refusing my request to pose for a picture with either Geoff Hurst or Kenny Dalglish, or even – to my horror – our '71 Double-winning captain Frank McClintock. 'He's like you dad,' said middle son (6), 'very old and boring.'

The game itself was pretty good. Mikael Silvestre headed United into the lead after 15 minutes but Thierry Henry replied soon afterwards with a low, curling free-kick from 30 yards that bobbled into the corner, literally a second after I had confidently declared, 'He's crap at these free-kicks, watch this one balloon over the top ...' Arsenal's supporters erupted with the predictable 'You're not singing anymore', to which United's bigger crowd replied quite amusingly with, 'You're not champions anymore.' Even funnier was a camera shot of United's new American goalkeeper Tim Howard screaming 'Sh*t!' as he picked the ball out of the net. This from a player who suffers from the swearing syndrome Tourette's, but fiercely denies it actually makes him curse a lot. I can't wait for him and Sir Alex to cross verbal horns. It will get bluer than Bernard Manning at the Moss Side working men's club.

It was bloody hot, but never more so than inside Francis Jeffers' head. He's a good player, who looked instantly sharp, and everyone in the stadium knew he had to prove a point to Wenger and the fans. But his brains appear to be firmly entrenched in the back of his shorts. And when Phil Neville – so aptly named a 'busy little c***' by Jaap Stam in the autobiography that got the big Dutch defender fired (I bought the serial rights for just £15K at the *Mirror*, and instantly realised on reading it he'd be gone by the end of the week) – tangled with him in the centre circle, Jeffers twatted him and was sent off. It takes a lot to get red-carded in a Community Shield game. A lot of stupidity. Wenger didn't look upset – just very irritated. A worrying sign. This was, incredibly, Arsenal's fiftieth red card since Wenger's appointment. Later Sol Campbell appeared to elbow Djemba-Djemba, who collapsed like he'd just been felled by a howitzer.

Penalties came, and I love them. Fans talk so much guff about penalties, when we all know there is nothing more exciting in the world than watching a world star make a complete arse of himself. Scholes scored for United, as did Edu for Arsenal. Rio Ferdinand then netted his, but Howard saved from van Bronckhorst. In the

third round, Lehmann instantly endeared himself to Arsenal fans
by making a full-stretch save to deny van Nistelrooy, and Wiltord
levelled matters by drilling a shot down the middle. Solskjaer
squeezed home his effort and Lauren jinked his shot into the corner.
That made it 3-3 going into the last round, and effectively sudden
death. Diego Forlan, or 'Forlorn Dago' as they like to call him at
Anfield, struck his home with confidence but Howard dived to his
left to deny Pires – handing United the meaningless trophy (even
more meaningless now we haven't won it, obviously). Consensus of
the fans afterwards was that both teams had good new keepers, van
Nistelrooy was off form, and there wasn't a match to strike between
the two teams.

**Arsenal:** Jens Lehmann, Ashley Cole (yellow card), Sol Campbell, Edu, Lauren, Ray Parlour, Robert Pires 45, Patrick Vieira (yellow card), Fredrik Ljungberg, Giovanni van Bronckhorst 64, Kolo Touré, Gilberto, Dennis Bergkamp, Francis Jeffers 60, Thierry Henry, Sylvain Wiltord 45
Subs Not Used: Stuart Taylor, Pascal Cygan

**Manchester United:** Tim Howard, Philip Neville (yellow card), Diego Forlan 78, Mikael Silvestre, Rio Ferdinand, Quinton Fortune (yellow card), John O'Shea 68, Ryan Giggs, Roy Keane, Paul Scholes (yellow card). Nicky Butt, Eric Djemba-Djemba 61. Ole Solskjaer, Ruud van Nistelrooy
Subs not used: Roy Carroll, Darren Fletcher, Kieran Richardson, David Bellion

**Thierry Henry 20, Mikael Silvestre 15**

## 12th August 2003

Vieira and Pires have both signed new contracts. Coming on the
back of Henry's new deal in July, this is fantastically good news.
With United losing Beckham, missing out on Ronaldinho, and
buying a bunch of unproven kids, we have definitely had the better
close season in the transfer market. By keeping our best players
we've sent a message to the rest of the Premiership that we are not
a selling club. Vieira will get £70,000 a week, Pires £65,000. They're
worth it. Vieira said: 'I'm really confident about this season as we
have a great squad here, with great team spirit and fantastic talent.
I really believe we will go from strength to strength.' I agree.
There's a feeling about this season, a feeling that won't go away.
A feeling that we can do something really special.

## Everton
**PREMIERSHIP, HIGHBURY**
**RESULT: 2-1 WIN**
My location: at game

It was hot but overcast. The freshly mown grass added to that surreal summer air of these first few games that always feels a million miles away from frost-bitten January clashes in places like Bolton. Arsenal always boast a few Premiership guarantees … the lushest turf, the worst burgers (comfortably), the quietest fans. Kolo Touré retained his new position as a centre-back at the expense of Martin Keown, who started on the bench. I love Keown, mainly because he always laughs when West Ham fans chant 'You've got a monkey's head' at him. But Touré is a sensational find – tall, athletic, powerful, fast, technically good and bursting with hyperactive energy. Sylvain Wiltord was pushed up front alongside Henry, with Dennis Bergkamp and Francis Jeffers keeping Keown company on the bench. The former will accept it as the model pro he is, the latter will be starting to really regret that Community Shield moment of madness.

The script seemed straightforward enough: Arsenal to come flying out of the traps, Everton to put up a bit of a fight, we score at least three and everyone goes home happy. Then Sol Campbell got sent off in the 25th minute for flooring Gravesen on the edge of the box. Campbell is not a dirty player, but he was the last man and there was little argument. The problem is that the FA are already looking at his Djemba-Djemba elbow last week so at this rate he might not play again this year … Nobody seemed overly concerned. Arsenal fans are relatively relaxed about going down to ten men. When you've been weaned on a disciplinary diet of Ian Wright, Martin Keown and Patrick Vieira then you get very used to it, and realise that it often increases your chances of winning. The remaining ten players get more fired up, the opposition side attack more than they

would ever dare against Arsenal normally, holes open up and
BANG, we often score. Sure enough, ten minutes later Stubbs hand-
balled it, Henry smashed the penalty in, and it was 1-0. Henry
celebrated by whipping his shirt off and charging straight over to
the Everton fans in an apparent revenge act for them repeatedly
chanting 'who the f***ing hell are you' every time he'd touched the
ball. The Scousers took it well, as you can imagine. On the hour,
Pires burst through and made it two. 'We've only got ten men'
crowed the Clock End. Hardly seemed to matter when they include
two of the world's best players. Ljungberg then hit the bar and the
onslaught continued. But Arsenal never fail to *fail* to hammer home
the six or seven goals their sensational play has deserved for two
years now.

We always seem to go easy on teams rather than go for the
jugular, and I don't like it. Rooney's arrival caused tension, mainly
because in the same match last year he nearly broke the net with a
wonder-strike past Seaman. Rooney is a cross between Gazza and
Shearer – a big, unhinged genius who puts his head down and runs
straight at goal. The hype is justified, he makes things happen. As
he began to run at our defence you could see nerves creeping in, and
when Tomasz Radzinski thumped home a lifeline for Everton with
six minutes left, we all braced ourselves for another totally
unnecessary nail-biting denouement. Fortunately Everton's Chinese
import Li Tie received his second yellow card and trudged off. What
made it so amusing was that he was only on as a substitute. A
simple but apposite chant of 'Bye bye Li Tie' filled the air. Everton
fans will be furious because his reckless indiscipline will seriously
harm their only way into Europe – through winning the 'Fair Play'
League. The only home concern is Gilberto. As one wag put it near
me: 'Rivaldo, Ronaldo, Ronaldinho … and we get the bloody
Brazilian nobody's ever heard of and who hasn't got a brilliant bone
in his body.' A bit harsh, but he does seem a little out of sorts.

**Arsenal:** Jens Lehmann, Ashley Cole, Sol Campbell (red card), Patrick Vieira (yellow card), Fredrik Ljungberg, Robert Pires, Ray Parlour 70, Lauren, Kolo Touré, Gilberto, Sylvain Wiltord, Martin Keown 30, Thierry Henry. Subs not used: Stuart Taylor, Francis Jeffers, Denis Bergkamp

**Everton:** Richard Wright, Steve Watson, David Unsworth, Li Tie 67 (yellow card), Alan Stubbs, Alessandro Pistone, Joseph Yobo, Thomas Gravesen, Tobias Linderoth, Wayne Rooney 57, Mark Pembridge, Gary Naysmith 67, Nick Chadwick, Tomasz Radzinski. Subs not used: Steve Simonsen, David Weir

Thierry Henry 35 (pen), Robert Pires 58, **Thomasz Radzinski 84**


## 17th August 2003

Wenger admits Henry 'got away with it' after escaping punitive action for his shirt-waving. Good. If you can't wind up a few Scousers, what *is* the world coming to?

## 18th August 2003

As usual, the Scousers get the last laugh. Henry *has* now been reported to the FA by referee Mark Halsley. Thierry, meanwhile, is insisting he was merely blowing kisses at his wife sitting in a box above the Everton fans. This seems rather implausible but hey … I'm prepared to buy it.

## 18th August 2003

Arsenal's all-conquering ladies team beat Tranmere 9-2. They are all huge, and utterly terrifying.

## 20th August 2003

Jermaine Pennant, our tempestuous but gifted young winger, punches an opponent in England's Under-21 game against Croatia and gets sent off. His manager David Platt says he has to 'grow up or else'. Or else what? Get transferred to Tottenham?

## 21st August 2003

It's worse than that – Pennant's going on loan to Leeds. Monsieur Wenger does not like naughty boys.

## Middlesbrough
### PREMIERSHIP, THE RIVERSIDE
### RESULT: 0-4 WIN

My location: playing cricket in Sussex, highlights on *Match of the Day*

OK, there are some days when it is just embarrassing how good we are, and this was one of them. Middlesbrough are a good side, with a good manager in Steve McLaren. But we just humiliated them. I always have the same bet on Arsenal: £100 to win both halves, £200 to win the match in normal time, and Henry for the first goal. I only bet, though, when we play a reasonable side and the odds are, well, reasonable. And I always seem to make a profit at the end of the season. Henry is so pumped up at the start of games, and the opposing defenders usually so terrified of what he's going to do, that he often sweeps past them and scores in the first ten minutes. He also takes all the free-kicks and penalties – which makes him a great bet even at odds of 3-1. I won my bet quite early today – Vieira put Ljungberg through, the Swede did one of his darting little runs into the area before shooting, and their keeper Schwarzer parried it straight to Henry, who scored. It was quick, ruthless, lethal and financially very nice, thanking you. Soon afterwards we were swarming at them again, a yellow-and-blue tidal wave engulfing a panicky Boro defence. Cole and Pires played some glorious one-twos down the left wing before Pires crossed to Gilberto who half-volleyed it in for his first Arsenal goal. So much for the early doubts, this was as good as anything his 3Rs countrymen could do.

As our forwards romped away, Sol Campbell was quietly celebrating his own milestone, his hundredth game for Arsenal. He has to be one of our greatest buys. I remember the moment we signed him, because as the news flashed up on the Press Association wire service, I instantly despatched a picture desk assistant (and fellow Arsenal fan) to the club shop to get me the first Campbell shirt off the press. And then wore it all afternoon. To land Spurs' captain and only world-class player was beyond joyous. It also showed he had balls of steel. And he has quickly become a titanic rock in our defence. Quiet, undemonstrative, but formidable.

The rampaging French boys soon conjured up a third, Pires sending Henry clear to thump a perfect cross into Wiltord for another cracking goal. And on the hour Wiltord added his second, Ljungberg unselfishly putting him on when he could have scored himself. Wenger sent on our supposed 'reserves', Bergkamp, Parlour and Edu, which offered the beleaguered Boro team little comfort. This is a great side, with great support acts ... I am starting to feel very excited about the season. Particularly as Henry still insists he's 'not fully fit'. Wenger was asked afterwards what he thought of his old foe Sir Alex Ferguson being sent off from the dugout for swearing at officials at St James's Park yesterday. 'I don't know what was said, but I think we can all guess,' he laughed. 'But the fact that Ferguson watched the rest of the game on television doesn't alter the result or the fact that United played better in the second half.' Quite.

**Arsenal:** Jens Lehmann, Ashley Cole, Sol Campbell, Edu 74, Robert Pires, Lauren, Kolo Touré, Gilberto, Patrick Vieira, Fredrik Ljungberg, Ray Parlour 74, Thierry Henry, Sylvain Wiltord, Dennis Bergkamp 74. Subs not used: Stuart Taylor, Martin Keown

**Middlesbrough:** Mark Schwarzer, Colin Cooper (yellow card), Alan Wright, Gareth Southgate, Chris Riggott, Andrew Davies 66, Doriva, Juninho, Stuart Parnaby, George Boateng, Malcolm Christie, Szilard Nemeth, Stewart Downing 85. Subs not used: Carlo Nash, Robbie Stockdale, Mark Wilson

**Thierry Henry 5, Gilberto 13, Sylvain Wiltord 22, 60**

**WEDNESDAY**
**27**
**AUGUST**

## Aston Villa
**PREMIERSHIP, HIGHBURY**
**RESULT: 2-0 WIN**
My location: a bar in Cyprus

Unchanged team for the third game running. But Villa are well organised, as you'd expect from their manager David O'Leary – who despite becoming one of the most annoying men in world football, still retains adoration at Highbury for his fantastic playing record in our defence for so many years. Henry and Pires were soon charging at them like uncoiled gallic cobras. Henry, loose, fluid, unbelievably fast and supremely cocky; Pires, supremely flat-footed but deceptively quick. Villa held firm, though, few sides proving as effective in snuffing out our musketeers like this. Half-time was livened up by a spectacular altercation in the tunnel between Pires and Mellberg, provoked by a grotesque dive our man had committed just before the whistle. There's simply no excuse for Pires doing this but nothing seems to stop him. Not even Villa's coach Roy Aitken shrieking some very Anglo-Saxon tributes at him as they all had to be pulled apart outside the dressing room.

Twelve minutes into the second half and the deadlock broke with a mess in the penalty box and a final header from Campbell – who should score so many more goals with that granite head of his but who never seems to know quite where he's nutting it. Bergkamp came on but looked, dare I say it, 'past it'. Is the King on the wane? I was editor of the *News of the World* when we broke the story that Bruce Rioch had smashed the club transfer record to sign him for £7 million from Inter Milan. It was the only decent thing Rioch did as our manager, but frankly that was enough. Forget Cantona or Zola, Bergkamp is the greatest Premiership player ever. The game meandered a bit towards the end, but Henry slipped away in stoppage time to score a late second goal and ensure we go to the top of the table. Early days, but that feeling remains.

**Arsenal:** Jens Lehmann, Ashley Cole, Sol Campbell, Patrick Vieira (yellow card), Fredrik Ljungberg, Ray Parlour 78, Robert Pires, Lauren, Kolo Touré (yellow card), Gilberto, Sylvain Wiltord, Dennis Bergkamp 67, Thierry Henry. Subs not used: Stuart Taylor, Martin Keown, Edu

**Aston Villa:** Thomas Sorensen, Mark Delaney (yellow card), Ronny Johnsen, Gareth Barry, Jlloyd Samuel, Olof Mellberg, Ulises de la Cruz, Mark Kinsella, Darius Vassell 60, Lee Hendrie (yellow card), Peter Whittingham (yellow card), Juan Pablo Angel (yellow card). Subs not used: Stefan Postma, Alpay, Thomas Hitzlsperger, Hassan Kachloul

**Sol Campbell 57, Thierry Henry 90**

## 28th August 2003

The one thing you want to avoid in the Champions League group stage is a Russian club, because these grounds are always the freezing hell-holes of Eastern Europe and such God-awful places to go and play football. So, with shocking predictability, Arsenal draw Dynamo Kiev *and* Lokomotiv Moscow. Which means Kanu will have to buy some extra-strong gloves. It also means Bergkamp won't be able to play in two away games because he can't fly. It's a tough draw, as usual, with Inter Milan making up the four.

## Manchester City
**PREMIERSHIP, CITY OF MANCHESTER STADIUM**
**RESULT: 1-2 WIN**
My location: a bar in Cyprus

I watched this game propped up against a dodgy bar in Southern Cyprus with eight burly – and rather vocal – Mancunians. More worrying, disturbing new details have emerged about madman Lehmann. Apparently he was so crazed in one 5-1 defeat Dortmund suffered that the fans began openly laughing at him and calling him Fliegenfänger – or flycatcher – for his habit of charging out of the goal and missing crosses completely. On the positive side, he also scored from a thumping header in the last minute of a fierce local derby with Schalke, and has another penalty goal and two assists to his name too. Off the field he is reputed to be an intelligent man, and a fine amateur painter with an eclectic style whose most innovative recent work was given an English title: 'Lots Of Dots'. Let's hope he enjoys lots of dot games in goal too.

Anyway, today was a good day to compare him with 'Safe Hands' Seaman who received a stunningly affectionate ovation from the Arsenal away fans. Thirteen years and nine trophies, not to mention seventy-five England caps, count for a lot in this part of the world. Certainly a lot more than that achieved by his new City colleague Nicolas Anelka, surely an early candidate for greediest and surliest player of all time. We made a shaky start when Lauren lost the plot in a chase back with Sinclair. His first touch was bad, and his second catastrophic as he slid it left-footed past Lehmann for a hideous own goal. General bemusement followed at Lauren's ridiculous behaviour. Even he appears to have no idea what the hell he was doing, although the fact the entire squad were apparently standing outside their hotel at 4 a.m. after a fire alarm went off might offer some excuse.

At half-time, it emerged later, Wenger read the riot act: 'Do you want to win the Title this year?' he barked. 'Because if you do, this is where it starts.' His rally cry worked. They did appear to want to win the Title, which was something of a relief, I must say. Two minutes into the second half, Wiltord capitalised on some poor defending to whip a Cole pass under a rather laborious looking Seaman. 1-1. We perked up a bit after that and 17 minutes from time we got the winner, thanks to a dreadful clanger from our old keeper. It was one of those moments, like when Ali fought Holmes and got battered senseless, that you wish professional sportsmen knew when to quit and kept to that decision. Seaman was painfully slow off his line as Pires burst through and compounded the horror by trying to reach the ball with his knees rather than his 'safe' hands – letting it bounce back to Freddie Ljungberg who scored. It was great to win, but very sad to see Wenger's opinion that Seaman had had his day so cruelly vindicated. Keegan called the clangers 'laughable'. Wenger simply observed: 'David Seaman was staying at the same hotel as us but obviously the alarm didn't go off in his room!' Cruel but fair.

**Arsenal:** Jens Lehmann, Martin Keown, Ashley Cole (yellow card), Patrick Vieira, Fredrik Ljungberg (yellow card), Ray Parlour 76, Robert Pires 83, Lauren (yellow card), Kolo Touré, Gilberto, Sylvain Wiltord, Dennis Bergkamp 76, Thierry Henry. Subs not used: Stuart Taylor, Pascal Cygan, Edu

**Manchester City:** David Seaman, Sylvain Distin, David Sommeil (yellow card), Jihai Sun, Joey Barton (yellow card), Antoine Sibierski, Danny Tiatto 68, Michael Tarnat (yellow card), Paul Bosvelt, Robbie Fowler 79, Trevor Sinclair, Shaun Wright-Phillips, Eyal Berkovic 79, Nicolas Anelka. Subs not used: Nicky Weaver, Richard Dunne

**Sylvain Wiltord 48, Fredrik Ljungberg 72, Lauren 10 (own goal)**

# SEPTEMBER

'Who put the ball
in the Arsenal net?
Half of f***ing Europe'

MANCHESTER UNITED FANS

**1st September 2003**

Francis Jeffers returns to Everton on loan. He did live to regret that sending-off. And I'd lay even money we never see him play for Arsenal again.

## Portsmouth
**PREMIERSHIP, HIGHBURY**
**RESULT: 1-1 DRAW**
My location: at game

Forget every other clash this season, this is the game every Arsenal fan *really* wants to win. Or, rather, doesn't want to lose. Because should we lose this, Teddy Sheringham will gloat. And Sheringham knows how to gloat better than any gloater in the history of gloaters. When he went to United, he won nothing in his first season and we all chanted 'Oh Teddy Teddy, she went to Man United and she won f*** all'. Next season he won the Treble … and the chant was modified to 'Oh Teddy Teddy, she went to Man United and she's still a c***'. When asked how he'd spend his summer, Sheringham said: 'I'm going to walk up and down Islington High Street trying to find as many Gooners as I can to show my medals off to …'. At that year's Charity Shield, he made even more friends at Highbury by warming up at our end of the ground waving three fingers at us all and sparking a near riot. Little. Twat.

It was a roasting hot day, and our midfield appeared to be suffering from sunstroke with disastrous consequences because 25 minutes into the game they lost the ball yet again and Stone beat Cole to whip a cross into … you've guessed it. Bloody Sheringham. He ran, naturally, straight to our fans with a quite revoltingly smug grin on his face. There's only one way to respond to that, and Pires knew it. Dancing into the box, he deliberately thrust his leg into one of their defenders and collapsed like a sack of spuds. Even the Clock End were shaking

their heads in embarrassment. Pires is now an Olympic-standard
diver, no question. Henry took the 'penalty', scored, and was then
ordered to retake it for no reason that anyone could see other than
the long theatrical pause in the middle of his run-up. He retook it and
scored again. 1-1 at half-time, and it was clear from the way we came
out that Le Boss had given another one of his rare bollockings. Edu in
particular appeared to have been awakened from his mogadon stupor.
The funniest moment came when the referee had to change his shirt
halfway through the first half because it clashed with Portsmouth's.
He was, therefore, genuinely playing for the other team, and took
plenty of stick for that, obviously. And the most heroic moment was
Lehmann decking Sheringham with a suspiciously low blow. He
clearly already hates Sheringham as much as the rest of us and he's
only just met him. A very special mention too, to one particular
member of the superb and very loud army of travelling Portsmouth
fans. This guy brought a huge bell with him that he kept ringing to
our great collective annoyance. The police eventually told him to stop
but he carried on. So they came back and led him and his bell away,
giving us the opportunity to sing the memorable chant: 'You're not
ringing any more'.

**Arsenal:** Jens Lehmann, Sol Campbell (yellow card), Ashley Cole, Edu, Fredrik Ljungberg 70, Robert Pires, Lauren, Kolo Touré (yellow card), Ray Parlour, Patrick Vieira, Dennis Bergkamp, Sylvain Wiltord 74, Thierry Henry. Subs not used: Graham Stack, Martin Keown, Jeremie Aliadiere

**Portsmouth:** Shaka Hislop, Arjan De Zeeuw (yellow card), Dejan Stefanovic (yellow card), Boris Zivkovic, Sebastien Schemmel (yellow card), Amdy Faye, Nigel Quashie, Steve Stone, Patrik Berger, Alexei Smertin 34, Teddy Sheringham, Tim Sherwood 90, Yakubu, Aiyegbeni, Jason Roberts 72. Subs not used: Harald Wapenaar, Hayden Foxe

Thierry Henry 40 (pen), **Teddy Sheringham 26**

## 15th September 2003

Freddie had a crash today in his new £50K BMW. Sol Campbell and
Vieira arrived on the scene soon afterwards and helped him. He's not
hurt but the car is – and it reminds me of the fragility of footballers'
lives. I often think of the Munich air crash that wiped out that great
Manchester United side and wonder how it must have felt for their
fans. The whole nation was in mourning, obviously, but for the fans

it must have been ten times worse. To see virtually every one of your heroes killed at the same time, unbelievable.

## Internazionale
### CHAMPIONS LEAGUE, HIGHBURY
### RESULT: 0-3 LOST
My location: at game

My favourite theatre review ever was by a guy called Clive Hirschorn who wrote of one play: 'Hand on heart, and without fear of contradiction, this unfathomable farrago is the worst thing I have seen in my entire life.' I tried desperately to get tickets but it closed before I had a chance. I knew how he felt after this game. This was the worst performance I have *ever* seen from an Arsenal team. Not just because we got hammered by a very good Inter side – there's no shame in that. But because we just gave up. Against a team that has been really struggling recently, and was missing their star striker Christian Vieri. Italian papers were predicting before the match that Inter's manager, the Argentinian Hector Cuper, would be gone by Christmas, so badly were they playing. So how in God's name did we get so criminally stuffed out of sight? Well, some players just had appalling off days. Campbell, for instance, has been astonishingly consistent since jumping from the Lane, but tonight he was abominable. Yet he was positively masterful compared to Pires, who had one of the all-time great shockers. It is rare that you can say 'I could do better than that' and it's actually true, but tonight was one of them. There are lots of rumours flying around about his personal life, suggesting his wife's left him. This would probably put a dampener on most blokes' moods so I want to be kind and charitable. But he shouldn't have played in the obvious state he was in. It was so transparently terrible that when the half-time whistle went, with us losing 3-0, Ljungberg lost it completely and ran over to literally scream abuse at Pires – gesticulating wildly and quite openly calling his team-mate every European swear-word he could think of. Pires just stood there and took it. Pathetic.

Inter's first goal came after 22 minutes when Cruz lobbed it over a lethargic Lehmann with most of our defence appearing to have taken simultaneous overdoses of valium. A few minutes later they were two up, courtesy of a stupendous volley from the Dutchman Andy Van der Meyde. He looked brilliant all night, but the technique on this strike was world-class, the sort of thing Bergkamp might do. Or rather used to do. Some respite appeared when Freddie fell over in their box and we, wrongly in my view, got a penalty. Henry struck it well but when you have a keeper as good as Toldo in goal then there's a good chance he'll save anything, and sure enough he tipped it wide at full stretch to his left. The ground was silent. Completely and utterly silent. Like the studio audience when David Icke first appeared on Wogan in that purple suit. Three minutes before half-time it is, horrifically, 3-0, as Martins holds off a half-dead Campbell and cracks it into the goal – then somersaults his way back to his own half. Our players are booed loudly off the pitch and I honestly can't remember the last time we did that. Arsenal fans are usually a supportive lot even when things aren't going well. But there is a mixture of disgust at the lack of effort out there and stunned amazement at the sheer quality of Inter's play. We thought we could mix it with the big boys of Europe now. We were, I'm afraid, suffering from a massive delusion.

I toy with leaving early and seeking solace in a large bottle of Jack Daniel's, but you can't, can you. We come out a bit chastened, and a bit livelier. But it quickly becomes a depressing pattern of an infuriated Henry winning the ball, running towards their goal, getting tackled, Inter clearing and Henry getting the ball again to have another go. Pires was put out of his misery after 64 minutes but it was too late for his replacement Bergkamp to do anything. I can't be bothered to detail any more about the match. Suffice to say Kanu fell over his own gangly legs a few times, Henry huffed and puffed and blamed everyone but himself, as usual when things don't go right, and Toldo saved anything that even looked like threatening their goal. We looked shattered at the end, like a large hurricane had just descended on Highbury and wiped out vast swathes of our homes.

I slip away a minute before time to be confronted by a rather aggressive Arsenal fan who took exception to us claiming he was a hooligan in the *Mirror* a couple of years ago and makes it his business to 'have a word' with me every now and again: 'Well look who it is sneaking out early, what sort of f***ing fan are you then eh? Revealed your true colours tonight, haven't you, you f***ing w***er.' I can't summon up the energy to say anything, but it rounds off a great night in appropriately unpleasant fashion. I turn my mobile off. I don't care if the Queen gets gunned down by Al Qaeda tonight, they can get on with it themselves at work. I need some quiet time on my own to reflect on the devastation wrought on my team tonight. We've got United at the weekend, so there is no time for feeling sorry for ourselves or bitter recriminations. Sometimes a good beating can lift the blinkers off a bit and kick complacent arses into gear. I sincerely hope this is one of those occasions.

**Arsenal:** Jens Lehmann, Ashley Cole, Sol Campbell, Patrick Vieira, Fredrik Ljungberg, Robert Pires, Dennis Bergkamp 64, Lauren, Kolo Touré, Gilberto, Nwankwo Kanu 64, Sylvain Wiltord, Ray Parlour 78, Thierry Henry. Subs not used: Graham Stack, Pascal Cygan, Martin Keown, Edu

**Internazionale:** Francesco Toldo, Fabio Cannavaro, Ivan Cordoba, Javier Zanetti, Marco Materazzi, Belozoglu Emre, Sabri Lamouchi 66, Kily González, Cristiano Zanetti, Andy van der Meyde, Thomas Helveg 69, Julio Cruz, Mohammed Kallon 84, Obafemi Martins. Subs not used: Alberto Fontana, Daniele Adani, Siqueira Luciano, Okan Buruk

**Julio Cruz 22, Andy van der Meyde 24, Obafemi Martins 41**

**SUNDAY**
**21**
**SEPTEMBER**

# Manchester United
## PREMIERSHIP, OLD TRAFFORD
## RESULT: 0-0 DRAW
My location: a pub in Dublin

One of the greatest pieces of boxing commentary I have ever heard came from Reg Gutteridge after Thomas 'Hitman' Hearns slugged it out for three amazingly brutal rounds with 'Marvelous' Marvin

Manchester United, Community Shield: **Friendly? You've got to be joking. Scholes clatters into Freddie like it's the last minute of the Champions League Final**

Everton, August:
Pires makes it two
after Campbell's
red card '… and
we've only got ten
men', crow the
Clock End

Manchester City, August: Seaman had a mare of a game for Man City, but he'll always be 'Safe Hands' at Highbury

Inter Milan, September: Um ... we're not going to win it like this now are we Sol?

Inter Milan:
The final nail, a
diabolical night ...
Henry misses his
penalty

**Manchester United, September:** 'Aaaaggghhhhhh!' Keown lets van Nistelrooy know how sorry he is that he missed his penalty

**Manchester United:** The fuse is lit as Vieira lashes out at Big Nose and gets sent off

**Newcastle, September:** You're quick, Kieron … but not quick enough, my friend

Chelsea,
October:
**Still The King –
Bergkamp
stamps his
uniquely
special class
on a very
classy game**

Chelsea:
'Oh, what a terrible cockupski …' Cudicini lets Henry in with one of the season's great howlers

Dynamo Kiev, October:
Kiev score, and we crash back down from our domestic pedestal to the reality of European mediocrity

Leeds, November: 'Merci beaucoup!' Pires races through for our second as Leeds crumble

Inter Milan, November: 'Ooh, Aaagh,' what a laugh. 3-1, and Ray just can't stop giggling

Inter Milan: This can't be happening! Edu makes it 4

West Brom, December: **Kanu, the forgotten man, scores again in the League Cup, but does anyone care?**

Wolves, December: **The master of all he surveys … Vieira patrols and controls the midfield**

Bolton, December: **Get him out of here! Cygan does his usual impression of a rabbit in the headlights**

Hagler for the world middleweight title. Gutteridge observed the
165 punches, endless knock-downs, and general barbarism before
concluding simply: 'That was three rounds of ... absolute mayhem.'
The same, it can be safely said, might apply to this match. I watch
it in a Dublin pub full of howlingly drunk local United fans. (To be
fair to them, most live nearer Old Trafford than the majority of
United supporters). The first 75 minutes were irrelevant really.
Very much the canapés before the 18-inch T-bone. Though the
Stretford End kept our spirits up with a chorus of 'Who put the ball
in the Arsenal net, Who put the ball in the Arsenal net, Who put
the ball in the Arsenal net, Half of f***ing Europe!' And they've
developed a hilarious new chant for their troubled keeper which
goes, 'F**k off, he plays in our net, f**k off Timmy Howard, f**k off,
he's got Tourette's.' The pot boiled over when Vieira was deservedly
booked for a late tackle. Seconds later he jumped with van
Nistelrooy for a high ball near our box and they tumbled to the
ground with the United striker clearly fouling our Senegalese titan.
Vieira then seemed to kick out at the squealing Dutchman – but
comfortably failed to connect. This didn't stop van Nistelrooy flailing
backwards as if he'd been garrotted. Both got booked, and Vieira
was off, lighting the tinder box. Arsenal reacted strongly to having
ten men, as usual, until injury time when Gary Neville crossed in
from the right, and Keown pulled down Forlan. It was 50/50, but at
Old Trafford that is always more than enough for a penalty.

Van Nistelrooy, now almost Sheringham-like in the hatred he
provokes from Arsenal fans, stepped forward to take what would
surely be a bitter last-minute winner. Say what you like about the
ugly little turd, he can take a penalty. Lehmann dived the wrong
way, but the ferocious shot smashed back off the crossbar. Cue
'absolute mayhem' as Keown led the Arsenal boys on a hilarious
verbal and physical handbags-at-dawn assault on poor Ruud. They
literally queued up to give him a smack, or 'tap' as I believe it is
known in parts of North London, making it rather clear what they

thought of him. It's easy to criticise this behaviour, and I'm sure many will, but I can only judge it on the basis of my own reaction. Watching in the pub as van Nistelrooy stepped up to the plate, I had my head buried in my hands and waited for the inevitable nightmare to unfurl. When I realised what had happened, from the appalled reaction of 95 per cent of the pub's shocked clientele, I leapt off my chair and embarked on a raging, drunken one-man conga repeatedly screaming, 'Yes, you CHEATING DUTCH BASTARD' at the top of my voice. For safety-conscious antics, it was right up there with marching into a Rangers bar with a green shirt and asking where the local Catholic church was. And I could see at least one bloke saying to his mate, 'That's no way for the editor of the *Daily Mirror* to behave now is it?' He was right, of course. But had van Nistelrooy been in front of me right then, I would have done exactly what Keown did and jumped above him shouting terrible things about his parentage. And probably followed through with a little 'tap'. It's called PASSION. That dreaded word that is now banned in school playing fields, abhorred in our national sporting legends, decried by the 'Establishment'. Well, I say there's nothing wrong with getting over-excited when Ruud van Nistelrooy misses a dodgy last-minute penalty after getting your captain sent off. Nothing at all. And as I watched the Arsenal players marauding around Big Nose at the end of that game, with not even Roy Keane stepping in to have a go back, I realised we were going to win the League. Because we want it more than they do.

**Arsenal:** Jens Lehmann, Martin Keown (yellow card), Ashley Cole, Ray Parlour, Patrick Vieira (red card), Fredrik Ljungberg, Lauren, Kolo Touré (yellow card), Gilberto, Dennis Bergkamp, Edu 82, Thierry Henry. Subs not used: Graham Stack, Pascal Cygan, Robert Pires, Sylvain Wiltord

**Manchester United:** Tim Howard, John O'Shea, Diego Forlan 76, Gary Neville, Philip Neville, Mikael Silvestre, Rio Ferdinand, Quinton Fortune (yellow card), Ryan Giggs, Roy Keane (yellow card), Cristiano Ronaldo (yellow card), Ruud van Nistelrooy (yellow card). Subs not used: Roy Carroll, Eric Djemba-Djemba, Darren Fletcher, Nicky Butt

## 24th September 2003

The FA have announced the list of players facing charges following
the post-match events at Old Trafford on Sunday. And, in a dramatic
reversal of the League Cup defeat at Highbury in 1990, Arsenal have
won this match 6-2. And we win the tie-breaker too, since the club
have also been charged for 'failing to ensure the proper behaviour of
their players'.

The full inglorious charge list reads: Ashley Cole: 'Improper
conduct' for confronting Ronaldo at the final whistle. Martin Keown:
'Violent behaviour' for hitting van Nistelrooy on the back of the head
at the whistle, and 'Improper conduct' for confronting him after the
penalty miss. Lauren: 'Violent behaviour' for kicking out at Fortune
following the penalty award and pushing RvN in the back at the
whistle, plus 'Improper conduct' for confronting RvN after the red
card and confronting Giggs at the whistle. Jens Lehmann: 'Improper
conduct' for confronting the ref after the red card and 'persistently
seeking to confront' RvN. Ray Parlour: 'Violent behaviour' for
'grabbing at Gary Neville from behind' (!) and confronting RvN at the
whistle. Patrick Vieira: 'Improper conduct' for failing to get off the
pitch quickly when sent off. Ryan Giggs: 'Improper conduct' for 'his
involvement in a confrontation' with Lauren at the whistle.
Christiano Ronaldo: 'Improper conduct' for confronting Keown at the
whistle. In addition, Phil Neville has been warned for 'confronting'
Lauren after the red card. All parties have fourteen days to respond.

## 25th September 2003

Kolo Touré has given us a fascinating insight into his very special
relationship with a very special influence: 'When Ramadan starts
and we have a game I don't do the Ramadan. Come on, if you have
to do the best for your club you have to eat and be strong. God
understands I have a big game, of course.' Of course he does, Kolo.

**26th September 2003**

Alan Smith, legendary 'Smudger' of Arsenal folklore, has torn into
the team for their brawling antics. He is, broadly, right. It was
completely over the top, absurd, ghastly – totally unacceptable. But
the main problem for 'Smudger' is that it is also almost certainly the
catalyst for us winning the League and most Arsenal fans love it.

**FRIDAY**
**26**
**SEPTEMBER**

# Newcastle United
## PREMIERSHIP, HIGHBURY
## RESULT: 3-2 WIN
My location: at game

We flew out of the traps like greyhounds on acid, clearly very pumped
up by the Battle of Old Trafford. Even the fans were; many sporting T-
shirts showing the already iconic picture of Keown climbing over van
Nistelrooy with the words 'JUMP UP IF YOU HATE MANC CHEATS'.
But, not for the first time, our exhilarating play was curbed by a referee
who just couldn't keep up with the speed of our attacks. Mike Riley is
one of those refs who just looks annoying. All his mannerisms shout
'TWAT' at you. The kind of guy who grasses you up at school for selling
illicit sweets in the corridor, and smirks as you get led away for a
beating. Three times we were away when he blew for fouls rather than
give us the obvious advantage. Then Titus Bramble casually waved a
boot at a cross from the right, missed it and turned to see Henry
steaming in for the tap-in. You cannot be casual with Henry around –
he doesn't do casual. It all looked good until Vieira went off injured, and
torrential rain battered down – reducing our thoroughbreds to a
suddenly less thorough state. Newcastle got amongst our midfield, and
equalised through Robert at point-blank range. It was scrappy after
that until Parlour went off for Pires, Freddie switched to the right
wing, and soon got hacked down by Bernard. Pires drilled in the free-
kick straight onto Gilberto's head and it was 2-1. But Freddie was hurt,

and was to spend the rest of the game limping and moaning, trying to avoid the ball but unable to go off because we'd used all our subs. Newcastle sensed his unease, and piled the pressure on. Dyer, who looked sharp and dangerous, put Bernard through and he rocketed it past Lehmann. 2-2. Highbury started murmuring. It's never a real whine, more a disgruntled murmur of discontent. But with 12 minutes left, Jenas jumped up and inexplicably handled it. One of those real 'why the hell did he do that?' moments. Henry saw Given move to his left and chipped his penalty softly and arrogantly down the middle. 'I didn't do it to be a little bit cheeky,' he said later. Hmm, well, it was Thierry, old son, it was. A win, with effectively ten men again. How good will we be when we have eleven fit guys?

**Arsenal:** Jens Lehmann, Martin Keown, Ashley Cole, Pascal Cygan 52, Ray Parlour, Robert Pires 62, Patrick Vieira, Edu 25, Fredrik Ljungberg, Lauren, Kolo Touré, Gilberto, Thierry Henry, Sylvain Wiltord. Subs not used: Graham Stack

**Newcastle United:** Shay Given, Andy O'Brien, Titus Bramble, Aaron Hughes, Olivier Bernard, Laurent Robert (yellow card), Darren Ambrose 81, Jermaine Jenas, Shola Ameobi 89, Lee Bowyer, Gary Speed 72, Kieron Dyer, Alan Shearer, Craig Bellamy. Subs not used: Tony Caig, Andy Griffin

Thierry Henry 18, 80 (pen), Gilberto 67, **Laurent Robert 26, Olivier Bernard 71**

TUESDAY
## 30
SEPTEMBER

# Lokomotiv Moscow
## CHAMPIONS LEAGUE, LOKOMOTIVI
## RESULT: 0-0 DRAW
My location: a pub at Labour Party conference, Bournemouth

I had a comical moment over a cup of tea in the sun with the Prince of Darkness, Peter Mandelson, before kick-off when he asked what I'd be doing later. 'Watching Arsenal on TV,' I replied. He honestly looked like I had just told him I was going to vote Conservative, as his whole face screwed up into an exaggerated frown of epic proportions. 'Why would anybody on earth want to do that?' he eventually sneered. I explained that Association Football was an interesting game, and quite a few of his subjects rather liked it. 'Well, I will be attending a Labour for Europe party and that I can assure you will be a lot more fun,' he said. I reflected on this for a moment and realised he was

actually right. There was a definite likelihood that even a meeting of
that spellbinding tedium would be more entertaining than what lay in
front of us tonight. Before the game I would have bet my car that this
would be a 0-0 draw. Russia ... cold, miserable, horrible to get to. No
'fear-of-flying' Bergkamp to pierce those crafty local defenders with
unpronounceable names. No Sol, as he mourns the death of his father.
No Vieira or Ljungberg through injuries. The game didn't disappoint
those like me who were totally prepared to be bitterly disappointed.
What was totally bizarre was Wenger's resolute refusal to use any
substitutes. If Kanu can't get a game when Pires and Wiltord play
that badly for 90 minutes, what *is* the point in keeping him on the
books at £40K a week? And why have all these brilliant youngsters
like Bentley and Aliadiere if we don't spring them late-on in games
like this where their youth and enthusiasm might just do the trick?
They, after all, are the only ones genuinely thrilled to be out there.

Wenger's reluctance to experiment was only marginally more
irritating than the TV commentary of ITV's Jon Champion who must
have thought he was attending a Thomas the Tank Engine
convention, judging by the sheer volume of 'off the rails', 'on the right
track' and 'steaming ahead' analogies we had to endure. The game is
relentlessly dull, with a lot of robotic, gaunt Russians called things like
Maminov and Ashvetia running rings round us but never really
looking like scoring. Neither team had won a game in their last six
European matches and it showed. Henry tried his best but was
woefully supplied and by the end the only noise being made by anyone
was the whining bazooki being strummed somewhere in the crowd.
Sure enough, it ended 0-0 and I suppose a point away in Russia is
not a bad result. But our European performances so far are even worse
than usual, we're bottom of the group, and I just can't understand
why, given the obvious amazing talent in this side.

**Arsenal:** Jens Lehmann, Efstathios Tavlaridis, Martin Keown, Ashley Cole, Robert Pires, Ray Parlour, Lauren, Kolo Touré, Gilberto, Thierry Henry, Sylvain Wiltord. Subs not used: Graham Stack, Pascal Cygan, Justin Hoyte, Edu, Nwankwo Kanu, Jeremie Aliadiere, David Bentley

**Lokomotiv Moscow:** Sergei Ovchinnikov, Vadim Evseev, Gennadi Nizhegorodov 73, Sergey Gurenko, Sergei Ignashevich, Dmitri Sennikov, Oleg Pashinin, Vladimir Maminov, Marat Izmailov, Dmitrij Khokhlov, Dmitri Loskov, Mikhail Ashvetia, Rouslan Pimenov 65. Subs not used: Ruslan Nigmatullin, Malkhaz Asatiani, Narvik Sirkhayev, Jorge Wagner, Lessa Leandro

# OCTOBER

'You don't expect me
to commit suicide,
do you?'

GÉRARD HOULLIER

## Liverpool
**PREMIERSHIP, ANFIELD**
**RESULT: 1-2 WIN**
My location: watching TV at home

It used to be Fortress Anfield, where a draw was considered a great result for visiting teams. But not any more. Good to see Sol Campbell back after the death of his father. Sol's a big family man and it will have hit him hard. But he played like a rock again today, what a signing he's been. And what a class act, on and off the pitch. Harry Kewell opened the scoring for Liverpool, but Edu quickly equalised off Hyypia's leg. Then Robert Pires scored with a piece of genius that indicated his marital woes might be easing slightly. Picking up the ball 30 yards out, he took two steps and curled it straight inside the far post. His feet are extraordinary. Flat, but electric. He just seems to steam past defenders whilst looking less mobile than me after five pints of Harvey's bitter. Owen missed some great chances, then got injured again late on. He's got brittle bones, that boy. And he's wasting his time at Liverpool. Slotted in next to Henry and Pires he'd be devastating. One of the funniest things about playing Liverpool is what happens every time their assistant manager Phil Thompson leaps out of the dugout for one of his many remonstrations. The Clock End normally wait about half a second before, to a man, booming 'Sit down Pinocchio' to the tune of 'La Donna E Mobile' from Verdi's *Rigoletto*. It is harsh, entirely accurate in its descriptive power, and almost always induces seething rage from Big Nose himself – which of course merely serves to encourage yet more chants. Thompson can't stop jumping up, and the Clock End can't stop taunting him for his giant proboscis. 'Get your nostrils off the pitch', sung to 'Bread of Heaven', 'It's here, it's there, it's every f***ing where, Thompson's nose, Thompson's nose.' And my own favourite ... 'Sneeze in a minute! He's gonna sneeze in a minute!' – to the tune of 'Guantanamera'. All

very childish, but very, very funny. Unless you are Phil Thompson
of course. Or someone with a very big nose yourself.

We were lucky to win this game, but the quality of Pires' goal
deserved to win any game. 'He does that all the time in training'
sighed a relieved Wenger. 'To win after going a goal down tells you
a lot about the mental strength of this team.' And he's right, it does.
Houllier was more to the point: 'Arsenal are top because they are
very clinical.' He was right too. We work hard and score goals even
when we are not playing at our best. That is the mark of a great
side. Houllier, under mounting pressure at Anfield, reacted sharply
to be being quizzed about his future: 'You don't expect me to commit
suicide, do you?' Looking at the faces of some Liverpool fans
afterwards, I would imagine that would actually be something they
wouldn't be massively averse to.

**Arsenal:** Jens Lehmann, Sol Campbell, Ashley Cole (yellow card), Edu, Lauren, Kolo Touré, Gilberto, Robert Pires, Ray Parlour (yellow card),Thierry Henry, Jeremie Aliadiere, Sylvain Wiltord 73. Subs not used: Graham Stack, Pascal Cygan, Martin Keown, Nwankwo Kanu

**Liverpool:** Jerzy Dudek, Sami Hyypia, Steven Gerrard, Vladimir Smicer, Anthony Le Tallec 42, Harry Kewell, Steve Finnan, John Riise, Salif Diao, John Welsh 83, Igor Biscan (yellow card), El Diouf, Michael Owen, Emile Heskey 72. Subs not used: Chris Kirkland, Stephane Henchoz
Sami Hyypia 31 (own goal), Robert Pires 68, **Harry Kewell 14**

## 9th October 2003

Sol gets off that Djemba-Djemba 'flick' with a £20K fine for
'improper behaviour'. He can earn that tomorrow, literally, so it's
hardly a crippling financial burden for the big man. It's the right
decision too. He's built like Frank Bruno and his elbows are great
chiselled lumps that can't help but break anything they connect
with. It is never, though, deliberate.

## 10th October 2003

I have been asked by *GQ* magazine to interview Freddie Ljungberg.
As I point out in the piece, 'this is a bit like a Catholic priest being
asked to have a private audience with the Pope ... there is a lot of
love in the room.' We meet at the offices of his management in

Central London, and he is bang on time. To my surprise his PR girl
leaves us alone. I literally cannot remember the last time a major
star allowed me to interview them solus. But it says something
about the confidence of the guy, although he probably knows a
season ticket holder at Highbury is not exactly going to stitch up
one of his favourite players. We chat for over an hour, and Freddie
is smart, polite, funny, and revelatory. No question fazes him (not
even 'Why is Robert Pires such a big girl's blouse?') and he is candid
and frank about the state of our national game. It's obvious that
Freddie abhors the drinking, 'roasting' mentality so adored by many
English players. And it is soon apparent why it doesn't happen at
Arsenal any more. 'There are a lot of players earning a lot of money at
a young age going out and behaving badly because nobody stops them.
If you did it at Arsenal you'd be out, Arsène wouldn't let you play.'

He worships Wenger, and tells the hilarious story of his first
bollocking from the great man. 'I'd just joined the club and we had
dinner one night in the team hotel at 7 p.m. and were told not to eat
again. But by 10 p.m. I was starving so I ordered a spaghetti
bolognese on room service. The next morning he was waiting for me
with the bill and gave me a terrible bollocking. He checks
everything and trust me, it isn't worth doing it twice.' I ask him who
his favourite player in the world is but he refuses to say in case his
team-mates get upset. When pushed he admits 'Zidane' but you can
tell that he is really worried this will piss off Henry and Vieira. He
confesses that scoring a goal *is* better than sex, insists he could
never sleep with Swedish compatriot Ulrika Jonsson, and laughs off
the gay rumours. I suspect he keeps them going deliberately
because it sells more merchandise. There's a lot of money in
androgyny at the moment. The funniest moment comes when I ask
him a question specifically at the request of his PR, intended to
confirm he's a cut above the average thick footballer. 'So Freddie, I
hear you read a lot.' 'Yes, I do, I like Wilbur Smith – do you know
him?' I look at the PR, who has now returned to the room. She at

least has the good grace to blush. Freddie is more intelligent than most who kick a ball, though. And I enjoyed his company. He signs a couple of photos for my sons at the end, and says he will try and score a good goal for them. Classy guy.

### 12th October 2003

The England game against Slovakia erupts into a ridiculous mass brawl as the teams come off. Ashley Cole, in the thick of it naturally, says later: 'Even the guys with the stretchers were giving me abuse.'

### 15th October 2003

Arsenal have pleaded guilty to all charges in the Battle of Old Trafford. This can only mean one thing – they think they'll get off lightly. Lehmann, incredibly, had his charge dropped. He will be furious. And Roy Keane, not even accused of anything and openly seen trying to calm things down on the day, will feel humiliated.

**SATURDAY**
**18**
**OCTOBER**

## Chelsea
**PREMIERSHIP, HIGHBURY**
**RESULT: 2-1 WIN**
My location: at game

Chelsea come to Highbury packed with their new all-stars and brimming with even more of their usual modesty, which has been substantially increased by the arrival of Abramovich and his billions. 'Shall we buy a ground for you' was their first new chant, which got a few laughs – and the devastating response, 'Shall we win the League for you' followed by 'Sh*t team in Fulham, you're just a sh*t team in Fulham'. Chelsea, not known for their deep-rooted love of our players, give up the jokey line of attack and resort to personal racist abuse. 'Vieira-ooooh! Vieira-ooooh! He comes from

Senegal, His dad's a cannibal!' There have been few more chilling statements in football history than Roman's claim that 'Thierry Henry is my favourite player'. Bit like Henry VIII announcing he fancies your wife.

Abramovich is a fascinating, menacing character. I watched him 30 yards away in the directors' box and he exudes the air of a young man who has acquired fabulous wealth and power by a mixture of charm, a ready smile, and fearsome 'business practice'. I, for one, would not wish to cross him, and the sight of his armed, mean-faced bodyguards doesn't improve the sense of unease he creates around him. Whether he is here for the long term or using Chelsea like some luxurious toy remains to be seen. But I don't think he will ever be viewed as a force for good in this country or by football worldwide. Nobody should be able to buy the title, and it would be a travesty for our game if he ruins the entire marketplace in his extravagant quest to do so.

After a ferocious first five minutes, we won a free-kick and, unusually, Edu stepped up to drill it low at Cudicini, who was wrong-footed by a big deflection and watched it slip inside his left-hand post. But three minutes later the Brazilian undid his good work by giving it away cheaply; Crespo pounced, cut inside Lauren and scorched it into the top corner. Fantastic goal by a great striker. This lot are serious contenders after all. Arsenal fans bayed for a penalty when Melchiot shouldered Henry off the ball but Thierry immediately shook the defender's hand to say well tackled, which didn't improve our chances of getting one, frankly. He's an honest player Henry. And if he's really honest, he wants Bergkamp out there threading those amazing passes at him. Which is what happened the moment Dennis came on. He set Pires free, who fired in a low cross which Cudicini decided to try and be clever with, rather than just falling on safely. Never be clever with Thierry Henry, would be my advice to any goalkeeper. The ball slipped between his legs and Henry flew through to knock it in. Cudicini looked crushed, as if he'd heard too many stories of what happens to those who upset Russian oil tycoons. Chelsea's fans didn't seem too perturbed. As the players trooped off into the tunnel they sang Andy Williams' 'Can't Take My Eyes Off You' with the chorus of 'We're f***ing loaded'. Very good. Arsenal, unbelievably, are at the top of the Fair Play League as well as the Premiership. Now that really is something special.

**Arsenal:** Jens Lehmann, Sol Campbell, Ashley Cole, Robert Pires, Pascal Cygan 90, Ray Parlour (yellow card), Nwankwo Kanu 66, Lauren, Kolo Touré, Gilberto, Edu, Thierry Henry, Sylvain Wiltord, Dennis Bergkamp 66. Subs not used: Graham Stack, Jeremie Aliadiere

**Chelsea:** Carlo Cudicini, Wayne Bridge, Mario Melchiot, Glen Johnson, Robert Huth, Geremi, Jimmy Floyd Hasselbaink 78, Claude Makelele (yellow card), Damien Duff, Joe Cole 71, Frank Lampard, Adrian Mutu, Jesper Gronkjaer 67, Hernan Crespo. Subs not used: Marco Ambrosio, Mario Stanic

**Edu 5, Thierry Henry 75,** **Hernan Crespo 8**

**TUESDAY**
**21**
**OCTOBER**

## Dynamo Kiev
### CHAMPIONS LEAGUE, OLYMPIYSKI
### RESULT: 2-1 LOST
My location: a pub in London

What *is* the matter with us in Europe? We beat Chelsea, Liverpool and Newcastle, and draw well with United – all powerful European sides. Then lose to a pretty mediocre Russian team. Domestically we swagger with the arrogance of Cote D'Azur playboys, seducing all in our wake. But abroad we tiptoe like timid British tourists in a Hamburg sex shop: nervous, unconfident.

Kiev took the lead against the run of play when Shatskikh volleyed home from eight yards and, as usual when we go behind, Arsenal looked suddenly shaken rather than stirred. None more than Lehmann, who chose to play tricksy football instead of hoofing it into the ether, and passed it straight to Belkevich who smacked it 45 yards back into Lehmann's chest. The keeper, now well out of his area, saw it bounce to Shatskikh who knocked it back to Belkevich who scored. All totally unnecessary and all rather alarming for

Seaman fans who are simply not used to these Grobbelaar-style antics. The boys kept trying and Henry eventually scored. But too little, too late. Touré missed an absolute sitter in the last minute of extra time, whacking the bar when it was genuinely easier to whack the net. He falls to his knees and starts praying for forgiveness, but I hope his rather understanding spiritual leader makes him wait a bit because some crimes need a period of contemplation before they can be repented, and this was one of them.

Another grotesque European failure, we're down at rock bottom again and almost certainly out of the Champions League. I think Vieira is the big problem. When he plays, he protects the back four and they look impregnable. When he gets injured or suspended and doesn't play for a bit then they get exposed and look a lot more vulnerable. We have shown we can win without Henry, but we really struggle without Vieira. He is our turbo, and unless he's charging we don't seem to run at all. As if I wasn't unsettled enough, I realise I have to spend three hours tomorrow interviewing Jordan in a penthouse flat for my TV series *Tabloid Tales*. Honestly, the awful things you sometimes have to do in this job ...

**Arsenal:** Jens Lehmann, Sol Campbell, Ashley Cole, Robert Pires, Ray Parlour, Fredrik Ljungberg 74, Lauren, Kolo Touré, Gilberto, Nwankwo Kanu 74, Edu, Patrick Vieira 61, Sylvain Wiltord, Thierry Henry. Subs not used: Graham Stack, Justin Hoyte, Pascal Cygan, Gael Clichy.

**Dynamo Kiev:** Olexandr Shovkovskiy, Yuriy Dmytrulin, Goran Sablic 33, Serhii Fedorov, Andrii Nesmachnyi, Goran Gavrancic, Jerko Leko, Valiantsin Belkevich, Tiberiu Ghioane, Aleksandr Khatskevitch 79, Maksim Shatskikh, Oleg Gusev, Diogo Rincon 64, Georgi Peev. Subs not used: Vitaliy Reva, Badr El Kaddouri, Roberto Nanni, Artem Milevski

**Thierry Henry 80, Maksim Shatskikh 27, Valiantsin Belkevich 64**

**SUNDAY**
**26**
**OCTOBER**

# Charlton Athletic
## PREMIERSHIP, THE VALLEY
## RESULT: 1-1 DRAW

My location: watching TV at home

Paolo Di Canio is one of my favourite opposing players. Mad as a brush, brilliantly talented, and with a temperament that makes

Lehmann look like a choirboy. Charlton got an extremely dubious penalty when Matt Holland 'fell over' Lauren's leg after half an hour and Di Canio took it in an unbelievably cheeky way – charging in, then chipping it down the middle before haring round the ground kissing his badge, ring, and anything else he could get his sweaty Italian lips on. Henry, not to be outdone, equalised with a brilliant curling free-kick ten minutes later. He is getting better at these now. In fact he's getting better at everything and becoming a very, very special player. For Charlton, Scott Parker lived up to his growing reputation. He's strong, fearless, direct and ambitious. So he'll be almost certainly be heading up the river to Chelsea, then. Both managers moaned about the other side's goals, with Wenger's complaint about Holland's 5.9 artistic impression dive sounding a bit hollow in the wake of Pires's recent activities.

But the truth is that we were pretty average today and appear to be badly missing Vieira. 'My players are jaded,' said Wenger. But how? Why? We're only in October, for Christ's sake. Surely their pampered legs haven't given way already? What would Bobby Moore have thought of players whining they were tired a quarter of a way through a season? Hang on. OK, I sound like my father. It doesn't matter what Bobby would have thought because today's game is so much faster etc. Or *is* it? When I watch old footage of the Brazilians back in 1970, they seem just as quick as their current team. No, our problem is that we find excuses for these modern players too often. They really are overpaid, overfed, overpreened. My answer to them being 'jaded' would be extra training. But I suppose Wenger will give them a day off and extra massages. And it will probably work better. Damn him.

**Arsenal:** Jens Lehmann, Sol Campbell, Ashley Cole, Robert Pires, Fredrik Ljungberg, Nwankwo Kanu 70, Ray Parlour, Lauren (yellow card), Kolo Touré, Gilberto, Thierry Henry, Dennis Bergkamp, Sylvain Wiltord 70. Subs not used: Graham Stack, Pascal Cygan, Edu

**Charlton Athletic:** Dean Kiely, Mark Fish, Chris Perry, Hermann Hreidarsson, Radostin Kishishev, Jonatan Johansson, Jamal Campbell-Ryce 76, Matt Holland, Claus Jensen, Graham Stuart, Scott Parker (yellow card), Paolo Di Canio, Jason Euell 45. Subs not used: Simon Royce, Chris Powell, Jonathan Fortune

Thierry Henry 39, **Paolo Di Canio 28 (pen)**

**TUESDAY**
**28**
**OCTOBER**

# Rotherham
**LEAGUE CUP, HIGHBURY**
**RESULT: 1-1 DRAW**
My location: watching TV at home

A mixed bag of experience (Wiltord, Kanu, Edu) and young blood
(including Aliadiere and Clichy). The League Cup may be devalued,
but it is a great opportunity for our kids to strut their stuff. Our
goal was brilliant to watch – swift passing between young and old
with Kanu finally laying off Aliadiere to score. He might be earning
£40K a week to sit in the reserves like a very expensive spare
gearstick but Kanu never complains and always tries his best. And
he is invaluable for helping bring the youngsters through in games
like this. Their keeper was sent off in extra time for handling
outside the box, despite claiming he had headed the ball. Clearly not
used to being exposed to too much damning TV evidence up there at
Rotherham ...

**Arsenal:** Graham Stack, Pascal Cygan, Efstathios Tavlaridis, Justin Hoyte, John Spicer 117, Gael Clichy, Edu, Nwankwo Kanu, Sylvain Wiltord, Jeremie Aliadiere (yellow card), Jerome Thomas, Ryan Smith 73. Subs not used: Francesc Fabregas Cesc, Quincy Owusu Abeyie, Craig Holloway, Olafur-Ingi Skulason

**Rotherham United:** Michael Pollitt (red card), Paul Hurst, Chris Swailes (yellow card), Shaun Barker (yellow card), Carl Robinson, John Mullin 93, Christopher Sedgwick (yellow card), Gary Montgomery 101, Stewart Talbot, Julian Baudet 105, Martin McIntosh, Paul Warne, Richie Barker, Darren Byfield. Subs not used: Andy Monkhouse, Mark Robins

Jeremie Aliadiere 11, **Darren Byfield 90**

## 29th October 2003

Nelson Vivas is retiring, and there won't be a dry eye at Highbury.
I've never known a player who started so few times but who
attracted such a devoted following. He was a gutsy Argentinean
full-back who came off the bench many times to do his bit, and
always got a good few chants, by stark comparison with someone
like Lee Dixon who barely got one at his own testimonial yet was
massively more successful for us. Vivas' career has ended sadly with
his own side's fans at River Plate booing him so badly that he asked

to come off at half-time, walked out of the ground and has now said he'll never play again. He deserved better.

Another Arsenal legend, Ian Wright, managed to get into trouble again watching his son Shaun Wright-Phillips play for Manchester City. Wrighty reacted badly to a racist member of the crowd insulting his boy and police had to calm everyone down. You get the feeling with Wrighty that he has a go at his own reflection sometimes. What a guy though, and what a clever new career he's built for himself on TV.

### 30th October 2003

The *Guardian* says we've been tapping up other Russian billionaires to see if they'll bung us some of their cash. Clearly Chelsea have got all the big boys rattled. There was a rumour that Abramovich wanted us first but was deterred by the ongoing uncertainty over our new ground. But most Arsenal fans I've spoken to don't fancy this funding route. There's a sense that it will all blow up soon, that Putin will put the clamps on these mysterious oil tycoons and they'll all be led away to help the KGB with their enquiries. With someone as astute as Wenger running the side, we don't need a load more money anyway, we just need to let him keep buying young guys nobody's heard of and turn them into superstars worth millions of roubles. Keeping Arsène Wenger alive strikes me as a much more worthwhile exercise than trying to find a billionaire with too much money and not enough sense.

# NOVEMBER

'You see Henry's name on
the team sheet and think:
"Oh no, not him again"'

STEVE BRUCE

## 1st November 2003

Sir Alex has blown a gasket (again) and lambasted the FA for daring to suspend Rio Ferdinand. It's everyone's fault but United's, of course, as ever with Ferguson. I'm sorry, but he is such a complete dickhead. He also has a shockingly poor sense of humour, which is usually the only get-out for tyrants like him. When he got off driving on the hard shoulder, because United's club doctor conveniently confirmed he was racing to the loo with urgent diarrhoea, I sent him a box of Immodium and a note saying 'We Gooners knew you were full of sh*t, and now we know for sure.' His PA, who sounded even more ferocious than the old growler, rang in a state of apoplectic fury saying she had 'never been more offended, ever'. I suggested she should get out more and perhaps listen to some of her angelic boss's press conferences – which sent her even further off the dial. Eventually she slammed the phone down saying she was throwing the Immodium away. I gave it ten minutes, then rang back to say it was my property and if she didn't retrieve it ASAP then I would be consulting my lawyers. It arrived back by return of post. Ferguson is a great manager, no question, but he should have quit when they won the Treble and before the team he built fell apart. Everything with him is personal now, from his racehorse feud with John Magnier, to his rows with the BBC, Beckham and Brian Kidd – and endless former friends and associates. He thinks he's an emperor, and at Old Trafford he is.

But emperors who behave like him are only any good as long as they keep winning. And he ain't winning much that matters any more. He has hated me, and the *Mirror*, ever since we ran our campaign to get United back in the FA Cup after they pulled out to spend some time on the beach at the ludicrous World Club Championships in Rio. But most of their fans agreed with us, as did most of Britain. At the height of that battle he rounded on one of my reporters at one public event and shouted: 'Tell your f***ing editor Morgan to f*** off back to Highbury and stagnate.' I was amused, and laughed even louder when he later banned us from the stadium. I don't know what he thought that would achieve, but we banned him from the *Mirror* anyway to show him who's really boss ... Anyway, he accused us today of cheating, doing a deal with the FA and generally conning the entire world to the detriment of his own virtuous side. 'I don't know how Arsenal got away with this,' he raged, 'I just know we wouldn't.' Said the manager of a team that last had a penalty awarded against them at home in 1912.

**SATURDAY**

**1**

**NOVEMBER**

## Leeds United
**PREMIERSHIP, ELLAND ROAD**
**RESULT: 1-4 WIN**
My location: La Manga, Spain

I was in La Manga, that well-known haunt of footballers with too much money and not enough brains, for a short golfing holiday with friends. The Leeds game was on Sky so we timed our round to catch kick-off, then forgot about the time difference and missed the first half, thereby confirming that we are just as stupid as most of the footballers who come out here – but without their millions.

Leeds are desperate, there's no other way to describe it. I had lunch with Peter Ridsdale a year ago and it was clear that a) he was a very nice bloke, b) he was a massive Leeds fan, and c) he didn't have a clue how to run a business like a football club. Nobody like him should ever be let loose on a big club because their love for the team makes them rule their head with their heart and do stupid things financially.

Things are so bad here now that Viduka marched off before today's kick-off after a row with Peter Reid. £60,000 a week, and this selfish Aussie upstart thinks he can just throw his toys out of the pram and go home when 35,000 Leeds fans have paid hard-earned money to see him play. It is *pathetic*. Viduka has never been the sharpest tool in the box. Who could forget his memorable observation, 'I would not be bothered if we lost every game so long as we won the league'? But he is getting away with this Naomi Campbell-like behaviour because Leeds are desperate and need him more than he needs them. If an Arsenal star did that now, he'd never play for us again. Because neither Wenger nor the fans would stand for it. But what can poor old Peter Reid do about this terrible mess his club is in – a mess, by the way, that has nothing to do with him. I've loved Reid ever since he was caught cheering a brilliant Bergkamp goal when he was in charge at Sunderland and admitted, 'I started clapping until I realised I was the home manager.'

To be fair to Leeds, they came out fighting but their Dunkirk spirit left them cruelly exposed at the back and we whacked them three times in the first half. Ashley Cole lobbed Henry through on his own as he hovered menacingly by the halfway line. He sped past Camara like a cheetah overtaking a bull elephant. Not a fair fight. Forty yards (and about two seconds) later he calmly slotted it past Robinson. Henry makes it look *so* easy. Ten minutes later, we counter-attacked again, Ljungberg squaring it for Pires who scored even more nonchalantly than Henry. Is it 'cos they're French? On the half-hour, Henry scorched past Batty – onto Freddie, then Dennis, who hit the post but Thierry was still running and just smacked it in the top corner. What do you say at half-time when you're 3-0 down to a rampaging Arsenal? Well, whatever Peter Reid said, I suspect it wasn't 'Tell you what boys, put your feet up during a Bergkamp free-kick after five minutes, yawn as Pires crosses the misfire in, and roll over as Gilberto scores.' Which is what they did. They looked beaten men, except Alan Smith who never stopped trying. Your heart aches for this guy. Viduka isn't fit to lace his admittedly rather ostentatious white boots.

**Arsenal:** Jens Lehmann, Lauren, Sol Campbell, Ashley Cole, Robert Pires, Fredrik Ljungberg, Edu 71, Ray Parlour, Kolo Touré, Gilberto, Thierry Henry, Dennis Bergkamp, Jeremie Aliadiere 77. Subs not used: Graham Stack, Pascal Cygan, Sylvain Wiltord

**Leeds United:** Paul Robinson, Gary Kelly, Zoumana Camara, Jose Roque Junior, Jermaine Pennant, Salomon Olembe (yellow card), David Batty (yellow card), Seth Johnson, Michael Bridges, James Milner 45, Alan Smith, Lamine Sakho, Aaron Lennon 61. Subs not used: Scott Carson, Ian Harte, Michael Duberry

Thierry Henry 8, 33, Robert Pires 17, Gilberto 50, **Alan Smith 64**

# Dynamo Kiev
## CHAMPIONS LEAGUE, HIGHBURY
## RESULT: 1-0 WIN

My location: first half, *Mirror* party, second half, at game

I missed the first half because I had to attend a *Mirror* centenary
party at the Science Museum, where the Prime Minister was going
to make a speech eulogising the paper that's berated him daily over
Iraq for a year now. Blair looked shot to pieces when he arrived,
just stumbling along beside me like a zombie. This war has sucked
all the life out of him, and I suspect it's as much to do with his
making a massive mistake as the realisation that he is a No.1 target
for Bin Laden's assassins. David Blunkett once told me that anyone
who read the intelligence threats against his life that Blair had to
read every single day would never leave a reinforced underground
bunker. He's also had this heart rate scare which was apparently
brought on by swigging too much caffeine, so this is not a good time
to be buying shares in TB. I moaned to Blair that I was having to
miss the match and normally he'd exchange a bit of footie banter
but he barely heard me this time. The other guests were pretty
shocked by what they saw too. His speech was rambling, incoherent,
and rather churlish given that the *Mirror* had played a massive part
in helping him win two elections. Perhaps he'd been a bit put out by
my opening line that it was great to see the Prime Minister alive
tonight. But there seem much more deep rooted problems than that
going on. Even his aides all looked stressed, depressed and nervous.

I rushed out to catch the second half, expecting to watch the final
ghastly death throes of our latest European disaster. But it turned
out to be one of those 'not so fast, Mr Bond' moments I so enjoy in
the 007 movies. Most of the second half was agony, pure ecstatic
agony. We had to win, but nobody thought we would as the match
went on. End-to-end, relentless chances, great saves on both sides,
but no goal. We shouldn't be in this position. We are too good not to

be beating up mediocre Russian teams like this. How can we rip teams like Liverpool to pieces but stutter against players nobody has ever head of – even in their own country?

With ninety minutes on the clock, fans began heading for the exit believing that was exactly where the team was going in the Champions League. But every serious football fan knows there are only two rules to observe: 1) Never change your team, 2) Never leave before the end. There is an amiable old guy who sits in front of me who always, always leaves five minutes before the end. I've seen him miss last-minute winners, penalties, sendings-off, fights, drama on a breathtaking scale. But nothing will ever stop him leaving before the final whistle. What's bizarre is that his twin brother always stays behind. Sure enough, he rose and left with a last disgruntled 'every bloody time' sigh as he ambled off. Seconds later Wiltord raced down the left, crossed it over, glanced off Henry's head and landed on a diving Cole who nutted it into the goal. Oh yes, oh yes, oh (to borrow a phrase from Meg Ryan) YEEEESSSSSS! They thought it was all over, but it ain't yet. The fat lady has her apron on and is cooking her doughnuts but this League is still alive. 'Lenin, Trotsky, Kruschev, Popodopolov … your boys took one hell of an unlucky beating.'

**Arsenal:** Jens Lehmann, Sol Campbell, Ashley Cole, Robert Pires, Fredrik Ljungberg, Sylvain Wiltord 69, Ray Parlour, Nwankwo Kanu 75, Lauren, Kolo Touré (yellow card), Gilberto (yellow card), Thierry Henry, Dennis Bergkamp, Edu 90. Subs not used: Graham Stack, Pascal Cygan, Gael Clichy, Jeremie Aliadiere

**Dynamo Kiev:** Olexandr Shovkovskiy, Serhii Fedorov, Andrii Nesmachnyi, Goran Gavrancic, Jerko Leko (yellow card), Denys Onischenko, Goran Sablic 21, Tiberiu Ghioane, Valiantsin Belkevich, Maksim Shatskikh, Roberto Nanni 71, Oleg Gusev, Diogo Rincon 60, Georgi Peev. Subs not used: Vitaliy Reva, Badr El Kaddouri, Alessandro, Olexandr Melashchenko

**Ashley Cole 88**

**SATURDAY 8 NOVEMBER**

## Tottenham Hotspur
**PREMIERSHIP, HIGHBURY**
**RESULT: 2-1 WIN**
My location: at game

It never really matters if you're home or away in these games, or if your best players are fit or injured. Nothing normal applies to this fixture. It is always a vicious, frenzied, nasty little kick-about and frankly, there is a sound argument for resting thoroughbreds like Henry and Pires and inserting the Rollerball boys like Ray Parlour who've been weaned on hating Spurs and know what it means to the fans to lose against them. Ironically, that's just what Wenger did. And how does Parlour reward him? He only gives away a soft throw-in in the first five minutes, which is hurled to King, who finds Keane, who ricochets it to 'Sicknote' Anderton, who only bloody scores. Cue intolerable chanting from the equally bemused but thrilled Spurs fans along the ludicrous lines of 'There's only one team in London', 'Are you West Ham in disguise' and the inevitable 'Campbell, what's the score, Campbell. Campbell, what's the score.'

This is not an easy day for Sol and never will be. Nobody crosses that North London divide oblivious to the tidal wave of venom that will come your way forever after. But that doesn't make it any easier to deal with. Men and women who once cheered your every move now spit at you, and genuinely wish you a slow painful death from a terminal disease that preferably involves some form of dismemberment. There is one particularly vile chant involving Vieira, Campbell's backside and an allegation of what the *News of the World* would call an 'unnatural' nature. But that's nothing compared to all the 'Arsène Wenger is a paedophile' nonsense. This started when a bored Spurs fan heard we'd signed him and thought it would be funny to start an internet rumour saying Wenger had been arrested for molesting children. It was a hideous, monstrous lie, but led to Wenger actually having to formally deny it. Since then Spurs fans have delighted in reminding him of the incident, rewriting things like Pink Floyd's 'Another Brick In The Wall' to include the line 'Please, Arsène ... leave our kids alone.' I think it crosses a line, like the Leeds fans chanting about Munich at Old Trafford, or United fans taunting Liverpool about Hillsborough. It's just not funny, it's horrible. Wenger, though – who has a beautiful wife and children – has never seemed too bothered. He endeared himself to every Arsenal fan on his first day in office by saying: 'I went back to my hotel and intended to watch Tottenham on television – but I fell asleep.' Spurs fans have real psychological issues. When George Graham became their manager, they couldn't bring themselves to chant his name because of his Arsenal heritage so they would sing 'Man in the raincoat's blue and white army ...'

Henry soon began to torment the Spurs defence. But Kasey Keller was just fantastic in goal, the best I have seen from any keeper for several seasons. Everything we threw at him he saved until he finally parried yet another Henry rocket straight to Pires who banged it home. Ten minutes later Freddie shot from 30 yards and it looked distinctly unthreatening until it struck Stephen Carr's foot and looped up over the desperately unlucky Keller. Now it was the Clock End's turn for a bit of merriment. 'You'll never play here again' was followed by another old favourite, 'You're sh*t and you know you are' and then something altogether less jocular: 'Heeeeeyyyy Yiddo, you SCUM, I wanna know-ow-ow ... where your captain's gone.' Amazingly the tannoy promptly crackled into life and a firm voice demanded that the offensive Jewish slur not be repeated. The Clock End thought for a second, then responded with 'Heeeeeyyyy scumbags, you SCUM, I wanna know-ow-ow ... where your captain's gone.' And I didn't hear any more 'yiddo' chants. Which has to be a really quite historic victory for the war against racism in football grounds – and a blow against absurd hypocrisy. Because a lot of those chanting 'Heeeeeyyyy Yiddo' in Arsenal's seats are, of course, Jewish themselves.

**Arsenal:** Jens Lehmann, Sol Campbell, Ashley Cole, Robert Pires, Fredrik Ljungberg, Ray Parlour (yellow card), Lauren, Pascal Cygan 61, Kolo Touré, Gilberto, Dennis Bergkamp 61, Thierry Henry, Nwankwo Kanu, Edu 82. Subs not used: Graham Stack, Justin Hoyte

**Tottenham Hotspur:** Kasey Keller, Paul Konchesky (yellow card), Mbulelo Mabizela 73, Anthony Gardner, Stephen Carr, Mauricio Taricco (yellow card), Dean Richards (yellow card), Ledley King, Darren Anderton (yellow card), Stephane Dalmat, Rohan Ricketts 82, Helder Postiga, Bobby Zamora 82, Robbie Keane. Subs not used: Rob Burch, Gary Doherty

Robert Pires 69, Fredrik Ljungberg 79, **Darren Anderton 5**

**SATURDAY**
**22**
**NOVEMBER**

## Birmingham City
**PREMIERSHIP, ST. ANDREWS**
**RESULT: 0-3 WIN**

My location: watching TV in London

England won the Rugby World Cup in the morning with a stunning last-minute drop goal from Jonny Wilkinson, who will now temporarily replace Beckham as the nation's sporting icon. But it won't last, because rugby will never replace football as our national game. It's a class thing. You get a few working class rugby fans and you get a few upper class soccer fans. But not many of either. And if you doubt this then either go to Anfield one day and shout 'Anyone for a glass of Chablis' or head down to Twickenham in your shell suit and cry 'Who the f***ing hell are you' at Martin Johnson.

This was one of those games where you can quickly come unstuck. Steve Bruce has done well at Birmingham and they are a well-run, well-resourced club. But it's all relative and only applies if you don't have Thierry Henry in your side, and when he flicked it through to Freddie in the fourth minute for a sweet opener you suspected the floodgates may have just been pushed ajar. Bergkamp, captain for the day, was on fire – refuting my early concerns about his current worth, and reminding us yet again how big a blow it is that he can't fly. This man should be striding the world stage like the footballing colossus he is, not staying at home and doing the gardening. But as someone whose mother shares Mr Bergkamp's terror, I can testify to the appalling sensation it induces in sufferers. Trapped on a flying object for hours is a living hell for those who fear it. Dennis, who has to put up with opposing fans waving their arms like wobbly jets whenever he takes a corner and chants of 'taxi for Mr Bergkamp', deserves our sympathy, not our derision. A lot of celebrities who fly all the time end up scared stiff because in their heads they are constantly reducing the odds of crashing. That's why Bill Wyman never flies now, for instance. Ever.

Anyway, Bergkamp was metaphorically flying today and tore Birmingham to pieces. With ten minutes to go he charged into the box, three defenders failing to keep up with his decrepit old legs and as the keeper rushed out, Dennis just chipped it gently over his head and let the ball roll into the goal. Masterful. Minutes later, Henry set up Pires who took it down brilliantly with two sublime touches and in a flash sent both the ball and defender sliding into the back of the net.

United and Chelsea win too, but we stay top and with this win we set a new Premiership record of thirteen games unbeaten at the start of a season. I suspect this won't be the first record we set this year. This team looks the business. Steve Bruce, whose team had battled hard, sighed: 'Henry's so consistent now, you see his name on the team sheet and think: 'Oh no, not him again.'

**Arsenal:** Jens Lehmann, Sol Campbell, Ashley Cole, Pascal Cygan, Gael Clichy, Nwankwo Kanu 59, Edu (yellow card),Kolo Tourè (yellow card), Robert Pires, Justin Hoyte 90, Fredrik Ljungberg, Dennis Bergkamp, Jeremie Aliadiere 90, Thierry Henry. Subs not used: Graham Stack, Efstathios Tavlaridis

**Birmingham City:** Maik Taylor, Jamie Clapham, Kenny Cunningham, Aliou Cisse (yellow card), Stern John 64, Matthew Upson, Stephen Clemence, Robbie Savage, Stan Lazaridis, Bryan Hughes 85, Damien Johnson, David Dunn, Mikael Forssell, Clinton Morrison 87. Subs not used: Ian Bennett, Olivier Tebily

**Fredrik Ljungberg 4, Dennis Bergkamp 80, Robert Pires 88**

## Internazionale
### CHAMPIONS LEAGUE, STADIO GIUSEPPE MEAZZA
### RESULT: 1-5 WIN
My location: watching TV in London

I had planned to fly out to Milan for this game, but our situation in the Champions League seemed so dire, and the chances of beating a team that had hammered us 3-0 at home so slim, I decided to save the plane fare and watch it on the box. It has to rank as the worst decision I have made since running that headline ACHTUNG SURRENDER during Euro '96, thinking everyone would enjoy a little joke about the Germans ...

I woke up feeling twitchy and it had nothing to do with Fiona Phillips' rather lurid new latex bra on GMTV. This was a massive day for the development of Arsenal Football Club. If we could get a good result against Inter then we might just scrape through to the next round of the Champions League. And the way we are beginning to play, that could be just the catalyst we need to do something really special in Europe. Wenger wants the players to remember our 3-1 massacre of Roma in Rome last year to inspire another great Italian job. 'We've shown we are capable of doing it in Italy, so why not again?' But inside, he must be doing emotional cartwheels at the prospect of crashing out of Europe yet again. He takes failure badly. Asked whether he beats himself up whenever Arsenal go out of the Champions League, he said with a smile: 'Unfortunately I do that every season and it's getting rather painful.'

Work seemed utterly irrelevant as various heads of department rattled through their schedules. Who gives a toss about famine, pestilence and war when there's a game of this importance looming in a few hours' time? The assistant sports editor Dominic, a Watford fan usually sent in by his bosses to 'amuse' me in conference, predicted we'd lose 2-0 – with a big grin on his face. I thanked him for his thoughts, made the usual P45 gags, and dismissed him without hearing anything else about the day's sports events. He laughed again; his game plan of diverting attention from the lack of any good stories that morning had worked marvellously. I left the office at 6.30 p.m., earlier than I had to but I knew I'd need some sustenance to get through the ordeal. Beer, curry, a few like-minded Gooner mates – and the obligatory United fan to howl abuse at if we won. Or do the washing-up if we lost. We looked nervous at the start and who can blame us ... going to the San Siro for a result is like going bull-fighting without your sword. It's never going to be easy. But on the 24th minute, Cole steamed into their half, passed to Pires and carried on steaming forward. Pires to Henry, to Cole, back to Henry and *whack* – 1-0. What passing, what movement, what speed, what finesse! Inter look stunned. Nobody does this to them in their own backyard. We took the game to them after that, with Kanu excelling in that holding way of his. I guess it is easier to 'hold' the ball when you've got size 19 paddles like Kanu and are 6ft 6in tall. What I love about him, though, is that he never complains, and always laughs. A rare specimen indeed for a Premiership star. He also had one of the greatest chants ever when he scored that unbelievable hat trick to beat Chelsea when we were 2-0 down with 20 minutes left ... 'Chim chimminee, chim chimminee, chim chim cheroo, who needs Anelka when we've got KANU.' The only problem is that his usual chant is 'Kanuuuuuuu', which always sounds like he's being booed by his own fans. 'Eduuuuuuu' has it too. On the upside, when they *are* being booed they smile and wave, thinking we are cheering their name.

Just when we were getting a little carried away, Vieri got the ball on the edge of our box and his shot deflected off Campbell over Lehmann's head for the equaliser. Half-time came, and it was tense. But three minutes after the restart Freddie and Henry linked up to flick passes to each other down the left wing before waltzing into their penalty area for Freddie to knock it past Toldo. Inter came at us again and again but from yet another corner, Henry set off from his own half, and kept on running until he arrived in their box and blasted a low shot into the corner. He is becoming the human Arkle, a dazzling athlete with a head for the finishing line. It was an explosive, sumptuous goal by a striker on top of his game. As the Renault adverts he stars in tell us, va va VOOM! Three minutes to go and Henry's off again, slipping it through to Edu who makes it 4-1. This is unbelievable, we are hammering one of the world's greatest sides in their own stadium. Aliadiere came on for Henry, who got a gladiatorial ovation from the travelling fans, and the French youngster promptly set up Pires for the fifth. One of the more alarming facts for Inter's proud tycoon owner Massimo Moratti to dwell on was that Toldo, supposedly the world's best keeper, cost more than our entire starting team. Jens Lehmann (£1m), Kolo Touré (nominal fee), Sol Campbell (Bosman free), Ashley Cole (homegrown), Cygan (£2m) Robert Pires (£5m), Ray Parlour (homegrown), Edu (£5m), Freddie Ljungberg (£3m), Kanu (£4.5m) and Henry (£8m).

Yes, Thierry was magnificent. But the unsung heroes of this match were Lehmann, Edu, Kanu, Cygan – guys who rarely get a headline but who stepped right up to the plate tonight. Lehmann apparently got all emotional in the dressing room afterwards, telling his colleagues that 'this is the biggest team spirit of all the teams I have played with ... I played for Schalke 04 and we won the UEFA Cup here in Milan, and at Dortmund where we won the Bundesliga, but this is more special. We were written off, but we are aware we have the power to play very good football. We didn't only win in Milan, we had a great win, and that put us back on Europe's map.' At which point he was led away to a large cold bath to restore some steel to his overwrought emotionally-ravaged German torso.

As Arsenal boarded the team bus after the game, I swear they all looked two inches bigger. This win didn't just restore their confidence, it pumped them up to believe that not only can they compete at this level, they can win the competition. A scary night for Inter. An even scarier one for Arsenal fans. I lie awake sweating at 3 a.m., reliving the goals and gulping with nervous anxiety at the dreams of cups to come. Even when we beat Inter Milan 5-1 at the San Siro it is agonising.

**Arsenal:** Jens Lehmann, Pascal Cygan (yellow card), Sol Campbell, Ashley Cole, Robert Pires, Fredrik Ljungberg, Ray Parlour, Kolo Touré, Edu (yellow card), Thierry Henry, Jeremie Aladiere 89, Nwankwo Kanu, Gilberto 73. Subs not used: Graham Stack, Justin Hoyte, Gael Clichy, Martin Keown, Michal Papadopulos

**Inter:** Francesco Toldo, Fabio Cannavaro, Giovanni Pasquale 59, Jeremie Bréchet, Ivan Cordoba, Javier Zanetti, Marco Materazzi, Sabri Lamouchi, Matias Almeyda 57, Cristiano Zanetti, Christian Vieri, Andy van der Meyde, Julio Cruz 69, Obafemi Martins. Subs not used: Alberto Fontana, Daniele Adani, Siqueira Luciano, Kily González

**Thierry Henry 25, 85, Fredrik Ljungberg 49, Edu 87, Robert Pires 89, Christian Vieri 33**

## 26th November 2003

I wake up at 5.30 a.m. Oh *no*, it wasn't a bloody dream was it? For a few unsettling moments I am convinced it never happened, that we didn't actually thrash one of the world's greatest clubs 5-1 in their own backyard. But I hurriedly turn on Sky News, and there it is flashing constantly on the sports section of their digital coverage. ARSENAL HAMMER INTER 5-1. If our 3-0 defeat at Highbury was the worst I had seen us play then this had to be the best. And Henry has surely stamped his reputation as the world's most dangerous striker now. He was just fabulous, toying with them by the end like a lion toys with a small group of trapped antelope. I'll have to go into work early, there are so many people to gloat to. Arsenal were 80-1 to win the Champions League after that defeat in Kiev. Now they're 9-1 and plummeting. Who the hell wants to play us now?

# Fulham
**PREMIERSHIP, HIGHBURY**
**RESULT: 0-0 DRAW**
My location: at game

Just when you think you can beat Real Madrid 4-0 (and people
actually believe you) along comes a mediocre bunch of journeymen
like Fulham to wind your neck in for you. But there's a pattern
emerging here. We're thrashing teams away, but struggling a bit at
home. Why? Because we are playing so breathtakingly well that
opposing teams come to Highbury, cower in the marbled dressing
rooms like naughty kids in the headmaster's study with just one
thought in mind: How bad is this going to be? Hence the desperately
negative, tedious and usually self-defeating tactic of packing nine
behind the ball, kicking lumps out of anything in a red and white
shirt, and praying for something, anything, less than a humiliation.
It's not easy managing a club like Fulham, with all the pressure
Mohammed Al Fayed and his millions bring to the commercial
party. Chris Coleman summed it up hilariously: 'I can't sleep, I can't
nod off, I can't go out for a beer with the lads like I used to, I think
about the job all the time and I'm losing my hair and losing all my
mates.' But that's his problem today, I'm afraid. We thrashed Inter
because the more we scored the more they had to come and attack,
and the more spaces appeared for us to do what we do best –
counter-attack. But it is a different game against a resilient side
like Fulham with a goalkeeper who plays as well as Van der Sar.

We had a good go at it – Henry, Bergkamp, Freddie and Pires all
coming close. The latter actually scored but was ruled offside –
something that often happens to us because the linesmen simply
can't keep up with the speed of our breaks. You're going to need
Dwayne Chambers running the flag soon, *with* stimulants. Van der
Sar was just superb, endlessly making saves from Henry and Pires
in particular. The second half was much the same, we launched

wave after offensive wave – and Van der Sar made save after save, from Kanu, Pires, Bergkamp. We kept shooting and he kept blocking, like Geoff 'Occupation of Crease' Boycott snubbing out the West Indies pace attack for hours on end. Emboldened by the extraordinary activities of their keeper, Fulham started attacking themselves towards the end and that admirable old warhorse Barry Hayles came nearest to scoring, something that would have been entirely appropriate given the context of the game.

We should have won 12-0, ought to have settled for at least 5-0, but ended up drawing 0-0. Most of the crowd looked vaguely bemused. Chris Coleman admitted: 'I had set our stall out all week on stopping them scoring and it worked. I know it wasn't pretty but I'm not bothered by that.' We hadn't failed to score at home in forty-seven consecutive games. But we didn't lose and the unbeaten run goes on. Worryingly, though, Chelski go top after beating United 1-0 at home. I don't like what's going on there. There is an aura of the Romans – literally – about Mr Abramovich: 'We don't do meetings, we kill everything that gets in our way.' Ironically, this very motto used to be pinned on former Chelsea supremo Ken Bates' door. How that ridiculous, festering old bore must be regretting bringing the Russians in now ...

**Arsenal:** Jens Lehmann, Sol Campbell, Ashley Cole, Pascal Cygan, Kolo Touré, Gilberto, Nwankwo Kanu 67, Edu (yellow card), Robert Pires, Fredrik Ljungberg, Jeremie Aliadiere 79, Dennis Bergkamp, Thierry Henry. Subs not used: Graham Stack, Gael Clichy, Justin Hoyte.

**Fulham:** Edwin Van der Sar, Zatyiah Knight, Andy Melville, Jerome Bonnissel, Moritz Volz, Junichi Inamoto, Sylvain Legwinski (yellow card), Steed Malbranque, Lee Clark, Sean Davis, Louis Saha, Barry Hayles 76. Subs not used: Mark Crossley, Alain Goma, Martin Djetou, Facundo Sava.

# DECEMBER

'I do not booze, Morgan.
I treat my body as a temple
and I do not let anything bad
like alcohol inside it'

THIERRY HENRY

## 2nd December 2003

Ryan Giggs and Christian Ronaldo pleaded not guilty to the
Handbag-gate offences, were then found guilty as charged, but now
get just a fine and a warning instead of bans. And they are *still*
bloody moaning. Arsenal as a club got fined £175,000 for 'failing to
control their players' and the individual badges of honour went to:
Lauren: 4-match ban + £40,000 fine; Keown: 3-match ban + £20,000
fine; Vieira: 1-match ban + £20,000 fine; Parlour: 1-match ban +
£10,000 fine. It could have been worse, and for the depth-charge it
clearly gave our season I'll take that happily. When you consider
that the banned games include Birmingham, Fulham and Wolves
you can start to work out why the Arsenal management seem pretty
relaxed. Good chance to rest some of our top boys when they are
least needed. It reminded me of Vinny Jones telling me when I
employed him on the *News of the World* that he always tried to
clock up four bookings by mid-December, then get himself
deliberately booked in the last game before Christmas so he could
get banned for the entire festive season and put his feet up. Never
as stupid as people assume, our Vinny.

## 2nd December 2003

The phone rang in my car as I was on my way to interview Shane
Richie for his *Tabloid Tale*. 'Allo, is that Morgan?' The accent was
thick French, and the tone slightly hysterical. 'Er, it might be, who's
this?' I replied, rather irritated that some mad Gaul had tracked
down my number. 'This is Thierry.' I nearly said 'Thierry who?' but
we both knew that would have been ridiculous. There's only one
Thierry, even if many Arsenal fans still insist on calling him Terry.
I would imagine they vote for the UK Independence Party. This had
to be a wind-up. Why on earth would the world's greatest striker be
phoning me in my car? As I always do when confronted in this way
by a celebrity, I flicked quickly through that morning's paper for
clues. And there it was, on page 13. An exclusive report on Thierry

joining other superstars in Spain for an advertising campaign, and partying in a nightclub. Not a big deal though, just a laugh. Not for Monsieur Henry it wasn't. 'Listen to me, Morgan. Why 'av you written all these lies about me today. Why 'av you said I was 'boozing' until 4 a.m., why 'av you said I was drinking bottles of champagne, why?' I was taken aback by the scale of his ferocity, but managed to stumble a 'Well, Thierry, are you saying you weren't there or something?' 'Not there? NOT THERE? I was THERE, Morgan, but I was not boozing. I do not booze, Morgan. I treat my body as a temple and I do not let anything bad like alcohol inside it. I am an athlete, and I look after myself ... And I take my responsibility as a role model seriously – I don't want children reading this sh*t and thinking it is cool to be a boozer because Thierry boozes. OK?' 'So you didn't drink anything then?' I stuttered, trying to maintain a modicum of editorial dignity in the face of this Gallic onslaught. 'Not. A. Thing. You hear me Morgan, not a drop of alcohol passed my lips. I DO NOT BOOZE.' This seemed fairly unequivocal to me. 'OK, OK, Thierry. Look, I am an Arsenal season ticket holder and you're my favourite player. So let's try and calm down here, shall we, and sort things out ...' 'Calm down? CALM DOWN? If you're such a fan, they why do you print this sh*t about me?' He had a good point, I must say. After twenty more minutes of ranting, he eventually did calm down. We agreed a new story to run the next day correcting any impression that he was a boozer. It read like one of the longest apologies ever.

I tell this story purely because it gives such a fascinating insight into the mind of the greatest footballer I have ever seen. Henry is a man on top of his game, a game that is simply beyond the reach of most players. A game of electrifying pace, phenomenal skill, awesome finishing, unspeakable arrogance and divine finesse. The guy has got it all. Yet in his hour of glory, he can still find time to call a tabloid editor and berate him for saying he had a couple of drinks in a club. As he said when we finished speaking, 'Morgan, I am not like those British players who like boozing and behaving badly, please understand that.' He doesn't just want to trailblaze on the pitch, he wants to do it off the pitch too.

Henry. He was languishing at Juventus on the wing, unloved and unhappy. Wenger, who knew him from Monaco, bought him for £8 million, made him play centre-forward and still he struggled for a bit. Then, in a game against Southampton, away, which I was lucky enough to be at, he got the ball, charged to the edge of the box and smashed it in the top corner. And BANG. The legend was born. Since that moment, Henry has grown into the most lethal striker in the world. Quicker than Ronaldo, more skilful than Raul, less selfish than Vieri. To watch him every week is like watching Mick Jagger do a Stones tour. Each gig he gets more daring, more experimental, more confident. Henry doesn't do simple goals. He likes great big spectacular firecrackers. And when he scores one like the thunderbolt that nearly beheaded Roy Carroll in the United game, you see an explosion of passion to rival anything Richard Burton unleashed on Liz Taylor.

Wenger urges him on, always supportive, never critical. For three years he has talked up Henry as the world's No.1 until Thierry believed it – and now everyone else believes it. And therein lies Wenger's real genius. He takes these players, works on them, on and off the pitch, until they are fully honed to his specification, and then lets them fly, free to roam the game how they see fit. And they, in turn, feel an extraordinary duty of care towards Wenger. Hence Henry's fury at that story in the *Mirror*. I suspect he wasn't so worried about upsetting the kids who revere him, so much as the boss who he owes it all to.

# Wolverhampton Wanderers
## LEAGUE CUP, HIGHBURY
## RESULT: 5-1 WIN
My location: at game

Our kids, propped up by Vieira, Wiltord and Kanu, gave Wolves such a stuffing that the crowd began chanting 'Are you Inter in disguise?' towards the end. If you can deliver beatings like this with a team including Simek, Tavlaridis, Hoyte, Skulason, Stack, Cesc, Bentley, Papadopoulous and Smith, then the future surely looks rather rosy for this club. After Kanu missed a hat-trick of relatively easy chances, proving why Wenger daren't risk him in the first team any more, he finally got one – squeezed in between two quick-witted Aliadiere strikes. Wiltord made it four before Cesc became the youngest player ever to score for Arsenal. It all looks very, very good.

**Arsenal:** Graham Stack, Efstathios Tavlaridis, Justin Hoyte, Olafur-Ingi Skulason 55, Gael Clichy, Frankie Simek (yellow card), Francesc Fabregas Cesc, Patrick Vieira, Nwankwo Kanu, Sylvain Wiltord, Jeremie Aliadiere, Michal Papadopulos 83, David Bentley, Ryan Smith 78. Subs not used: Rami Shaaban, Quincy Owusu Abeyie.

**Wolverhampton Wanderers:** Andy Marshall, Lee Naylor, Paul Butler, Jody Craddock, Alex Rae, Keith Andrews, Dean Sturridge 68, Henri Camara, Shaun Newton 73, Johannes Gudjonsson (yellow card), Paul Ince, Nathan Blake, Kenny Miller, Mark Kennedy 60. Subs not used: Michael Oakes, Silas

Jeremie Aliadiere 24, 71, Kanu 68, Sylvain Wiltord 79, Francesc Fabregas Cesc 88, **Alex Rae 81**

## 3rd December 2003

The next morning I was back in my car on the way to work when the phone rang again. 'Morgan? What 'av you done NOW?' It was Thierry, sounding even more enraged than he'd been the day before. He then started shrieking about some tiny point in paragraph nine. I let him run out of steam, then shouted back: 'Thierry, shut up.' 'WHAT? You tell me to 'shut up?' 'Yes. You may well be a brilliant footballer, and I may worship the ground you spit on, but I have had enough of this nonsense. I gave you the greatest apology in newspaper history yesterday and all you can do is complain. I don't know who you're used to treating like this, but it isn't going to work

with me, mate, so either shut up or go away.' There was a long
silence. Then laughter. 'OK, OK, OK, OK, Morgan. Sorry for
shouting. I just care, you know, I just care.' We had a bit of fun after
that and he ended up thanking me, and agreeing to wear a T-shirt
with 'MORGAN – L'IDIOT' under his shirt in the weekend game if
he scored, which tragically he didn't.

## 4th December 2003

Sol Campbell is a great guy, marvellous player, and incredibly brave
for making the move from Spurs. *But*, even I get a bit worried when
he gives interviews like one today in which he says: 'I'm going to go
for it with the acting. I really want to do it.' – Sol mate, I love you to
bits, but Denzel Washington you ain't, mate. Now get back into that
penalty area and concentrate on what you're good at, please.

## 6th December 2003

Worrying news about Henry, who has picked up a leg injury in
training and may miss the unprecedentedly massive game against
Lokomotiv. I can't even bear to think how I'd feel if he got a bad
injury. Football fans are always haunted by the Marco van Basten
experience. Arguably the greatest natural striker ever, at the peak
of his powers at 28, then his repeatedly battered leg finally gives
way and he never plays again. One moment of madness and he's
gone for all time. If Henry did that I fear I would actually break
down and sob like a baby. He is now *so* good, *so* spellbinding, *so*
unstoppable, and *so* obviously getting better all the time – it would
be just heartbreaking to see him stretchered off. In fact, the mere
thought of is making me feel so ill I'm going to book a room in the
Priory Clinic just in case.

## Leicester City
### PREMIERSHIP, WALKERS STADIUM
### RESULT: 1-1 DRAW
My location: watching TV at home

I thought Fulham was bad, but unlucky. This was just bad.
Leicester are not a good side. They never have been. They are just
annoying, which is why Robbie Savage was so keen to play for them,
presumably. And why they attract fans who think it's funny to sing
'Who let the frogs out, who? who? who? who?' as we ran out. (OK, it
was quite funny ... but as a confirmed Europhile I just think we
should be better than this.) But they comfortably outplayed us for
the first half, and even had the brazen gall to be quite positive.
Henry wasn't playing, which is a reasonable excuse for our inertia.
But Bergkamp, Freddie, Wiltord and Pires all were – and frankly
I've seen better performances from Spurs upfront this season. It was
*that* damning. Ironically, former White Hart Lane reject (and that
takes some doing) Les Ferdinand nearly scored twice. And looked
the sharpest player on the pitch. But to everyone's surprise, we
scored on the hour through Gilberto, who buried a classy Bergkamp
cross with a bullet header. Least sharp player of the day, if not
decade, was Ashley Cole who with 15 minutes to go was sent off for
a quite ridiculous, indefensible two-footed lunge at Ben Thatcher.
I watched the replay several times and it actually looked worse each
time. Thatcher was miles from anywhere, and threatening the
dugout more than the goal. But Cole tore into him like he'd been
watching too many Razor Ruddock videos. This provoked several
Leicester players to come and 'ave a word in his shell-like. Howey
even raced 50 yards to join in the rather unseemly fray and shove
the offending left-back. I don't blame him, to be honest. If someone
did that to an Arsenal player then I would be appalled. It was a
deliberate, leg-breaking challenge. People's careers end like that. He
then made it considerably worse by arguing with the referee as if it

had all been some terrible misunderstanding. Coming on the back of Handbag-gate, it was not a clever move by a great young player with a rather suspect temperament. I hope Arsenal fine him properly and Wenger has a stern word.

**Arsenal:** Jens Lehmann (yellow card), Pascal Cygan, Sol Campbell, Ashley Cole (red card), Robert Pires, Fredrik Ljungberg, Martin Keown 88, Kolo Touré, Gilberto, Edu, Jeremie Aliadiere, Sylvain Wiltord 67, Dennis Bergkamp, Gael Clichy 74. Graham Stack, Nwankwo Kanu

**Leicester City:** Ian Walker, Jordan Stewart, Ben Thatcher, Andy Impey, Steve Howey, Callum Davidson, Riccardo Scimeca, Billy McKinlay, Craig Hignett 59, Marcus Bent, Paul Dickov 67, James Scowcroft, Les Ferdinand (yellow card), Keith Gillespie 76. Subs not used: Danny Coyne, Matt Elliott
**Gilberto 60, Craig Hignett 90**

### 7th December 2003

Judging by Cole's abject apology after the game, Wenger clearly did just that. He will miss at least three games, so he gets Christmas off. Wonder if he's a mate of Vinnie Jones.

### 8th December 2003

Interestingly, referee Rob Styles now says the reason Cole stayed on the pitch remonstrating for so long was because he was 'trying to apologise'. He explained: 'His reaction was one of disappointment as well as apology, things are not always what they seem ...' Quite. Sorry, Ashley.

WEDNESDAY
**10**
DECEMBER

# Lokomotiv Moscow
## CHAMPIONS LEAGUE, HIGHBURY
## RESULT: 2-0 WIN
My location: at game

The big one (again – aren't they all these days?) We thought it was all over with one point from the first three Champions League games, and it still might be if we trip up again. An exit now wouldn't just be very annoying, it would be financially disastrous. We need the millions that going through a few knock-out rounds will bring because we need a new stadium, and we need to pay for it without spending every penny. (We shall need some new players.)

The atmosphere at these games is weird, mainly because UEFA reduce the capacity by 6,000 seats for advertising hoardings (why the hell do we let them?) and ban drinking in the ground. Arsenal didn't endear themselves to the highest-paying season ticket holders in the upper East Stand by re-directing them to the ceiling of the North Bank where you need a telescope to see the front row, let alone the players. It is not a good way to treat people paying £1,700 for their seats, and it's not the first time they've done it. Yet there is, I suppose, another way of looking at it. Why shouldn't the most expensive seat-holders rough it once in a while? It might just remind us how lucky we are, and how removed we are from the reality of how football was once watched by everyone. When my dad first took me, back in the eighties, we stood in the North Bank in peeling terraces with high odours of urine, sweat, beer and rank hotdogs. But it seemed much more real and exciting then. You'd literally sway with this heaving mass of a chanting, swearing, always potentially violent crowd, and when a goal was scored it would be complete and utter pandemonium. Now, I just punch the air in a rather Alan Partridge-like way, and exchange high-brow knowing smiles with those around me as if watching a particularly thrilling game of crown green bowls. It is a tad phoney, and we all know it.

Anyway, the main result of the no-booze rule is that nobody turns up until five minutes before kick-off, because they are all guzzling down four last pints for the road, and so a huge scrum develops outside and nobody can get in on time. Since there is never any trouble at Arsenal, even when we play emotive local teams like Chelsea and Spurs, I cannot see the logic in this absurd regulation. And even as a Europhile, it irks me that it is being foisted upon us by some bureaucratic European organisation who just don't *get* what it is to watch football in this country. Or perhaps they do get it, very well indeed, and it is payback for all the beautiful European towns and cities our ghastly hooligans have trashed over the years. I still remember watching Arsenal 'fans' destroy a nice little square in Copenhagen, supposedly defending themselves against evil Turks from Galatasaray. It was just vile, really vile. And the obvious pleasure many of them took in it defied belief. The police have made most grounds safe in this country and I salute them for years of hard, painful work. But let's not kid ourselves that we have got rid of the hooligans. They are still there, waiting for any lapse in security to unleash their very special brand of violence.

Back to the game, and Henry showed his rising genius by charging over to their penalty area to nick the ball off the toe of a Russian defender, then hover with the ball by the corner flag until he spied Pires sneaking in unmarked and drilled it perfectly to him. Two neat touches and it was 1-0. The dream start. We looked up for it. I like night games because they are more intimidating to visiting teams. The fans are closer to the pitch at Highbury than almost anywhere else in the world and they can seem very near indeed on a dark cold tense night like this. Henry's only real problem is a tendency to sulk when things aren't going his way, or another player doesn't pass when he thinks he should. And a habit of showboating when he's scored or made a great goal. It's not odious, just irritating. He starts giving it the full Gallic repertoire of shoulder shrugs and chest-beatings, then drifts around trying to see how many defenders he can humiliate with his box of tricks when a quick ball in might produce another easy, if not his preferred choice of spectacular goal.

The second half was much like the first, Arsenal dominant and Lokomotiv oddly defensive for a side who had to win and were losing. Amusement came from a rare Dennis Bergkamp header. He must be the worst header of a ball for a man of his technical genius that there has ever been. Truly awful. He always looks the part, rising like a gazelle to knock it in the corner. Only when the ball connects with his bonce, it flies off in completely the wrong direction. Or as one radio commentator put it, 'Bergkamp rose like a salmon and finished like a tart.' After 65 minutes, Vieira lost the ball in midfield then hared back to reclaim it, passed quickly to Bergkamp, who in turn found Henry on the edge of their box. With his back to the goal, he spotted Freddie running in behind him and hooked it beautifully over his shoulder into the path of the flying Swede who poked it home. 2-0. Two more assists for Thierry, who now makes as many goals as he scores. The Clock End began to sing 'We've got the best player in the world' which seems about right – though if there has ever been a better all-round player than Zidane, I'd like to see him play. Wenger even acknowledged a 'one Arsène Wenger' chant which was very unusual and indicated the warm front blowing in from the deep Champions League chill of a month before.

This was a great performance by a team determined to prove they can hack it with the big boys of Europe. The players look meaner than normal, leaner too. They have matured this season from rookies to real contenders. Perhaps the best accolade is that nobody will want to draw us in the knock-out stage.

**Arsenal:** Jens Lehmann, Ashley Cole, Pascal Cygan, Sol Campbell, Patrick Vieira (yellow card), Fredrik Ljungberg, Kolo Touré, Robert Pires, Gilberto, Dennis Bergkamp, Nwankwo Kanu 74, Thierry Henry. Subs not used: Graham Stack, Martin Keown, Ray Parlour, Edu, Jeremie Aliadiere, Sylvain Wiltord

**Lokomtiv Moscow:** Sergei Ovchinnikov, Sergei Ignashevich, Dmitri Sennikov, Vadim Evseev (yellow card), Oleg Pashinin, Vladimir Maminov, Dmitrij Khokhlov, Dmitri Loskov, Jacob Leksetho (red card), Mikhail Ashvetia, Winston Parks 45, Maksim Buznikin, Sergey Gurenko 45. Subs not used: Ruslan Nigmatullin, Gennadi Nizhegorodov, Malkhaz Asatiani, Jorge Wagner, Lessa Leandro

**Robert Pires 12, Fredrik Ljungberg 67**

## 11th December 2003

A disappointing day for Arsenal fans – Pascal Cygan has extended his contract at the club. I'm sorry, but he is Frank le Boeuf without the talent. A big, bald French lump with a good heart but a clumsy slow style that spells trouble against anyone half decent. Wenger needs to buy a new centre-half soon. Either that or Touré needs to show he can step up a gear. His improvement is amazing, but he's still an over-excitable pup.

**12th December 2003**

We've drawn Celta de Vigo in the last sixteen of the Champions
League which is fantastic news because they are third from bottom
in La Liga and having a mare of a season. The only names in their
team I recognise are Silvinho, who was axed from Arsenal when
Ashley Cole erupted into the first team, and Edu. He's not our one
but this will be very, very tricky for the commentators. Particularly
if Edu brings down Edu in the box and Edu takes the penalty as
Edu gets sent off. United have drawn Porto, who are dangerous and
have a hilariously arrogant manager in Mourinho.

**13th December 2003**

Freddie Ljungberg's PR woman rings me to say his Calvin Klein
pictures are all over Times Square in New York. They won't have a
clue who he is, of course, but I suspect they will all react the same
way anyway: 'Christ, look at the size of that.'

SUNDAY
**14**
DECEMBER

**Blackburn Rovers**
**PREMIERSHIP, HIGHBURY**
**RESULT: 1-0 WIN**
My location: at game

We came out looking way off the pace, lethargic and generally
disinterested. Not a clever mindset against any side managed by
Graeme 'You's looking at me son?' Souness. Dwight Yorke, who always
laughs however bad his form is, missed a fantastic chance in the first
minute, shooting wide after Campbell missed a ball into the box. Three
years ago Yorke would have buried that, but too much Jordan has
clearly dimmed his powers somewhat. A few minutes later Lehmann
came out to snatch one off Yorke's head, one of many good catches he
made in the match. And yet there is still a permanent sense of unease
about our mad German. He looks fit, strong, determined and has a lot

of obvious ability. But every time he comes out for the ball we all grab our rosary beads and say a few Hail Marys. Even the atheists. Perhaps we are just too used to 'Safe Hands' Seaman who was almost invisible most of the time, so easy did he make his work seem.

After the early wake-up calls, we stepped it up a gear and began to dominate the game completely. We were helped by scoring in the 11th minute. There is no doubt that if we score quickly against teams like Blackburn then they have to be more attacking, and have to actually venture into our half occasionally, if only to admire the well-mown grass. If we don't score early on then the opposition sniff a draw, pack their defence with their whole team, and it becomes the Alamo – with our boys raining down on eleven trembling opponents and trying to scramble a goal through an impenetrable wall.

Our goal came when Touré, playing at right-back today, got the ball on halfway and to a great cry of 'skin him' proceeded to do just that and storming past Gresko like he was a snowman. When he runs like this Touré looks awesome, an electric, ox-like human force. The potential is incredible. He could be the best defender in the world in three years, he is that good. And in any position at the back. He's also a quiet, God-fearing, polite young lad who smiles a lot and can't believe his luck. Wenger doesn't just pick great players, he picks great attitude. They all fit the new Arsenal brand. Lean, mean, athletic, and utterly professional in every way. Touré careered into their box and found Bergkamp who brought it down, nutmegged their defender and slotted it past Freidel. Great skill from a player who is now playing better this season than for several years. We should have had a couple more in the first half, Pires fluffing a good ball from Freddie, then Vieira doing the same after a neat Freddie/Henry one-two. Pires hit the post with one of his now trademark curlers, Bergkamp was the victim of two ridiculous offside decisions when he was clean through – and Freddie then hit Pires on the head, which is the politest way of describing what happened to another absurd attempt at a header by the Frenchman. Hardly anyone in this wonderteam can head the ball at all, quite bizarre.

In the second half Blackburn had a goal disallowed, which stunned the home fans as it was turned down by referee Andy D'Urso, who is pretty universally loathed at Highbury. Souness was enraged, as ever: 'If that had happened in front of the North Bank, Stretford End or the Kop for the home team it would have stood.' But he reserved his real ire for Pires, who he claimed got two of his players booked with his diving. 'He just goes down too easily,' he sneered. Which is what Pires certainly would have done had he accepted Souness' invitation to come and have a word in the dugouts about the second incident. Lehmann dropped one on the six-yard line just to hasten the heartbeats towards the end but we hung on, and with Chelsea losing at home to Bolton, we went back to the top. It is going to be a rollercoaster season, no question. But we are still unbeaten, and we are beginning to look like we know how good we are.

**Arsenal:** Jens Lehmann, Pascal Cygan (yellow card), Ashley Cole, Sol Campbell, Patrick Vieira, Fredrik Ljungberg, Edu 84, Robert Pires, Kolo Touré, Gilberto (yellow card), Dennis Bergkamp, Ray Parlour 74, Thierry Henry. Subs not used: Graham Stack, Martin Keown, Nwankwo Kanu

**Blackburn Rovers:** Brad Friedel, Craig Short, Andy Todd (yellow card), Lucas Neill, Markus Babbel (yellow card), Dino Baggio 82, Vratislav Gresko (yellow card), Steven Reid 46, Brett Emerton, Kerimoglou Tugay, Barry Ferguson (yellow card), Dwight Yorke, Paul Gallagher, Andy Cole 57. Subs not used: Peter Enckelman, Garry Flitcroft

**Dennis Bergkamp 11**

## 15th December 2003

Thierry Henry comes second to Zinadine Zidane in the FIFA World Player of the Year contest. The voting went: Zidane 264, Henry 186, Ronaldo 176. And although there may be cries of fury from parts of Islington, I think it is the right result. Our man is playing out of his skin, but Zidane has been doing that for five years now *and* winning major trophies including the European Cup. Thierry knows in his heart that Zidane is better, for the moment. But the gap is closing, and Henry is certainly now the world's best striker, of that there can be little doubt. To put things in perspective, he didn't even win the *French* competition for European player of the year, losing to the Czech midfield genius Pavel Nedved.

## West Bromwich Albion
**LEAGUE CUP, THE HAWTHORNS**
**RESULT: 0-2 WIN**

My location: *Mirror* features party

With a trophy looming, more of the big boys played tonight –
Lauren, Parlour, Keown, Edu. But there were still six kids out there
and they again gave a Premiership team a good stuffing in
appalling conditions of howling gale-force wind and rain. Kanu
scored a simple tap-in, then came a ridiculous ten-minute addition
to half-time while an injured linesman was replaced. The rules state
that whoever takes over as 4th official must be qualified to be a
linesman and of course nobody had thought this might ever be
necessary so there was nobody to do it. Step forward top referee
Dermot Gallagher, who was watching in the stands, to fill in. It all
then got very exciting when the existing referee himself got injured
and nearly had to go off – which would have led to Gallagher
possibly running the line in his smart suit. Alas it wasn't to be and
the ref recovered. Aliadiere made it two and we move onto the semi-
finals. Wenger likes trophies even more than he likes talented
young kids. Stand by for the A-team cavalry …

**Arsenal:** Graham Stack, Efstathios Tavlaridis (yellow card), Martin Keown, Gael Clichy, Edu, Ray Parlour, Lauren, Jeremie, Aliadiere, Francesc Fabregas Cesc 73, Nwankwo Kanu, Sylvain Wiltord, David Bentley, Jerome Thomas 81. Subs not used: Rami Shaaban, Frankie Simek, Michal Papadopulos

**West Bromwich Albion:** Russell Hoult, Neil Clement, Ronnie Wallwork, Joost Volmer, Phil Gilchrist 65, Bernt Haas, Thomas Gaardsoe, James O'Connor, Artim Sakiri 71, Sean Gregan, Andy Johnson, Lee Hughes 39, Scott Dobie, Rob Hulse. Subs not used: Joe Murphy, Adam Chambers, James Chambers

**Kanu 25, Jeremie Aliadiere 57**


## 17th December 2003
We've drawn Middlesbrough in the semi-final which will be tricky
because they will play their first team and be desperate to win.

## Bolton Wanderers
### PREMIERSHIP, REEBOK STADIUM
### RESULT: 1-1 DRAW

My Location: hungover after work party – London

Bolton, like the appalling hangovers I suffer after office Christmas parties, are always bloody awkward to shift. I still have sweat-drenched nightmares about our game at the Reebok last season, watching in a Barbados bar at 7 a.m. local time, going 2-0 up over three coffees and a banana split, then sinking into a sea of Pina Colada as Bolton scored twice in the last 15 minutes, kicked us to pieces, and wrecked our entire season.

This year they've been playing well and they tore into us from the start. Campbell and Touré held them off well, and 12 minutes into the second half we scored thanks to Bergkamp slipping another perfect pass through to Henry, who flicked it on to Freddie who shot – Jaaskelainen dropped the save and Pires scored the rebound. Quick, clinical, 1-0. But Bolton didn't give up and kept at us, and finally got a well-deserved equaliser when Pedersen volleyed home from a Cygan-headed clearance (he is not getting any better).

It pissed with rain all night, which it always seems to do in Bolton whatever sunny gloss the locals try and put on it. But that was no excuse for our poor performance. Too many of our big names go missing when it rains, or snows, or when the wind gets up or it's just freezing cold. I only have to see those mittens come on to know what kind of day we are going to endure. I would always pick a team for bad weather that included Parlour and Keown. They *love* it when it gets dirty and horrible.

We are now seventeen games unbeaten – our second best start to a League season ever since 1947–48. The only longer run was in 1990–91, and we won the title in both those years. But United have gone top after beating Spurs, and we are only ahead of Chelsea for alphabetical reasons. Could it be that we might go the whole season unbeaten and not win the title, or not even come second? It could happen.

**Arsenal:** Jens Lehmann, Pascal Cygan, Gael Clichy, Sol Campbell, Patrick Vieira (yellow card), Fredrik Ljungberg, Kolo Touré, Gilberto, Robert Pires, Dennis Bergkamp, Ray Parlour 69, Thierry Henry (yellow card). Subs not used: Graham Stack, Martin Keown, Edu, Nwankwo Kanu

**Bolton Wanderers:** Jussi Jaaskelainen, Simon Charlton, Emerson Thome, Ivan Campo (yellow card), Ibrahim Ba 78, Nicky Hunt, Jay-Jay Okocha, Youri Djorkaeff, Kevin Nolan (yellow card), Henrik Pedersen 75, Per Frandsen, Ricardo Gardner, Kevin Davies. Subs not used: Kevin Poole, Anthony Barness, Stelios Giannakopoulos

**Robert Pires 57, Henrik Pederson 83**

FRIDAY
**26**
DECEMBER

# Wolverhampton Wanderers
## PREMIERSHIP, HIGHBURY
## RESULT: 3-0 WIN
My location: at game

I like the festive games. There's always a party atmosphere in the grounds, and usually a lot more kids watching. And the matches often produce a glut of goals. Presumably as a result of all that pent-up fury in the players for having to train on Christmas Day. Though I have never been too sure how bad they feel about that. On the various newspapers I have worked on, there was a huge stampede to work Christmas Day and get away from all the chaos and enforced familial 'fun'.

Cygan was given another start today and looked even dodgier than usual. Wenger has been loyal to him, but he just isn't up to the job of winning a major title and never will be. As soon as Lauren is fit, Touré should go back next to Sol in the centre and stay there. In the 13th minute Freddie won a free-kick, Henry forced a diving save and from the resulting corner Vieira knocked it in off Jody Craddock, who stood, rooted to the spot, like he'd just been asked to sleep with Edwina Currie. Wolves had been an astonishing 20-1 against beating us today but even those odds looked ungenerous when the dozy Craddock let Vieira rip the ball off him in midfield and watched our captain rampage into the penalty area, setting up Henry, who fell as he hit it but still banged it in. Just to compound

his misery, Craddock then sliced high and wide with an easy shot at
the other end. Near the end, Henry was left one-on-one with Oleg
Luzhny, currently on loan from Arsenal to Wolves. Now Oleg,
nicknamed 'The Horse' at Highbury because he never stops running
– albeit in a manner more suited to the prefix 'cart' than 'wonder' –
is a great guy who never gave anything but his best for us. But Oleg
against Thierry is up there with Mike Tyson and Julius Francis in
the 'shall we take him straight to the hospital and forget about the
fight' school of challenges. Luzhny went one way and then the other
(without actually going anywhere in the end), and was left helpless
as Henry smashed an angled shot into the left-hand corner.

As if to emphasise the enormous gulf in quality between the teams,
there was still time for a Dean Sturridge cameo where he soared to
head in a cross from eight yards out and managed to drill it right
back to the guy who had crossed it instead. Manager David Jones
said afterwards that his team had to 'keep believing'. Keep believing
what, though, Dave? That they are the worst team in the Premiership
by quite a long way? Because that's exactly what they are. United
won, but Chelsea got stuffed by Charlton. It's getting interesting ...

**Arsenal:** Jens Lehmann, Pascal Cygan, Kolo Touré, Gael Clichy, Sol Campbell, Ray Parlour, Patrick Vieira (yellow card),Fredrik Ljungberg, Edu 71, Robert Pires, Jeremie Aliadiere 71, Dennis Bergkamp, Thierry Henry. Subs not used: Graham Stack, Martin Keown, Nwankwo Kanu

**Wolverhampton Wanderers:** Michael Oakes, Oleg Luzhny (yellow card), Lee Naylor (yellow card), Paul Butler (yellow card), Jody Craddock, Alex Rae (yellow card), Colin Cameron, Henri Camara, Dean Sturridge 85, Mark Kennedy, Paul Ince (yellow card), Kenny Miller, Shaun Newton 76. Subs not used: Andy Marshall, Mark Clyde, Steffen Iversen.

**Jody Craddock 13 (own goal), Thierry Henry 20, 89**


## 27th December 2003

Wenger says he is not intending to buy anyone when the transfer
window reopens in January. But he did suggest he had money to do
so if he changed his mind – so the usual rumours have begun about
Trezeguez, Kluivert, Ronaldo and Totti. None of these will be true
because Wenger doesn't buy expensive proven stars. He prefers
cheap gold nuggets, and Arsenal fans have grown to appreciate this
and eagerly await the signing of someone we have never heard of.

## Southampton

**PREMIERSHIP, ST MARY'S STADIUM**

**RESULT: 0-1 WIN**

MONDAY

**29**

DECEMBER

My location: a sports bar, Tenerife

Southampton are always a tough side to beat, and have in manager Gordon Strachan one of the game's greatest characters. Take his quote recently: 'I have discovered that when you go to Anfield or Highbury or Old Trafford, it pays not to wear a coloured shirt because everyone can see the stains as the pressure mounts. I always wear a white shirt so nobody sees you sweat.' His on-field tactics are just as clever as his *bon mots*, and this will be a massive test of our unbeaten record. It's utterly bizarre that we still haven't lost a game but are not top.

Our back four look suspect again. Touré stays at right-back, Lauren not playing yet, and Cygan's still there. What does this all mean? I just hope Lauren is still not quite ready, and that when he is he will return to right-back. The Cameroon star is one of our real unsung heroes. Like his predecessor Lee Dixon, nobody ever chants his name but he never lets us down. He is powerful, skilful, runs all day and has a great temperament.

The Saints are always a tricky side, their crowd are usually well up for it, and in Beattie they have a very dangerous British striker, who can mix it with the best defenders and who scores a lot of goals. Sure enough, he was all over our back four and came close to winning a penalty early on. After half an hour, Bergkamp spied Henry, who diagonally found a flying Pires who touched it once before slipping it past Niemi. It was nearly two minutes later when Freddie floated one onto Bergkamp's head. I say nearly not because it was intercepted just before it landed but because even if it had reached Dennis, the chances of him scoring with his cranium were somewhere south of zero.

As time ticked by, Southampton ran at us more but our defence was strong, Clichy in particular stifling several moves down the right. He is like Cole, small, quick and fearless. He also loves to attack. Its hard to imagine how worried we all were when Nigel Winterburn retired, especially given how ludicrously one-footed he was.

We hung on for a crucial win, and the joy was only slightly marred by a piece of rank idiocy from Lehmann, who fell to the ground catching the ball as the final whistle went and rather than celebrating took it upon himself to stand up and throw the ball straight into Kevin Phillips' back. Phillips did not appear to have done anything to deserve this, and it was a clear act of petulance from Herr Lehmann which went some way to showing why he's been sent off five times in his career. Because the whistle had gone, he couldn't be sent off … but he could be reported. Ominously, ref Steve Dunn said, 'Afterwards Lehmann came in and apologised to me – that's nice but it won't change what's in my report …' Southampton fans booed Lehmann off with cries of 'Same old Arsenal, always cheating,' to which our travelling support volleyed back: 'Same old Arsenal, always WINNING'. Game, set and match.

**Arsenal:** Jens Lehmann, Pascal Cygan, Gael Clichy, Sol Campbell, Ray Parlour, Patrick Vieira, Fredrik Ljungberg, Edu 73, Kolo Touré, Robert Pires, Lauren 87, Dennis Bergkamp, Nwankwo Kanu 74, Thierry Henry. Subs not used: Graham Stack, Martin Keown

**Southampton:** Antti Niemi, Danny Higginbotham, Michael Svensson, Fitz Hall, Leandre Griffit, Brett Ormerod 57, David Prutton, Rory Delap, Paul Telfer, Neil McCann 78, Kevin Phillips, James Beattie, Chris Baird., Darren Kenton 59. Subs not used: Paul Jones, Chris Marsden

**Robert Pires 35**

# JANUARY

'Are you coming
back for more?'

THE CLOCK END

## 4th January 2004

Apparently we are now 'definitely' signing Juan Pablo Angel from
Villa, presumably because he has had one or two reasonable games
lately. I reckon this all stems from Wenger saying 'I'd like an angel
on my Christmas tree', and there are the proverbial two hopes of
him signing this bandana-clad Columbian ... no hope and Bob Hope.
Kluivert has been seen 'eyeing houses in Avenell Road' and
Cameroon star Samuel Eto'o has entered the gossip frame, the
theory being that because Real Madrid still own a 50 per cent stake
in him they will use him as bait to get Henry. I haven't read yet
that Lauren is his secret half-brother but surely that's only a matter
of time.

SUNDAY

**4**

JANUARY

## Leeds United
### FA CUP, ELLAND ROAD
### RESULT: 1-4 WIN
My location: watching TV in London

The one thing we didn't need to do was gift Leeds an early goal, so
naturally the one thing we immediately did was gift Leeds an early
goal. Sol passed it back firmly to Lehmann, who pushed it forward a
little too hard with his first touch and then watched in horror as
Viduka, kindly consenting to play today, raced in with surprising
pace for such a vast Australian slug and challenged him. Panicky
Lehmann, whose first thought was probably to chin him, got his
boot there first and kicked it hard – unfortunately straight into
Viduka and straight back into the goal. Complete farce. But at least
it woke us up. In the 25th minute, Kanu set Freddie free, who raced
away and crossed to Henry who shot first time from the centre of
the box and scored a sublime goal. Rule No. 1 with Henry is 'don't
wind him up', but Bakke blatantly obstructed him a few minutes
later, the ref ignored it, Bakke had a few gloating words and Henry

then sprinted 60 yards back like an enraged gazelle to foil a
dangerous Leeds attack near our penalty area. His gander was up
and that spelled big trouble for already deeply troubled Leeds. Six
minutes later Vieira passed wide left to Henry who squared it
straight into Edu – who in turn slid and stretched to reach the ball,
and just got there to deflect it past their keeper. 2-0. Near the end,
we brought on Parlour, Touré and Pires just to really demoralise
our beaten opponents. Henry almost immediately laid on Pires for a
third goal, and the D'Artagnan lookalike returned the favour by
chipping in for Touré to jab it home with his foot raised high. One
for all and all for one! The scoreline was a bit flattering but we're
through and that's all that matters in the cup. Got to feel for Leeds
though, their fans were amazing again today – persistently loud,
positive and unbowed. Their players, Viduka in particular, don't
deserve them. Wenger was delighted afterwards saying: 'Some of
our passing today was brilliant and the goals we scored were
brilliant. You can see the players enjoy playing together.' He then
really stuck the knife into Leeds' tormented carcass by revealing
that Henry wouldn't even have played if Aliadiere had passed a
fitness test. It really has come to something when Leeds are not
considered a big enough team to justify our strongest side. But on
this showing it's true, they're not.

Henry showed his kind side by offering his shirt to 18-year-old
James Milner at the end of the match. I've noticed an increasingly
unseemly scramble for his shirt now, so it was a typically generous
touch from a guy who can be humble. When he really tries hard.
Continuing his magnanimous performance, Henry urged caution as
all around waxed lyrical. 'Last season, a lot of people were talking
about us winning this and winning that, and we only won the FA
Cup,' he said after the Gunners stretched their unbeaten run in the
competition to 15 games. 'Let's keep our feet on the ground, enjoy it
and see what we can do. But we are not trying to beat any records.
We are far from another FA Cup final. We have a lot of stuff to

focus on with the Premiership, then the Champions League and when the FA Cup comes around again we will focus on that.' He's right, but that won't stop the pundits lauding us from the hilltops. We are playing sumptuous stuff at the moment and everyone knows it. Lehmann's clanger was the only dampener on the day. 'I made the wrong decision, made a mistake and it was a freakish goal,' he explained. 'Unfortunately it happens and I am very sorry about it. I said sorry to my team-mates in the dressing room at half-time, but they told me not to worry.'

**Arsenal:** Jens Lehmann, Martin Keown, Sol Campbell, Ashley Cole, Patrick Vieira, Fredrik Ljungberg, Kolo Touré 81, Lauren, Gilberto (yellow card), Edu, Ray Parlour 80, Thierry Henry, Nwankwo Kanu, Robert Pires 81. Subs not used: Rami Shaaban, David Bentley

**Leeds United:** Paul Robinson, Dominic Matteo, Ian Harte, Michael Duberry, Frazer Richardson, Matthew Kilgallon, James Milner, Aaron Lennon 84, Eirik Bakke (yellow card), Lamine Sakho 70, David Batty, Alan Smith (yellow card), Mark Viduka. Subs not used: Scott Carson, Salomon Olembe, Seth Johnson

Thierry Henry 26, Edu 33, Robert Pires 87, Kolo Touré 90, **Mark Viduka 8**

## 5th January 2004

We draw Middlesbrough in the Cup. Which means we now have to play them four times in January. We play them at home in the league on the 10th, then home again on the 20th in the League Cup semi first leg. Another home game in the FA Cup on the 24th or 25th, and finally away in the second leg of the semi on the 28th. That's four January matches out of seven against the same team, including three in a row. Hard not to feel that the FA Cup tie is destined for a replay.

## Everton

### PREMIERSHIP, GOODISON PARK
### RESULT: 1-1 DRAW
My location: watching TV in London

We started brightly but then Everton began to get stuck into us, primarily through that great big growling prime cut of Scottish beef

Duncan Ferguson. He's just a menace in the air, genuinely one of the best players for mixing it in the clouds you could wish for. But against the run of play we took the lead after some smart thinking by Freddie who slipped in behind their defence and fed Kanu who scored a goal. He's doing this quite a lot at the moment but still looks out of sorts and too slow. But I will always love him. Ten minutes later we were ourselves caught cold when Kilbane whipped in a great cross to wonderboy Wayne Rooney. It was genuinely one of those moments where it was comfortably easier to score than miss but 'Britain's greatest player ever, or at least since Gazza anyway' headed it wide. I suspect there is not a lot going on in that head and it is therefore rather hard, which might explain the lack of control.

Cygan was, again, a total liability today. As the game went on he was more and more involved, and more and more unreliable. If he's not trying to dribble out of the box like Zidane then he's being beaten in the air by Ferguson or losing it on the ground to Jeffers. The latter took advantage of one such lapse and got a shot in which was parried only as far as Radzinski, who scored. Jeffers looked sharp and quick, and very much the Fox in the Box we thought we had bought for that £8 million. If he hadn't been so injury prone, and so stupid in that Community Shield match, then it might have worked. He and Henry linked up well in their few games together. A draw was about right today, but United won away to Bolton. So we are twenty games unbeaten but the Mancs are pulling away from us by either winning or losing and avoiding our numerous draws.

**Arsenal:** Jens Lehmann, Pascal Cygan, Sol Campbell, Ashley Cole, Robert Pires, Patrick Vieira, Fredrik Ljungberg (yellow card), Gilberto 89, Ray Parlour (yellow card), Kolo Touré, Lauren 20, Thierry Henry, Nwankwo Kanu, Edu 81. Subs not used: Rami Shaaban, Jeremie Aliadiere

**Everton:** Nigel Martyn, David Unsworth, Alan Stubbs, Gary Naysmith, Tony Hibbert, Li Tie, Tobias Linderoth 45, Lee Carsley, Kevin Kilbane, Francis Jeffers 70, Duncan Ferguson, Wayne Rooney, Tomasz Radzinski, Kevin Campbell 87. Subs not used: Steve Simonsen, Joseph Yobo
**Kanu 29, Tomasz Radzinski 75**

## 10th January 2004

Lehmann has been charged for his ball-throwing nonsense at St
Mary's and he will have to be banned. He was blatantly in the
wrong and made it even worse afterwards by saying: 'I don't have a
problem with communication but get frustrated by my lack of
communication with the ref.' We can hardly feign surprise, though.
If you sign someone with his extraordinary disciplinary record then
this kind of thing is going to happen. And some of it is quite
amusing. There's a touch of the Grobbelaar to his work, definitely.

**SATURDAY**

**10**

**JANUARY**

## Middlesbrough
### PREMIERSHIP, HIGHBURY
### RESULT: 4-1 WIN
My location: at game

'Are you coming back for more?' queried the Clock End to the hordes
from Teesside making the first of three trips to Highbury this
month. And the unfortunate answer for them was 'Yes, I'm afraid
we are.' Without Mendieta or Juninho, Boro looked pretty tame
today, and Southgate is beginning to look his age at the back. To be
honest, Schwarzer was man of the match in their goal and it could
have been eight or nine. I often think that, but it never happens.
This Arsenal team is really going to destroy someone soon, just rip
them to pieces for ninety minutes with no mercy. And the score will
be something like 11-0, with Henry getting six and laying on four.

Every few minutes we had another chance. And that Mensa-
brained quarter-wit Danny Mills decided to help his team by
winding up Henry after Ehiogu brought down Vieira in the box,
standing in front of Thierry and looking generally 'threatening'.
Words were had, Vieira ran over to split them up and Thierry
nearly broke the net with his kick. Henry laughed in Mills' face and
Pires trotted over to give him a little congratulatory nudge too,

followed by Campbell who also wished to proffer his thoughts to his England colleague. It is hard to imagine what goes on in a player's mind when he thinks: 'Oh, I know what I'll do, I'll really wind up Thierry Henry and see if that works'. The Arsenal boys don't even do that in training because they know he will only humiliate them. To compound Mills' misery, Pires nutmegged him beautifully a few minutes later, to general hilarity around the ground. As half-time approached, Henry smashed a free-kick which went in off Quedrue. 2-0.

Second half and much of the same. Twelve minutes in and Henry tried to put Kanu through, the ball fell nicely to Pires who passed it in for number three. Five minutes later and Freddie latched onto a partially saved Kanu shot to score the fourth. This was his fiftieth goal for the club, and earned him a big group hug in the centre circle. I love Freddie – he has the *corps d'esprit* of this team infused in his entrails. It was game over, but not before some last entertainment from Mills. Maccarone went down in the box in a challenge with Lehmann, and clearly wanted to take the kick himself. Mills, though, had other ideas – and was seen demanding to take it, as if in one last desperate effort to atone for his miserable antics all afternoon. With a minute to go, Henry raced to their corner flag and performed the move of the day – a fantastic back-heeled nutmeg to utterly humiliate the victim. Yes, you've guessed it ... taxi for Danny Mills, please.

So, two Boro games gone and its 8-1. Bet they're *really* looking forward to seeing us again. We go top again thanks to our position in the alphabet, reaffirming that very sensible decision to drop the word 'Woolwich' from our name all those years ago. But Aliadiere's out with medial ligament damage to his knee, and with Kanu away at the African Cup of Nations and both Bergkamp and Wiltord not back for two weeks we have a bit of a forward crisis. Well as much as a crisis can be when the one remaining fit striker is Thierry Henry, of course, but if he gets felled then we are in deep trouble.

Despite this, Wenger is still saying he's not looking to buy. I can't
believe this. If we are going to actually win the Champions League
then we've got to go and get ourselves a new forward who can help
Henry drive us home. Wenger's bluffing. Watch this space.

**Arsenal:** Jens Lehmann, Pascal Cygan, Sol Campbell, Ashley Cole, Patrick Vieira, Fredrik Ljungberg, Ray Parlour 72, Lauren, Robert Pires, Edu 67, Gilberto (yellow card), Jeremie Aliadiere, Nwankwo Kanu 45, Thierry Henry. Subs not used: Graham Stack, Martin Keown

**Middlesbrough:** Mark Schwarzer, Danny Mills, Gareth Southgate, Ugo Ehiogu, Chris Riggott 45, Franck Queudrue, Doriva (yellow card), Juninho 62, Stewart Downing, George Boateng, Boudewijn Zenden, Szilard Nemeth, Joseph-Desire Job, Massimo Maccarone 62. Subs not used: Bradley Jones, Stuart Parnaby

**Thierry Henry 38 (pen), Franck Quedrue 45 (own goal), Robert Pires 57, Fredrik Ljungberg 68, Massimo Maccarone 86 (pen)**

## 13th January 2004

David Seaman retired from football today. A sad postscript to a
brilliant career. Wenger knew he was finished at the top level which
is why he let him go, but Seaman – like so many before him –
thought he had a bit more in his tank and went to Manchester City
on a one-year contract. He looked old, wooden and immobile for
much of this season and in the end his recurring shoulder injury
became insurmountable and after he was subbed 14 minutes into
City's loss at Portsmouth that was enough for him and, probably,
for Kevin Keegan. He'll get a load of crap poured on his head now
which is unfair and unnecessary. Seaman was a class act. Big,
strong, reliable, and, when he had to be, a brilliant instinctive
keeper. His trick was to never get noticed much. He'd often go a
whole game at Arsenal without you realising he'd done anything.
He was always cool, unruffled, and ready with that disarming smile.
All right, the ponytail was a massive mistake, a really gigantic,
horrendous sartorial gaffe. And we could probably have done
without the *Hello* magazine spreads about his lovely family life
when we all know he barely has anything to do with his two sons by
his first marriage. And I could certainly have done with not being in
Paris when ex-Spurs irritant Nayim beat him from the halfway line
in the last seconds of the Cup Winners' Cup Final. But he played 75

times for England, 563 times for Arsenal, and won nine trophies, and was without any doubt one of the top five post-war English goalkeepers. Anyone that actually signs his name 'Safe Hands' obviously needs a little quiet lesson in ego-management. But that's what he was most of the time. A safe pair of hands. We were lucky to have him, and I wish him well.

## Aston Villa
**PREMIERSHIP, VILLA PARK**
**RESULT: 0-2 WIN**
My location: a sports bar, Tenerife

Angel will be up for this, to try and show Wenger he's the right man to play upfront with Henry. And David O'Leary will be equally up for it to prove he has what it takes to be the next Arsenal manager. Villa started well, Angel going close from a Hitzlsperger free-kick. Then Vieira began to boss the midfield in a way that suggests he is back to full fitness. What a monstrously powerful force 'Paddy' is when he's like this. He's so quick across the ground, so relentless in his pursuit of the ball, so hard to dispossess when he gets it, and so fluid when he breaks forward. Everything revolves around him when he's fired up and he has grown into a truly great replacement for Tony Adams as skipper. Someone the players revere and look to constantly on the pitch for advice and encouragement. He was a hothead for years but by giving him the armband Wenger cleverly realised the sense of responsibility that would bring. What's curious is that off the pitch you would be hard pushed to meet a kinder, more generous, gentle and lovely guy than Patrick Vieira. When my two older sons, then aged ten and six, met him in the players' lounge he treated them like they were his own without knowing who the hell I was. I was struck by his nobility and total lack of any aggression. Very hard to equate with his on-field image. But then all great warriors were usually softies off the battlefield.

Pires had a brilliant curling shot from 25 yards tipped over the bar, and forced another good save from Sorensen soon after. In the 17th minute Henry was clipped in the face by Samuel and got predictably booed and called a cheat by the Villa fans for looking hurt. The sad thing is that he *was* hurt, quite obviously and quite badly. It's too much to hope those boo-boys will feel a little churlish when they see pictures of blood streaming from Henry's busted lip on TV later. But it is a bit pathetic that someone as gracious and honest as Henry on a football field has to put up with this kind of nonsense. Then came one of the moments of the season. Vieira burst through and won a free-kick, a few yards outside the box to the left of centre. The ref, Mark Halsey, stood talking to Henry and Vieira as the Villa wall arranged itself. Angel, in one of the least impressive contributions to gaining a transfer ever seen, was actually kneeling down doing his bootlaces up. Henry suddenly looked up, asked Halsey if he could go, got the answer 'yes' and kicked the ball straight in the corner of the goal. Cue complete mayhem, with every Villa player having what appeared to be a spontaneous heart attack, and O'Leary looked like he wanted to kill everyone in sight. Which was fairly ironic given that it was O'Leary himself who was manager at Leeds when Ian Harte did just this to us at Highbury. Sitting in a bar in Tenerife as I was at the time, surrounded by Villa fans, it was clear that most of them thought they'd been served a terrible injustice. They hadn't. The truth is that Henry asked the ref for permission to take the kick, got permission, and took it. It was a piece of pure genius from a player whose confidence grows with every game and whose eye for creative artistry like this gets ever more vivid.

When Villa later got a similar free-kick from a similar position, Freddie stood over the ball to make sure there was no revenge attack. He got well jeered for it, of course, but I thought it was very astute of the Swede. A minute later Kanu weaved his way

Leeds, January: **Samba time as our Brazilian boys, Edu and Gilberto, enjoy themselves**

Middlesbrough, January:
**'You're crap and you know you are, Henry.' Danny Mills commits footballing suicide**

Aston Villa, January: **They shall not pass …** Sol, our rock, wins it again

Manchester City, February: 'What have we got here then?' Reyes makes a dazzling debut in the rain

Chelsea, February: 'Ole!' José Antonio fires in his thunderbolt against Chelsea, and even his teammates look impressed

Celta de Vigo, February: **'Anything Thierry can do …'** Edu scores a cracker

Blackburn, March: 'Come on then … if you're think you're good enough.' Henry and Cole throw down the gauntlet

Manchester United, March: 'Hey ref, I didn't mean to rest Thierry, can he come on now please?' Wenger isn't actually saying that but he should have been

Manchester United: Big, bad, German … the perfect goalkeeper for a team with our disciplinary record

Chelsea, April: 'Not again …' Vieira's hopes of winning the Champions League take another dent

Mark Thompson/Getty Images

Liverpool, April: 'We're not finished yet.' Henry celebrates his stunning hattrick

Tottenham, April: **'Unbeatable, unbelievable!'** Arsène finally lets his hair down at Spurs

Tottenham: **''71, we did it again, '71, we did it again.'** The ultimate nightmare for Spurs as our boys celebrate in their own back yard

Leicester, May:
'Phew! That was torture.' Henry with the Premiership trophy after we scrape home against Leicester

**Keown Testimonial:** In my dreams … Henry and Wright together for Keown's testimonial

**Keown Testimonial:** 'A monkey's head, but a lion's heart.' Farewell to Martin Keown

brilliantly into the box, knocked it forward and ran into Mellberg. It was a harsh penalty but there was definitely contact. The keeper nearly saved it from Henry but the ball slid in off his left-hand post. Villa fans took it well, chanting '2-0 to the referee'.

The win took us two points clear after United, incomprehensibly, lost to Wolves. Daylight, not much, but daylight. The row over Henry's first goal raged all night. David O'Leary, the Villa manager, reported that his players had been told to retreat the full ten yards and wait for the whistle, but the referee's recollections differed: 'I gave the option to Thierry Henry: Do you want to take it quickly or do you want the wall ten yards?' he reported. 'His reply was "a quick free-kick". I stood back and made a quick signal for him to go on and take it – I didn't say to the Aston Villa players "move back ten yards". I can understand their frustration at conceding a goal that way but I'm under no obligation to inform the Aston Villa players that Henry is going to take a quick free-kick. You are under no obligation to give a whistle for any free-kick.' Henry was more direct: 'It's happened against us before, so I tried my luck today.' But O'Leary was oddly vague about *that* goal ... saying 'That happened a long time ago on a very emotional night and I can't remember the ins and outs of it ...' Of course you can't, David. Terrible thing when age creeps in and the memory fades like that, isn't it?

**Arsenal:** Jens Lehmann, Pascal Cygan, Sol Campbell, Ashley Cole, Patrick Vieira (yellow card), Fredrik Ljungberg, Ray Parlour 76, Lauren, Robert Pires, Edu 77, Gilberto, Thierry Henry, Nwankwo Kanu, Kolo Touré 76. Subs not used: Graham Stack, Martin Keown

**Aston Villa:** Thomas Sorensen, Ronny Johnsen, Jlloyd Samuel, Gareth Barry (yellow card), Liam Ridgewell 86, Mark Delaney (yellow card), Olof Mellberg (yellow card), Thomas Hitzlsperger, Lee Hendrie, Ulises de la Cruz 86, Marcus Allback, Peter Crouch 86, Juan Pablo Angel, Peter Whittingham (yellow card). Subs not used: Stefan Postma, Dion Dublin

**Thierry Henry 29, 53 (pen)**

**TUESDAY**
**20**
**JANUARY**

## Middlesbrough
**LEAGUE CUP, HIGHBURY**
**RESULT: 0-1 LOST**

My location: watching TV at home

Well they had to win one of them, didn't they. I am really struggling to engage in these League Cup games. I know it's a semi-final, I know you end up with a trophy if you win it, I know all this. But the truth is no serious football supporter of a big Premiership team gives a rat's arse about it. Boro, though, do care because it is their one chance of silverware. So they pack their team with superstars like Mendieta and Juninho and we have our usual mishmash of first and second-team players. Inevitably their goal comes from a pass from the Spaniard to the Brazilian. But I feel utterly unfazed by the defeat, or the prospect of going out of the tournament at this late stage. For the simple reason that if we got to the final then we'd have to play Henry and co., and they might pick up an injury or knacker themselves out for an important match. It's just not worth it and I know this is typical Arsenal fan arrogance, but it is the reality of being as good as we are in the competitions we are still challenging for.

**Arsenal:** Graham Stack, Pascal Cygan, Martin Keown, Gael Clichy, Edu, Gilberto, Ray Parlour, Kolo Touré, Nwankwo Kanu, David Bentley, Ryan Smith 73, Quincy Owusu Abeyie, Jerome Thomas 64. Subs not used: Craig Holloway, Ashley Cole, Olafur-Ingi Skulason

**Middlesbrough:** Mark Schwarzer, Chris Riggott, Danny Mills (yellow card), Ugo Ehiogu, Franck Queudrue (yellow card), Doriva, Gaizka Mendieta, Stuart Parnaby 80, George Boateng, Boudewijn Zenden, Juninho (yellow card), Massimo Maccarone, Joseph-Desire Job 77. Subs not used: Bradley Jones, Stewart Downing, Michael Ricketts

**Juninho 53**

## 21st January 2004

Wenger says there is a 20 per cent chance of a transfer window signing. Which still makes it sound unlikely, but has moved up from 'no chance' so probably means we are stalking someone on the quiet and don't want to cock it up with a blaze of fee-enhancing publicity. We're not as bad as Chelsea, where the mention of their name doubles valuations, but any hint that we are after someone and the selling club inevitably lashes a premium onto the asking price. Wenger's confession provokes another storm of speculation. Kluivert is the favourite but I just can't see it. On and off the pitch he is trouble, and that's not Wenger's preferred type of player. He's also very expensive, a bit past his best, and apparently desperate to come here. Three more reasons I don't think he will. Arsenal vice-chairman David Dein, one of the great unsung heroes of this club, has apparently been 'seen in Spain' but that's probably because he has a boat and a villa out there rather than anything suspicious. One thing Dein *is* adamant about is that Henry's going nowhere. 'Our message is simple,' he said. 'Hands off.' Can't see that stopping people trying, but Henry does seem remarkably loyal to the cause.

### 22nd January 2004
'We have not made an enquiry for Jermaine Defoe, we have not made a bid and we have no plans to make a bid.' – Arsène Wenger

### 23rd January 2004
'Defoe is one of the targets, yes.' – Arsène Wenger
    ... And they accuse the press of being duplicitous.

**SATURDAY**
**24**
**JANUARY**

## Middlesbrough
**FA CUP 4TH ROUND, HIGHBURY**
**RESULT: 4-1 WIN**
My location: at game

God, this is getting boring. Not just playing Middlesbrough, but thrashing them. Henry was rested for this too, showing where the FA Cup now figures in Wenger's priority list. Not very high. Interestingly, Boro rested Juninho because they want him fit for next week's League Cup second leg, which shows their own rather different priorities. We took the lead after some brilliant work by Parlour, who chased the ball all the way down the right wing, just caught it in time and cut it back for Bergkamp to score via a deflection from Riggot. They equalised through the hilariously named Joseph-Desire Job, which might well be the case for him if Boro keep getting stuffed like this. Our second came from a Bergkamp free-kick that fell to Vieira who laid it back for Freddie to squeeze it under Schwarzer's legs. High comedy a bit later when Lehmann gratuitously shoved our old friend Mills – and won a free-kick for it, to the Boro player's utter incredulity. Freddie made it three by heading in a Pires corner. Boro were showing obvious signs now of being completely hacked off with playing us so often. Boateng was booked for dissent then promptly slid studs-up into Parlour and got sent off. A neutral observer would think he had just had enough. Bentley, a cocky little devil who invites comparison with his idol Bergkamp, came on as sub and scored a wonderful goal – two touches on the left of their box, and a delicate chip under the bar. A really great goal, and didn't he know it. I like Bentley immediately, he's got that Rooney-style self-belief that all young players need now to survive and thrive in the Premiership.

**Arsenal:** Jens Lehmann, Ashley Cole, Robert Pires, Ray Parlour, Patrick Vieira, Gael Clichy 75, Fredrik Ljungberg, Lauren, Kolo Touré, Edu, Dennis Bergkamp, David Bentley 84. Subs not used: Graham Stack, Martin Keown, Quincy Owusu Abeyie

**Middlesbrough:** Mark Schwarzer, Danny Mills, Chris Riggott (yellow card), Franck Queudrue, Stuart Parnaby (yellow card), Stewart Downing, Szilard Nemeth, Boudewijn Zenden (yellow card), Gaizka Mendieta, George Boateng (red card), Michael Ricketts, Massimo Maccarone 73, Joseph-Desire Job, Juninho 73. Subs not used: Bradley Jones, Andrew Davies

Dennis Bergkamp 19, Fredrik Ljungberg 28, 68, David Bentley 90, **Joseph Desire-Job 23**

## 25th January 2004

Our ladies' team join in the fun by dishing out a 6-1 thrashing to ... yep, Middlesbrough.

## 27th January 2004

Blimey. We've only gone and spent £17 million signing Spanish wonderkid José Antonio Reyes from Sevilla. This is going down in

Spain like a lead bullwhip. Reyes is gaining God-like status out there for regularly humiliating top sides. Sevilla thrashed Real Madrid 4-1 recently, and Reyes scored two. Zidane was reported to have said to Redondo at one stage: 'What's that kid on – a f***ing motorbike?' Further reports aren't quite so encouraging, though. Apparently Reyes gained international renown of a sort when team-mate Francisco Gallardo bit his penis during an unorthodox goal celebration in a 4-0 win over Valladolid. Gallardo was charged by the Spanish FA with 'infringing the dignity and decorum of sport'. Reyes seemed remarkably cool about it. 'I felt a slight pinch, but not until I saw the video did I realise what Francisco had done,' he said.

Reyes is an oddity in Spain because he never goes out, preferring to stay in with his Playstation and his family, going to bed by 11 p.m. and drinking water, just water. 'He trains, goes home to his family, eats, sleeps and comes back the next day, that's it,' says another former team-mate. Don't think he'll be rooming with Ray Parlour then.

### 28th January 2004

Turns out that Reyes might be banned for a few games because of outstanding disciplinary issues in Spain. Wenger jokes, 'This makes me think he has all the qualities to be an Arsenal player.' Certainly shrinking violets need not apply. Some worrying reports from the Spanish media suggesting Reyes may not be the sharpest tool in the box. They appear to be hinting that he is some form of mentally retarded gypsy who can't even spell his own name. But hey, if he scores the winner against Real in the Champions League final then who cares? I've never thought a high IQ was necessary for top-flight football. Look at the trouble Graeme Le Saux got into for revealing he reads the *Guardian*. It was seen as a greater crime than murder, and further evidence that he must be gay. This is not true, but that has never stopped the terrace jesters.

# FEBRUARY

**'José Antonio … José Antonio …**
**José Antonio … José Antonio'**

## Manchester City
**PREMIERSHIP, HIGHBURY**
**RESULT: 2-1 WIN**
My location: at game

What a game. And what a player we've got in Reyes. Things got off to a ridiculous start with the much-heralded 'Fans Day' pre-match entertainment. This is designed to turn Arsenal from the 'library' that many think it has become to something more, well, noisy. Quite why we need to change anything is beyond me. Most other grounds suffer constant appalling drumming or trumpet-blowing, or really irritating incessant chants. Arsenal fans are much more refined, choosing to shout when we have to – not because we think it's a vital ingredient to the day's enjoyment. So the frankly embarrassing 'entertainment' we had to endure was met with our usual indifferent silence which said it all really. You can't force people to behave in a certain way at football. It's an emotional thing and we behave according to our emotions at Highbury. Which is cool, calm, collected, a bit cocky, and occasionally up, pumping and passionate if we feel the team needs it. The only bit that meant anything was the farewell reception given to David Seaman who got an amazing ovation as he walked out through a line-up of the two teams. He is a true hero here, and it was nice he got the send-off he deserved.

There was a nasty scare early on when Henry looked like he had done his groin. The whole crowd went eerily quiet as he hobbled off in apparent agony. But a bit of magic sponge from our physio Gary Lewin and he was back to a rapturous reception. Watching Anelka was interesting. Still very quick, but still relentlessly caught offside, still very scowly, and still living in a bubble of self-obsessed frustration. A bigger threat came from Ian Wright's lad Shaun Wright-Phillips who looks and plays just like his old man used to. Frisky, very, very frisky.

Our first goal came after 39 minutes when Bergkamp played a

brilliant diagonal pass to Henry who crossed first time to a flying
Freddie. But just when he went to tap it in, Tarnat got there first
and scored an own goal. The match started on what seemed to be a
crisp winter's day but by half-time the heavens opened and we were
deluged. This slowed things down and Henry, in particular, looked a
bit out of sorts – hopefully not because of that groin twinge. He's
hilarious when things don't go well. We get the full range of Gallic
shrugs and sighs and arm-waving and chest-beating. It's never his
fault, it's always somebody else causing his poor play.

Lehmann, by contrast, had a stormer of a game. He is fearless,
not afraid to leave his box to clear or come storming out for corners
and crosses. He's not 100 per cent secure, but then which goalkeeper
is? He is, though, big and confident and aggressive – and the more I
see of him the more I like him. It was sad seeing Fowler and
McManaman going through the motions. They were both great
talents but you suspect all the gambling and partying did for our
Robbie, while McManaman will never again find the buzz he
must have got from celebrating a goal with Ronaldo, Carlos, Figo
and Zidane.

Twenty minutes to go and Reyes came on in terrible conditions to
a great cheer. He looked instantly sensational, getting the ball near
the halfway line, flicking it from left to right, slipping two defenders
in a flash and putting Pires through. It was truly one of those 'Wow
– what have we got here then?' moments. Henry seemed to view
him as a personal wake-up call, and the pair of them, linking up
remarkably well considering they've only just met, were running
through large muddy puddles which must have seemed far removed
from the sunny climes of Seville. As the crowd chanted 'José
Antonio' ... Henry decided to remind us all who Top Gun really is
with a fabulous 30-yard thunderball rocket straight into the top-
right corner that gave James no chance. It was a fantastic strike,
straight as an arrow, with none of his usual curve. Even Reyes
looked taken aback.

Cygan came on for Pires, and looked much better at left-wing than centre-back, which is not saying much. I feel guilty for loathing him like this, but he will cost us big games if Wenger doesn't get rid of him soon. Anelka, perhaps realising it could have been him up there with Henry in a world-class team if he just hadn't been so damn greedy, got into a senseless row with Cole near the end and raised his hands to his old team-mate's face. The red card was inevitable but why a yellow for Cole? He hadn't done anything wrong from where I was looking. Anelka was afforded a great ovation from the Arsenal crowd. Not. I haven't heard booing like that since I saw David Mellor turn up at a film premiere once.

Near the end, Reyes showed he is no soft touch by facing down Tarnat after getting a hefty barge. A phalanx of red shirts flew in to help him out, but he looked perfectly capable of looking after himself, thanks very much. Reyes, who speaks hardly any English, said afterwards that he didn't understand a word Tarnat or the ref were saying. One thing we understood about him afterwards, though, was that he's a quality player. I have rarely seen a more dramatic debut, given the atrocious weather and the fact that he had just 20 minutes to live up to the hype. He looked hard as nails, very quick, lightning feet and a great head for goal. Perhaps he did a bit of bullfighting when he was younger, but his instinct to just stick his head down and charge straight for goal was great to watch. Early days, but on this showing, Wenger's done it again.

**Arsenal:** Jens Lehmann, Sol Campbell, Ashley Cole (yellow card), Robert Pires, Pascal Cygan 84, Fredrik Ljungberg, Edu 59, Ray Parlour (yellow card), Lauren, Kolo Touré, Gilberto, Thierry Henry, Dennis Bergkamp, José Reyes 69. Subs not used: Graham Stack, David Bentley

**Manchester City:** David James, Richard Dunne, Sylvain Distin, Jihai Sun, Joey Barton (yellow card), Michael Tarnat, Paul Bosvelt, Robbie Fowler, Trevor Sinclair (yellow card), Claudio Reyna, Steve McManaman 76, Nicolas Anelka (red card),Shaun Wright-Phillips. Subs not used: Arni Arason, Antoine Sibierski, Jonathan Macken

**Michael Tarnat 39 (own goal), Thierry Henry 83, Nicolas Anelka 89**

## Middlesbrough

**TUESDAY 3 FEBRUARY**

### LEAGUE CUP, THE RIVERSIDE
### RESULT: 2-1 LOST

My location: watching TV at home

OK, we're out of the League Cup. Big deal.

**Arsenal:** Graham Stack, Ashley Cole, Pascal Cygan, Martin Keown (red card), Gael Clichy, Quincy Owusu Abeyie 81, Edu, Kolo Touré, Patrick Vieira, Ray Parlour, José Reyes, David Bentley (yellow card) Subs not used: Stuart Taylor, Olatur-Ingi Skulason, Justin Hoyte, Ryan Smith

**Middlesbrough:** Mark Schwarzer, Gareth Southgate, Danny Mills, Chris Riggott, Franck Queudrue, Doriva, Gaizka Mendieta, Boudewijn Zenden, Jonathan Greening, Stuart Parnaby 63, Juninho, Massimo Maccarone, Joseph-Desire Job 70. Subs not used: Bradley Jones, Stewart Downing, Michael Ricketts

**Edu 77, Boudewijn Zenden 69, José Reyes 85 (own goal)**

## Wolverhampton Wanderers

**SATURDAY 7 FEBRUARY**

### PREMIERSHIP, MOLINEUX
### RESULT: 1-3 WIN

My location: watching oldest son play a school football match

I spent the morning watching my oldest boy Spencer playing in a school match. And what was so inherently satisfying is that he played as a defensive midfielder, and gave every impression of wanting to emulate Vieira not Henry. Not many ten-year-olds would choose that route, and I am both surprised and delighted.

Bergkamp used to score beautiful goals. Now he scores ugly ones. But he still plays beautiful football, so that's OK. Nine minutes into this one-sided affair at Molineux, he hit a first-time shot from a Cole cross, and sliced it inside the far post. For a moment I thought he was going to try and claim it was deliberate but then he laughed and we all knew it was a mis-hit. Albeit a rather useful one. Unbelievably, they equalised when we left Ganea unmarked in the box at a corner and he volleyed it in. People like him should not be scoring against our defence from set pieces. No disrespect, but Crespo he ain't. We have got to sort this out before we get to the

really big games or we will pay for it. A quarter of an hour into the
second half Henry hovered in an offside position before suddenly
racing onside then forward again to take a Pires pass. He picked it
up on the edge of the box and fired it over the advancing Jones.
Their manager moaned about it afterwards, but this had nothing to
do with the admittedly absurd new laws about offside and more to
do with Henry's raw speed and quick brain. He often lurks offside
now, then sprints back before the pass is made before darting the
other way just as quickly to receive it. 'The stupid, bloody rule,'
fumed David Jones anyway. 'Is he offside or not? We don't know
what to do with it. You can't coach against it. It's rubbish.' The
truth is that few players can do it because they are just not fast
enough. Five minutes later, Touré – the only man who I reckon
could beat Henry in a 100 metre sprint, with the possible exception
of Cole – nodded in from two yards and it was game over. Henry
and Reyes linked up promisingly again. They are going to be just
incredible when they understand each other.

This win extended the unbeaten run to twenty-four, a new all-
time club record and a new Premiership record. We also stay top by
two points, though it would have been more if United hadn't hung
on against Everton to win 4-3 when they were 3-0 up at half-time.
They always score in the last minute – it is another incredibly
irritating facet of Manchester United that irks me beyond belief.
David Jones excelled even his earlier idiotic thoughts with this
assessment of the difference between the two sides: 'I can't fault my
players for effort today, but we missed that bit of quality Arsenal
had in front of goal.' Yes, I think you can safely say there's a bit of a
gap there, Davey sunshine.

**Arsenal:** Jens Lehmann, Sol Campbell, Ashley Cole, Robert Pires, Patrick Vieira, Lauren, Kolo Touré, Gilberto, Edu, Dennis Bergkamp (yellow card), José Reyes 55, Thierry Henry. Subs not used: Graham Stack, Pascal Cygan, Gael Clichy, Ray Parlour

**Wolverhampton Wanderers:** Paul Jones, Paul Butler, Lee Naylor, Denis Irwin (yellow card), Jody Craddock, Colin Cameron, Mark Kennedy, Alex Rae, Ioan Ganea, Carl Cort, Steffen Iversen 76, Kenny Miller (yellow card). Subs not used: Michael Oakes, Mark Clyde, Johannes Gudjonsson, Silas

Dennis Bergkamp 9, Thierry Henry 58, Kolo Touré 63, **Ioan Ganea 26**

**TUESDAY**
**10**
**FEBRUARY**

## Southampton
**PREMIERSHIP, HIGHBURY**
**RESULT: 2-0 WIN**
My location: at game

We looked instantly dangerous, Pires going close twice in the first
four minutes. But the biggest noise from the crowd appeared to be
for the presence of two favoured figures of ridicule: Le Saux and
Strachan. The former because, as stated earlier, he reads the
*Guardian* and therefore must be gay. And the latter because he is so
easy to wind up. Strachan spends most of the match leaping up and
down screaming at his players, our players, the officials, the crowd,
God. Anyone he can get enraged about, frankly. You can't but admire
his passion and determination. As my army officer brother would say
'you'd want him in the trenches ...' The more we informed Le Saux
that he 'takes it up the a**e', the better he played, of course. One
thing he does very well is take a good corner, perhaps encouraged by
all the 'advice' he gets from the touchline crowd ... and three fizzed
over to cause us real problems. Ironically, though, it was a Le Saux
free-kick that led to our first goal. Lehmann saved, fed it straight to
Pires who released Henry down the left wing. He looked offside, but
he wasn't. Just frighteningly quick to react. He raced into their box
and beat an out-rushing Niemi to make it 1-0.

Reyes seemed to be struggling a bit, regularly dispossessed as he
tried to find his colleagues. But they will find him soon enough. His
attitude is fantastic, constantly chasing and harrying and
scampering back to defend if he has to. He also has that touch of
haughty Spanish arrogance that suggests he knows what he can do,
and it won't be long before he does it. In the meantime, Henry *is*
doing it. In one sublime moment he headed over one defender,
chipped it over the next, then shot past a floundering Niemi. It
missed the far post by inches but Henry just shrugged and trudged
back to try again. I can't imagine anyone, not even Zidane, is

playing as well as Henry just now. Or that many players of the past have been able to unleash this kind of all-round firepower.

Our second was a bit lucky, and Southampton were rather aggrieved, judging by the hilarious war dance Strachan performed in the immediate aftermath. Parlour had caught Higginbotham with his arm ten yards into our half but we either didn't notice he'd gone down or conveniently chose to ignore it. Seconds later, Henry was pasting it into the goal. Higginbotham got up and didn't seem too hurt but the Saints players (and their demented Ginger Whinger manager) clearly felt we should have knocked the ball out of play. It reminded me of that dreadful FA Cup tie against Sheffield United when the ball was kicked out for an injury to one of our players, they threw it back to their keeper on the restart, Kanu intercepted it, and passed to Overmars who scored. It was the first and only time I have called a radio station, calling Talksport to say that if we didn't replay the game I'd cancel my season ticket. It was just so unsporting and so unlike Arsenal. The moment I had finished gabbling my fury on air, I heard David Dein on another station saying we had already offered a replay. And in that moment I thanked the Lord that I support a team that knows how to behave.

The lasting memory of this game was the incessant chanting by Southampton fans against Glenn Hoddle, widely tipped to be replacing the 'retiring' Strachan. It's amazing how unpopular Hoddle is, not just with their fans but with everyone. Because of his Tottenham link, every time they chanted abuse about him we all applauded. But I hardly ever hear anyone say a good word about the guy. Which is odd given that he was, I thought, a very good England manager, and one of the best players we have ever produced. There's just something about his aloof, 'I know best' attitude that winds everyone up. I heard that the England players used to get infuriated by Hoddle's habit of teaching them how to do tricks in training as if he was a circus ringmaster educating a bunch of unruly junior acrobats. Perhaps my own affinity for the poor bloke goes back to when I studied journalism at Harlow College in Essex, and lived with a family just 100 yards from his palatial residence. Now, most people grow up and spend their every waking moment trying to *leave* Harlow, one of those godforsaken new towns where every pub and bar is named after a butterfly or moth (Red Admiral, White Admiral etc, etc) and where there's more concrete than at a Corleone family cemetery. But Hoddle stayed there and had this great new pile in the town which made him an even bigger hero than he already was. People would literally pay homage to him, hanging around his gates hoping for a glimpse of the messiah or a few words of wisdom from the man who gave us such memorable phrases as 'I didn't say them things'. Perhaps all this hero-worship made it difficult for him to relate to mere mortals.

Strachan tried to 'get to' the officials at the end of the game, but was kept away. 'If I'm in London the next time and get mugged I hope the same number of policemen and stewards turn up,' he said. 'I couldn't get near them.' But he did calm down enough to say of Henry, 'A player comes around every ten years that's special and he's definitely one.'

**Arsenal:** Jens Lehmann, Ashley Cole, Sol Campbell, Ray Parlour (yellow card), Patrick Vieira (yellow card), Robert Pires, Lauren, Kolo Touré, Gilberto, José Reyes, Gael Clichy 74, Thierry Henry. Subs not used: Graham Stack, Pascal Cygan, Edu, David Bentley

**Southampton:** Antti Niemi (yellow card), Darren Kenton, Graeme Le Saux, Marian Pahars 82, Danny Higginbotham, Stephen Crainey, Michael Svensson (yellow card), Anders Svensson, Chris Baird 27, Paul Telfer, Rory Delap, Kevin Phillips, Brett Ormerod. Subs not used: Paul Smith, Fitz Hall
**Thierry Henry 31, 90**

## 14th February 2004

Injuries, the bane of any season. There you are, smashing all records, swarming round the Premiership unbeaten and apparently on an unstoppable path to infinite glory, when, one by one, your best players all go lame. Henry picked up a leg injury in the Southampton game, Wiltord and Aliadiere are still out, Freddie's not ready yet, Keown's having treatment, Sol's groin is playing up … This is where we will find out if we have a big enough squad to get through. I am worried that we don't.

## Chelsea
**FA CUP 5TH ROUND, HIGHBURY**
**RESULT: 2-1 WIN**
My location: at game

If it's the FA Cup, and we're playing Chelsea, then they will lose.
That, at least, must be what Claudio Ranieri thinks, given that it's
happened to him each of the four years he's been there. If he sticks
around long enough, he might be able to add 'And Reyes will score a
sensational goal', because after today that looks an increasingly
likely feature in most games.

There have been some fantastic opening goals in an Arsenal career
but none I suspect quite as good as this thunderbolt. It came after
Chelsea had got us on the run a bit. Gronkjaer had a perfectly good
header ruled offside by a dozy linesman, and then Mutu side-stepped
Touré to drive a left-foot shot in from the edge of the box. In the 56th
minute, Gilberto forced a corner on the right, it was cleared back to
Edu who rolled it in turn to Reyes. The Spaniard then just smacked
it straight in from at least 25 yards, a wonderfully clean, technically
perfect collision with the ball, that was hit with frightening power.
The sheer shock of it sent Chelsea into a meltdown of misery, and
the home fans into stunned ecstasy. A few minutes later, with the
crowd still chanting his name in one of those dreadfully predictable
Spanish-inflected 'José José' songs, he was slipped through by Vieira
and beat Sullivan from close range. It was another great goal, made
by a terrific run and quick thinking in the area. The boy's a natural.

That night I went to the BAFTAS and kept bumping into this
rather fetching blonde in a tight silver number. I thought nothing
more of it until I got the papers on the way home and realised it
was Scarlett Johansson. Now I know what Henry must feel like
when he slips one just past the outside of the post, or hoofs it over
the bar from three yards.

**Arsenal:** Jens Lehmann, Ashley Cole, Sol Campbell (yellow card), Ray Parlour, Edu 51, Patrick Vieira (yellow card), Robert Pires, Lauren, Kolo Touré, Gilberto (yellow card), José Reyes, Gael Clichy 82, Dennis Bergkamp. Subs not used: Graham Stack, Pascal Cygan, David Bentley

**Chelsea:** Carlo Cudicini, Neil Sullivan 60, Mario Melchiot (yellow card), John Terry, Wayne Bridge, William Gallas, Claude Makelele (yellow card), Jesper Gronkjaer, Joe Cole 69, Frank Lampard, Scott Parker, Jimmy Floyd Hasselbaink (yellow card), Adrian Mutu (yellow card), Eidur Gudjohnsen 64. Subs not used: Robert Huth, Hernan Crespo

José Reyes 56, 61, **Adrian Mutu 40**

## 16th February 2004

Parlour's now out for six weeks, after hobbling off against Chelsea.
But on the more positive front Lehmann's only been fined £10,000
for his pitiful behaviour at Southampton with Phillips. Wenger
pretends to read the Riot Act, saying, 'He knows he must learn to
keep his cool and I've told him that.' But *five times*, Arsène. You
knew he'd been sent off five times. What the hell do you expect from
that kind of CV – a ballet dancer?

## 19th February 2004

Ashley Cole left the field after only 17 minutes of England's 1-1
draw against Portugal, and Gilberto had to be subbed after just 14
minutes with a damaged ankle in Brazil's draw with Iceland. This is
not an injury list now, it's an epidemic ...

**SATURDAY**
**21**
**FEBRUARY**

## Chelsea
**PREMIERSHIP, STAMFORD BRIDGE**
**RESULT: 1-2 WIN**
My location: watching TV in London

Lehmann, not exactly humbled by his fine, has now offended the
whole German nation with a disgraceful slur against their hero (and
his rival) Oliver Kahn. Unhappy at not having replaced the brilliant
but ageing superstar already, Lehmann decided to go for the
jugular, or should I say genitalia, by openly attacking Kahn for
cheating on his pregnant wife with a sexy young blonde. Franz
Beckenbauer called him 'cheeky' and demanded a ban. 'Cheeky?

Cheeky? What is cheeky? I haven't done anything,' retorted
Lehmann, and explained that the reason he brought up Kahn's
mistress was because Kahn had accused *him* of behaving like he
was in kindergarten. All good dirty fun, and further indications that
our keeper is not quite the full ticket.

Perhaps all this domestic mayhem was preying on his mind
though, because Gudjohnsen put Chelsea ahead after just 28
seconds, capitalising on a Clichy slip after Mutu flicked on a Geremi
cross to power his shot past Lehmann. A shocking start but Vieira
got us back in the game quickly by taking on an exquisite
Bergkamp pass and striding through their defence in the 15th
minute to equalise. It was tremendous power-play from a player
back to his best fitness and form. Flapping Sullivan then committed
a terrible howler to let Edu score and we were actually ahead before
half-time.

Chelsea kept coming, but their desperation began to tell when
Gudjohnsen was booked for diving. The big striker made it much
worse a bit later when he clattered into Clichy from behind and got
sent off by Mike Riley. He couldn't complain, it was a crass challenge,
but he tried anyway, of course. His departure, though, was a telling
moment in the game and Chelsea never got back into us.

Wenger raved about Bergkamp after the game, saying, 'It is
surprising that you can think a player is dead and then he is alive
again'. One of the obvious benefits of his inability to fly is that
Dennis is able to relax whilst the rest of the boys toil away in
godforsaken places like Kiev. He can't score like he used to, and he's
never been able to head the ball. But Bergkamp, on his day, is still
the most technically gifted player in the league.

One Chelsea fan explained on TV why she still had a Zola shirt: 'I
just don't know who I really like among all these new players yet.'
And therein lies the problem for moneybags Chelski. They have too
much cash, too many players, too great an expectation. It doesn't
work because they don't gel as a team. Arsenal have a much smaller

squad but everyone knows his place in it. The first team picks itself. At Stamford Bridge it's as if Ranieri gets a pin out and takes his chance on wherever it lands. Manchester United drew 1-1 at home to Leeds, and that leaves Arsenal seven points ahead in the Premiership table.

**Arsenal:** Jens Lehmann, Sol Campbell, Gael Clichy, Edu, Kolo Touré, Gilberto, Lauren (yellow card), Robert Pires, Patrick Vieira, Dennis Bergkamp, Fredrik Ljungberg 78, Thierry Henry (yellow card). Subs not used: Graham Stack, Pascal Cygan, Nwankwo Kanu, José Reyes

**Chelsea:** Neil Sullivan, John Terry (yellow card), Wayne Bridge, Mario Melchiot, William Gallas, Geremi, Joe Cole 73, Claude Makelele, Scott Parker, Jesper Gronkjaer 62, Frank Lampard (yellow card), Eidur Gudjohnsen (red card), Adrian Mutu (yellow card), Jimmy Floyd Hasselbaink 73. Subs not used: Marco Ambrosio, Marcel Desailly

**Patrick Vieira 15, Edu 21, Eidur Gudjohnsen 1**

## Celta de Vigo
### CHAMPIONS LEAGUE, ESTADIO BALAÍDOS
### RESULT: 2-3 WIN
My location: watching TV at home

This lot should have been a walkover. They are lurking at the bottom of La Liga, and Deportivo caned them 5-0 recently at *home*. But we made heavy weather of this. After a scrappy start we took the lead in typically untidy fashion, with Edu poking it in from a yard after the keeper parried his weak header from a Pires cross. The keeper, Cavallero, emerged from the rubble with blood gushing from his nose just to compound his misery. Ten minutes later it was 1-1 thanks to a brilliant free-kick from ex-Arsenal left back Silvinho – headed in by the other Edu, Luis. The Brazilian lost his place to Ashley Cole after getting injured, but he was always a very good player and showed it again tonight. With both Edus scoring, the commentators are having the nightmare I predicted.

We went in level at half-time and came out again rather lethargically. Their Edu was livelier than ours, and Reyes missed a sitter to the delight of the taunting Spanish crowd. In the 58th minute, though, *our* Edu woke up at last and scored an absolute peach. Picking it up on the edge of their box, he switched feet, dummied one of their defenders with majestic ease, looked up and curled one from 25 yards into the top right-hand corner. The name *Edu* has now scored three times tonight. But as we sat back congratulating ourselves on finally leading in Europe, we conceded another goal from another set piece, Mostovoi slicing it in from a Lehmann half-save. It's an aggravating goal to concede at that time of the game, but just as I was screaming at the French 'superstars' to 'earn their bloody dough', they did just that. Pires and Henry linked up superbly for a lightning fast one-two that Pires slotted into the right-hand corner before any of their defenders had stirred enough to stop him. It was a great goal, created by two guys who have got the ability to win any match against any opposition.

So we won our first ever game away in Spain, by playing not very well. This, I think, has to augur well. Doesn't it? A relieved Wenger said our Edu was trying to pass it when he scored his brilliant goal but couldn't find anyone ...' so he had no option but to score with his right foot.' I think they should work on nobody being available for Edu to pass to in practice, so he runs out of options more often.

**Arsenal:** Jens Lehmann, Sol Campbell, Gael Clichy, David Bentley 89, Kolo Touré, Lauren, Robert Pires, Patrick Vieira, Fredrik Ljungberg, Pascal Cygan 90, Edu (yellow card), Thierry Henry (yellow card), José Reyes, Nwankwo Kanu 78. Subs not used: Graham Stack, Justin Hoyte, Martin Keown, Francesc Fabregas Cesc

**Celta de Vigo:** Pablo Cavallero, Silvinho (yellow card), Eduardo Berizzo, Juan Velasco, Sergio, Lopez Ángel, Vagner 64, Alexander Mostovoi, José Ignacio, Peter Luccin, Edu, Mauricio Pinilla 75, Savo Milosevic. Subs not used: Jose Pinto, Fernando Cáceres, Pablo Contreras, Sebastian Mendez, Jandro

Edu 18, 58, Robert Pires 80, **Edu 27, José Ignacio 64**

## Charlton Athletic
**PREMIERSHIP, HIGHBURY**
**RESULT: 2-1 WIN**
My location: at game

The worst possible start. We scored twice in the first four minutes.
Now this would normally be rather good news for a home side. But
Arsenal fans hate it because when the initial joy wears off, we know
we're going to have to sit there for another 86 minutes of tedium as
our boys give up trying too hard and sit on their lead as the
opposition launch fruitless attacks in between desperately trying to
cave in completely and lose 20-0. Then all you need is a late goal
from them, as happened here, and it's always panic stations and
bitten nails right to the end.

Our first goal came from Henry ghosting at high speed into their
penalty area, taking on a perfectly timed Ljungberg pass and sliding
it straight to Pires who gleefully accepted his early present. It was
too easy, especially against a side currently competing for a place in
Europe. A minute later Henry was in again like an invisible but
deadly spirit, latching onto a sharp pass from Vieira as Charlton
stood there wondering what the hell was hitting them. That was the
end of any real entertainment until the 59th minute, when Claus
Jensen suddenly unleashed a 30-yard volley that rocketed past a
thrashing Lehmann into the top of the net. It was a great strike
from a dangerous player, and suddenly Arsenal were having to
defend frantically and run around like blue-arsed flies – after
coasting along without a care in the world for most of the game.
Two minutes into injury time, sub Jonatan Johansson smashed an
overhead kick against our post. It was that close to being a draw.
And we would have kicked ourselves all the way home if it had gone
in. Why we don't just murder teams 10-0 when we start like an
express train is beyond me. We always seem to stop playing, almost
as if it's beneath us or we feel sorry for them. Well it's not, and I

never feel sorry for anyone we play. Ever.

Curbishley squealed like a pig afterwards about both goals being offside. Pires probably was, just, but it was so close, and the speed of passing up to that point so breathtaking that you can hardly blame the linesman. As for Henry's, Curbishley was bemused as well as suffused with fury. 'I'm completely at a loss over this offside rule,' he whined. 'I thought Henry was five yards offside when the ball was played in to Vieira. Then he was inactive but when it was crossed he suddenly became active.' The simple truth, Mr Curbishley, is that as the law currently stands it was a perfectly good legal goal. You just don't have any players who can take advantage of it like Henry. My only advice would be to always assume Thierry's 'active' because he usually is, in every sense.

So we remain unbeaten, with just eleven matches left. And we're still in the Champion's League too. Hmmm. Is it too early to start booking tickets for the double-decker bus trips to Islington Town Hall?

**Arsenal:** Jens Lehmann, Sol Campbell, Ashley Cole, Patrick Vieira, Fredrik Ljungberg, Gilberto 74, Robert Pires, Pascal Cygan 88, Lauren, Kolo Touré, Edu, Dennis Bergkamp, José Reyes 74, Thierry Henry. Subs not used: Stuart Taylor, Nwankwo Kanu

**Charlton Athletic:** Dean Kiely, Mark Fish, Luke Young, Hermann Hreidarsson, Jonathan Fortune, Radostin Kishishev, Jonatan Johansson 78, Graham Stuart, Matt Holland, Claus Jensen, Paolo Di Canio, Carlton Cole, Simon Royce, Paul Konchesky, Michael Turner, Shaun Bartlett
**Robert Pires 2, Thierry Henry 4, Claus Jensen 59**

# MARCH

'The result is wonderful,
but it is even more enjoyable
to hear opposition fans
cheering our team'

ARSÈNE WENGER

## Portsmouth
### FA CUP 6TH ROUND, FRATTON PARK
### RESULT: 1-5 WIN
My location: watching TV at home

This was just barbaric. Portsmouth have had a great season under Harry Redknapp and must have quietly fancied their chances at home against a team they knew didn't have the Cup as a priority. But we just destroyed them, there's no other way to describe the carnage that went on. Kick-off was delayed while Berkovic was ordered to remove his necklace, little lamb. But the only jewels on show here after that were our boys. In the second minute Reyes crashed one onto the bar, then Henry nearly scored direct from a vicious curling corner. Incredibly it took 25 mintes for us to actually score, Henry tucking it away after a swift break from midfield. We continued pressing, Henry and Reyes causing panic in their penalty area with their speed. Just before half-time Ljungberg stroked in a second after a neat one-two between Edu and Vieira. A minute later, it was three as Touré shanked it past Hislop from eight yards after some more appalling defending from a Pompey side now clearly in deep, deep trouble.

I don't know what the hell you say if you're losing 3-0 to a rampant Arsenal at half-time but whatever Redknapp came up with, it didn't work. On 50 minutes, Ljungberg broke forward again and nudged it to Henry on the edge of the box – from where he just curled it straight into the right-hand corner. He makes it look pathetically easy. The home crowd, far from leaving in disgust, started making more noise than ever and doing so with great humour. 'We're going to win 5-4' was one hilarious chant. Freddie was a livewire today and scored a great goal from a Henry through ball, only to see it ruled offside. Then Reyes had a blatant penalty rejected. But Freddie finally got his reward in the 57th minute when Touré ripped Pompey's defence open with one of those surging runs of his, slipped it to Ljungberg whose first-time shot was deflected off Primus past Hislop. The Portsmouth fans immediately started singing the theme tune from *The Great Escape*, but it was too late for any Steve McQueen antics now. With twenty minutes to go, Henry, Vieira and Ljungberg went off – to a standing, rousing and extraordinary ovation from the whole stadium. They looked genuinely shocked, and I haven't seen anything like it since Ronaldo scored that brilliant hat-trick at Old Trafford and they roared him off then.

Sheringham eventually came on, to a slightly different reception from the Arsenal fans, as you can imagine – and looked dementedly determined to mar things, if he could, by scoring. Sure enough, in the last minute he popped up to volley home a Hughes nod-down. Sheringham ran towards our fans looking sickeningly pleased with himself, as usual.

At the end of the match, the Fratton Park faithful cheered our team off. 'Their fans were outstanding,' Henry told BBC 1. 'I have never seen that in my life – even when they were four or five down they kept singing. I hope they don't get relegated, they deserve to stay in the Premiership with fans like that.' Wenger was equally amazed by what he'd heard. 'The result is wonderful,' said Wenger. 'But it is even more enjoyable to hear opposition fans cheering our team.'

**Arsenal:** Jens Lehmann, Ashley Cole, Sol Campbell, Patrick Vieira, Gael Clichy 72, Fredrik Ljungberg, David Bentley 72, Lauren, Kolo Touré, Gilberto, Edu, José Reyes, Thierry Henry, Nwankwo Kanu 72. Subs not used: Stuart Taylor, Pascal Cygan

**Portsmouth:** Shaka Hislop, Matthew Taylor, Linvoy Primus, Arjan De Zeeuw, Petri Pasanen, Alexei Smertin, Amdy Faye, Eyal Berkovic, Steve Stone 45, Nigel Quashie, Richard Hughes 70, Yakubu Aiyegbeni, Ivica Mornar, Teddy Sheringham 77, Harald Wapenaar, Kevin Harper

**Thierry Henry 25, 50, Fredrik Ljungberg 43, 57, Kolo Touré 45, Teddy Sheringham 90**

# Celta de Vigo
**CHAMPIONS LEAGUE, HIGHBURY**
**RESULT: 2-0 WIN**
My location: at game

I spent the afternoon having a benign cyst removed from my head.
Quite a weird experience as the doctor literally gouged my scalp
open under a local anaesthetic and scooped out this prawn-like
thing before stitching me back up again. He asked me not to do
anything too exciting later. I said I'm going to the Arsenal. 'Who are
they playing?' he asked. 'Celta Vigo.' 'Oh that should be OK,' he
replied, showing a sound knowledge of the current state of the
Champions League.

We needed a quick goal to ease the nerves and we got one.
Bergkamp, so good at the moment, threaded another pearler of a
pass through to Henry, who knocked it past Cavallero for,
incredibly, his first Champions League goal at Highbury in two
years. 4-2 on aggregrate and they needed at least three to beat us
now which was not going to happen unless the defence suddenly
decided to go walkabout. On the half hour it was definitely all over,
as Bergkamp won the ball and set up Ljungberg, who crossed it in
hard and low. Pires jumped and missed, but Caceres only managed
to clear it gently to a rampant Henry, who took it down and scored
from three yards. This signalled the cue for the habitual group
huddle, a lot of badge-kissing, and general euphoria. And why not?
We're through to the next round, playing superbly, and we have got
to have a serious chance of winning this damn thing at last – after
it seemed as if we'd never get past the group stage a month ago.
How important that last-minute Cole header against Kiev looks
now. At moments like that, not just seasons but careers and history
can be forever defined or shattered.

The most striking aspect of the game was the presence of Pierluigi
Collina as referee. It was my first time watching him live and he

really was as good as you would hope. He's tall, very fit, and has the world's most demonic eyeballs and stare. The players are clearly all terrified of him, and there is no backchat, no aggro, no nothing. He controlled the game with a mastery that fully earned him the title of world's best ref. The Clock End even afforded him a chant of 'Who's the genius in the black?', which was bizarre in the extreme. But then why can't all refs be like him? Why can't it be like rugby where the players fear the consequences of bad behaviour so much that they daren't even think about it most of the time. If it was ten yards further up for every swear word, then swearing would stop. It works in Saudi with their fixed link between thieving and hand severing. Collina's only fault came when he didn't give Bergkamp a fairly obvious penalty after Cavellero rushed out, studs up and gave him a full bootful in the chest. Dennis rarely gets penalties these days, I suspect because wise old birds like Collina have seen him con them out of officials for a decade. You reap what you sow in this game. That's why Pires won't get many either, and why people like Vieira and Keane always get sent off. The refs know their reputations and deal with them accordingly.

**Arsenal:** Jens Lehmann, Lauren, Kolo Touré, Sol Campbell, Ashley Cole, Patrick Vieira, Fredrik Ljungberg, Robert Pires, José Reyes 69, Edu, Gilberto 69, Dennis Bergkamp, Nwankwo Kanu 76, Thierry Henry. Subs not used: Graham Stack, Pascal Cygan, Martin Keown, Gael Clichy

**Celta de Vigo:** Pablo Cavallero, Fernando Cáceres, Sergio, Silvinho, Pablo Andres Contreras 21, Juan Velasco, Alexander Mostovoi, José Ignacio, Peter Luccin, Jesuli 29, Borja Oubiña, Gustavo López, Vagner 70, Mauricio Pinilla, Jose Pinto, Sebastian Mendez, Edu, Savo Milosevic
Thierry Henry 14, 34

## 12th March 2004

It was utterly inevitable of course: Arsenal have drawn Chelsea in the Champions League. I should feel supremely confident given our amazing unbeaten run against them stretching back the entire millennium ... but I have this awful sense of foreboding inside. They are a class side now, with pots of money and rising confidence, and they will know their turn must come eventually – and that all the other games would be forgotten if they could turn us over in this one. This is the biggest English club match for donkey's years and the most important Arsenal/Chelsea clash *ever*. I have so many Chelsea friends, and they have suffered so much for so long … so why do I feel so uneasy? The law of averages, that's why. On the upside, one of the papers instantly does a Bergkamp map guide to getting to Chelsea, at least this is one European away leg he should be able to get to quite easily, though frankly I wouldn't entirely trust London's transport system on that one. The winner will play the winner of Real Madrid and Monaco, so that's Real then. I am already mentally buying tickets for the Bernabeu, and imagining Ronaldo running out at Highbury. I know this thinking is fatal but every Arsenal fan will be doing the same.

**SATURDAY**

**13**

**MARCH**

## Blackburn Rovers
### PREMIERSHIP, EWOOD PARK
### RESULT: 0-2 WIN
My location: watching TV in London

This was a game we had to win, but didn't need to break a sweat winning. And that's exactly how it panned out. We were workmanlike, to the point, and got the job done on time and in budget. It was memorable only for another fabulous piece of skill from Henry, who nicked the ball with his foot from Friedel's hands as he went to punt it, and charged off to knock it in the goal. It was fantastic speed of mind and amazing to watch. But the referee Alan Wiley was forced to invoke a useless old rule that unless the ball touches the floor then it is still deemed to be in the keeper's possession. It's a stupid rule because Henry never physically touched Friedel, but rules are rules are rules, so they all trudged back to re-start with the crowd feeling rather deflated. It's one of those goals you want to be able to say you witnessed, in twenty years' time. Nobody ever remembers the disallowed ones really.

Our first goal came in the 12th minute of the second half when
Henry, enraged by not getting a free-kick for a blatant shirt-tug
from Andresen, went over spectacularly a few seconds later after
deliberately bumping into Short. Everyone went mad – Short,
understandably, Souness, the crowd, everyone. Except Henry, who
just waited for them all to calm down before slotting it cleanly
inside the left corner. 'It wasn't a free-kick and that poxy decision
changed the game,' spluttered Souness later. Well, he was right.
But the shirt-tug *was* a free-kick and I didn't see big-hearted
Graeme jumping up and down insisting we got one then, so all's fair
in love, war and football.

Blackburn lost heart after that – Cole and Jansen failing to make
much impact up front, and their midfield getting the runaround
from our bigger, more athletic powerhouses. Vieira eventually broke
free once again and found Gilberto whose shot was parried by
Friedel, only back to Pires who shot home the rebound. 'Our legs
were heavy, but our desire kept us going,' Arsène Wenger said. 'We
are solid defensively this year and even if we are not as fluent as
usual we always know we can score.' What he really meant to say
was: 'I can win games the George Graham way too if I have to, but I
just prefer winning them in style most of the time.'

**Arsenal:** Jens Lehmann, Ashley Cole, Sol Campbell, Patrick Vieira, Robert Pires, Pascal Cygan 89, Lauren, Kolo Touré, Gilberto, Edu (yellow), José Reyes, Gael Clichy 77, Thierry Henry. Subs not used: Graham Stack, David Bentley, Nwankwo Kanu

**Blackburn Rovers:** Brad Friedel, Michael Gray, Craig Short, Andy Todd, Markus Babbel 84, Lucas Neill, Kerimoglou Tugay, Brett Emerton, Jonathon Douglas, Vratislav Gresko 77, Martin Andresen (yellow card), Matt Jansen, Dwight Yorke 73, Andy Cole. Subs not used: Peter Enckelman, Nils Johansson

**Thierry Henry 57, Robert Pires 87**

## Bolton Wanderers
**PREMIERSHIP, HIGHBURY**
**RESULT: 2-1 WIN**
My location: at game

A horrible day, so gusty that the game was delayed 15 minutes because police feared scaffolding might fall on the crowd in the howling gale sweeping Highbury. Bolton made it clear they wouldn't be blowing any howling goals up front by playing just a lone striker, Kevin Davies, stuffing Campo in front of the defence, and presumably hoping the sensational Jay-Jay Okocha could weave some magic somewhere. It was not the greatest plan, and Henry soon began ruining it – smashing a rocket against the bar early on and generally tormenting them with his electrifying runs. After 15 minutes of fairly relentless fluent pressure, Edu played the ball into the box, Bergkamp deftly chested it back, and Pires (yet again) popped up to score. A few minutes later, Pires found Henry racing down the left, who swept inside and found Bergkamp, who hit it first time straight and true to make it 2-0. It was razor-sharp play, quite startling in its pace and precision. Never mind the gale, this was hurricane-force football from a team at the top of their game. Then, as so often happens when we are demolishing someone, we got a bit complacent and Campo snuck in to score when Lehmann misjudged an admittedly swirling corner. Giannakopoulos hit the bar soon after that and we were actually grateful to hear the half-time whistle when we should have been dancing to the tune of 'four nil to the Arsenal'.

Bolton came out looking primed for the fight, and we were lucky to hang on as Giannakopoulos gave Davies a free header which went wide, and the offending striker then fluffed it again from a Pedersen pass. A more in-form forward than Davies would have had a hat-trick and we'd have been buried long before the end. But the most in-form striker in the world is, of course, our boy Thierry and he thundered another cracker which brought a brilliant save from Jaaskelainen, then put Freddie through, only for the flying Swede to fall over himself and then seek, pathetically, to blame everyone else and ludicrously appeal for a penalty. There was a near miss at the end when Campo appeared unmarked again to hit a cross from the otherwise anonymous Okocha and volley over from close in. Even Wenger looked a nervous wreck by now, leaping out of his seat every few seconds to wave his arms pointlessly. 'I am not the master of relaxation,' he observed later, which is hardly surprising when you consider that he spends all his free time either watching, thinking, or talking about football.

'I think they should have let us have a point,' said Allardyce, hilariously, 'as it wouldn't have affected their unbeaten run.' Fair enough, Sam, but this isn't Battersea Dogs Home, my friend. And you wrecked our title bid last season by kicking us off the park when we were 2-0 up, so forgive us if we don't view you as a particularly deserving case for handouts anyway. 'The second half was a Hitchcock one – no one knew what was going to happen next,' Henry remarked of the unexpected tension. The same might apply to himself, of course. We have come to expect the unexpected from Henry this year. Sometimes we need to stand back and realise we are watching an unbelievably great player every week and get slightly less annoyed if he doesn't get five goals *every* game.

**Arsenal:** Jens Lehmann, Sol Campbell, Ashley Cole (yellow card), Robert Pires, Pascal Cygan 88, Patrick Vieira, Lauren, Kolo Touré, Gilberto, Fredrik Ljungberg 69, Edu, Dennis Bergkamp, Thierry Henry. Subs not used: Graham Stack, Nwankwo Kanu, José Reyes

**Bolton Wanderers:** Jussi Jaaskelainen, Simon Charlton, Emerson Thome, Ivan Campo, Bruno N'Gotty, Nicky Hunt, Stelios Giannakopoulos, Jay-Jay Okocha, Kevin Nolan (yellow card), Per Frandsen 76, Kevin Davies, Henrik Pedersen (yellow card). Subs not used: Kevin Poole, Anthony Barness, Ricardo Vaz Te, Dwight Pezzarossi

**Robert Pires 16, Dennis Bergkamp 24, Ivan Campo 41**

## Chelsea
### CHAMPIONS LEAGUE, STAMFORD BRIDGE
### RESULT: 1-1 DRAW

My location: Barbados

I'm in Barbados to watch the Test match. This is an ominous sign because I was here last year when Bolton effectively wrecked our league hopes. But we had a crap English cricket team then, and this year we're on fire, so I am hoping the omens have swayed back Arsenal's way. No drinking during the game because I am still reeling from a night out with Ian Botham, *Mirror* columnist, fantastic bloke and drinker extraordinaire. And I've got to save myself for a party at Jodie Kidd's house tomorrow. Admittedly there will be 500 other people there but as every Spurs fan will know, you can but dream, can't you?

I watched the game in Bubba's Sports Bar, Barbados. It was packed, with an even split of Arsenal and Chelsea fans – and a few disgruntled United supporters. You can always spot them these days by their deep frowns, short tempers, and heavy drinking. Oh what joy to see Wenger's 'shift of power' speech actually come true.

The game started tensely, neither side wanting to give anything away. Vieira had the run on Makelele, who has been nowhere near as strong in the Premiership as he was in La Liga. But otherwise both sides had chances, and neither came particularly close to scoring. The second half started more ominously. Chelsea looked really up for it, bayed on by their ferociously noisy crowd. Lampard, who played with growing authority and menace, went desperately close with a shot that deflected off Campbell's head past Lehmann but thankfully also past the post. But they came at us again and when our back four pressed forward to the halfway line, Mutu put Gudjohnsen through. Lehmann beat him to it, but only succeeded in smashing it into the striker who quickly shot into an empty net. It's tempting to blame Lehmann, and that's exactly what I'm going to do.

Because the German hothead didn't need to speed out like that, and his kicking in that kind of tight situation was execrable, and not for the first time. He dropped a Lampard shot a few minutes later, and was generally living up to the sobriquet of 'dodgy keeper' that was being howled at him from the Shed. Then we came up with a fantastic move to equalise, quick-fire passing all over the pitch until Cole raced into space on the left onto a Vieira pass and chipped it into the middle of the box where Pires jumped to head it low inside the left-hand post. In the 80th minute Desailly, looking several years too old for a game of this high-octane tempo, got booked for handling the ball – as Lehmann was throwing it out. Quite ludicrous, and an act of folly that was to prove rather costly when he promptly cracked into Vieira, got a second yellow card, and trudged off out of the game and the second leg at Highbury. I can't decide if I'm pleased or not. I think he's more of a liability when he plays at the moment.

The result was fair enough. Everyone assumes our away goal gives us the edge but if they score at Highbury then they only have to score once more and we've had it. So I think it's pretty even. Wenger afterwards was on top form, admitting he had watched the Deportivo thrashing of Milan because it was 'relaxing to watch someone else in trouble!' Then, asked again if he felt sorry for Ranieri with all the endless speculation about his job, he laughed: 'Yes, I feel sympathy for Claudio. But if you play tennis with your wife you can love her to death but still want to win.' The man's native tongue is French for God's sake, yet he is more eloquent and amusing in English than any English manager. I must remember to send David Dein another thank-you card. If he hadn't found Wenger then none of this would be happening.

**Arsenal:** Jens Lehmann, Sol Campbell, Ashley Cole, Patrick Vieira, Fredrik Ljungberg, José Reyes 78, Robert Pires, Lauren, Kolo Touré, Edu, Dennis Bergkamp, Gilberto 72, Thierry Henry. Subs not used: Graham Stack, Pascal Cygan, Martin Keown, Gael Clichy, Nwankwo Kanu

**Chelsea:** Marco Ambrosio, Marcel Desailly (red card), John Terry, Wayne Bridge, William Gallas, Claude Makelele (yellow card), Frank Lampard, Scott Parker, Joe Cole 72, Damien Duff, Eidur Gudjohnsen, Mario Melchiot 86, Adrian Mutu, Hernan Crespo 72. Subs not used: Neil Sullivan, Robert Huth, Jesper Gronkjaer, Geremi

**Robert Pires 59, Eidur Gudjohnsen 53**

## Manchester United
### PREMIERSHIP, HIGHBURY
### RESULT: 1-1 DRAW
My location: Barbados

This is always the game that gets the juices flowing fastest. I am once again at Bubba's Bar, this time a teaming mass of United fans with a small smattering of Gooners, most of whom are keen to share with me the new Rio Ferdinand joke: Have you heard about the latest in mobile technology? It's called the Rio Ferdinand, because it's big, it's ugly, has no memory, is vastly overpriced and takes three months to charge!

The atmosphere is fantastic, the screens are everywhere, and the action leaves nothing in the disappointment locker. Early skirmishes were intriguing: Touré snuffing out Scholes, Wes Brown making a stupendous tackle to stop Freddie careering onto a Henry pass, Edu spraying it around like a left-footed Beckham, Gael Clichy having a game at left-back to cause injured Ashley Cole sleepless nights, and a razor-sharp Reyes causing them endless problems in and around the box. Also on show were the pitiful antics of one Djemba-Djemba, who was fouled below the waist by Vieira and clutched his face as if Mike Tyson had just jabbed him hard on the nose. Then he collapsed in abject agony after a collision with Pires, but sprang straight to his feet and sprinted off the moment he realised the free-kick had been given against him.

The speed of the game picked up in earnest as soon as the second half started. And then came a moment of pure dazzling magic from Thierry Henry. Reyes squared a Henry header back to him, the Frenchman hit it first time and it went like a swerving exocet, straight over Carroll's head into the roof of the net. Dead centre and absolutely lethal. The goal kicked everything up a gear. Keane went ballistic at Giggs for not tracking back on a Lauren run, but then played bizarre peacemaker when Campbell appeared to drag down

Giggs for a certain penalty that wasn't awarded – restraining shop steward Gary Neville from losing it completely. Neville's a fascinating human being, and not just because his dad's called Neville Neville. He is always, always, being chippy. He must be one of those guys who, like a brilliant sports editor I once employed, throws a cup of steaming hot tea over his lap if he gets to work and feels too happy about life. For Neville, there is a deep pride to be had in relentless misery and agitation.

And, talking of relentless misery and agitation, our march to victory could only be spoiled by one man. Yes, my great idol Pascal Cygan, who let Solskjaer cross from the wing, past van Nistelrooy who missed his kick, into the path of Saha who had an easy goal. Cue a frenzied last five minutes with chances at both ends, the best falling to Lauren who was put through brilliantly by Henry only for the Cameroon star to show us just why he is a defender not a striker by making an almighty hash of it – first delaying his shot, then shooting into Carroll's legs when Henry was now free to score. The Frenchman screeched his anger, and quite rightly. No full-back should ever try and shoot when the footballing equivalent of a preying mantis is lurking nearby.

The final whistle ended a tight, exciting, deserved draw. We have now set a new top-flight record of thirty games unbeaten from the start of the season and are seven points clear at the top. 'We've shown everyone we're not dead yet,' snarled Sir Alex afterwards. Talking of twitching corpses, Wenger conceded that bringing Cygan on for Freddie 'didn't make things any better'. But all were agreed that Henry's goal was a masterpiece. Well, all except the United manager who said it had been down to the 'new modern ball which moves around too much'. He really is a world-class bad loser.

**Arsenal:** Jens Lehmann, Sol Campbell, Gael Clichy (yellow card), Edu, Kolo Touré, Lauren, Robert Pires, Dennis Bergkamp 85, Patrick Vieira, Fredrik Ljungberg, Pascal Cygan 82, Thierry Henry, José Reyes, Gilberto 77. Subs not used: Graham Stack, Nwankwo Kanu.

**Manchester United:** Roy Carroll, Mikael Silvestre, John O'Shea, Gary Neville, Wes Brown, Paul Scholes (yellow card), Ryan Giggs, Roy Keane, Eric Djemba-Djemba, Louis Saha 59, Darren Fletcher, Ole Gunnar Solskjaer 71, Ruud van Nistelrooy. Subs not used: Tim Howard, Philip Neville, Nicky Butt

**Thierry Henry 50, Louis Saha 86**

# APRIL

'The only way to
stop Thierry Henry
is to knock him out'

EDDIE GRAY

# Manchester United
## FA CUP SEMI-FINAL, VILLA PARK
## RESULT: 0-1 LOST
My location: watching TV at home

Ask any Arsenal fan what nightmares they have, and most will concur that a regular one is the memory of Bergkamp missing a last-minute penalty in an FA Cup semi-final against United at Villa Park, and Giggs promptly scoring that stunning solo goal before ripping his shirt off and baring his hideous Tom Selleck-style chestwig to the world in a goal celebration of equally irritating length. We returned here with that terrible night hanging over us like a very dark nimbus. And yet surely United should have been more fearful. *We* are the team of the moment, *they* are the fading has-beens. Well, United may have blown the big two competitions but they know they can still stop us emulating their Treble by winning this game, and they also know it's their only chance of silverware, especially as the winner of this match has a virtual walkover in the final. (No offence to Millwall, obviously. No, really, lads, didn't mean to say that … no, wait, don't hit me …) Our concerns were not helped by confirmation from the team sheet that Wenger was resting Henry. I just don't understand why. Henry is the fittest guy in the Premiership, he is playing superbly, and we are facing a week of huge games where we will need him fronting the attack and forcing the momentum on and on. Why give United such a huge boost? His replacement Aliadiere is a very promising player, but his time will come.

Ferguson had clearly ordered the hit on 18-year-old Gael Clichy, standing in for Cole at left-back, and it was down that flank that Neville broke clear and crossed to Giggs, who slid into the area before cutting it back for Scholes to romp in as he always does, and score. It was an easy goal, too easy for a game of this intensity. Perhaps the Arsenal players have taken their lead from the manager and relegated this match to something not very important. But it's the semi-final of

the FA Cup against United, for Christ's sake, not a League Cup game
at Rotherham. It could have been different if we had scored in the first
few minutes when we came out at a blistering pace and had four
chances – Bergkamp's shot saved by Brown on the line, Edu chipping
onto the crossbar, Touré's header clawed away by Carroll, and Pires
missing a free header. United played the second half determined to
hang on to their lead, and we didn't have the penetration to break them
down. Wenger accepted his gamble had failed by bringing on Henry
and Reyes on the hour but it was too late. Scholes pretty quickly
stopped the greater threat from José Antonio with a bestial tackle that
damaged his medial ligament and will put him out for three weeks.
Scholes has always had a nasty little streak in him, but this was a
horrible assault on a young player that did him no credit. Then, to
make things even worse, Ljungberg broke his hand. 'It is a big blow to
us not only to lose, but to lose players,' lamented a grim-faced Wenger.
'With such a short squad, that is a massive disappointment.'

Our dejection was in stark contrast to the extraordinary scenes of
jubilation from United. Banned Ferdinand ran on with injured van
Nistelrooy to join in the lap of honour and endless hooplas.
Considering they demeaned the FA Cup by not even participating
three years ago, it was pretty rich. But also pretty revealing that
underneath all that Old Trafford arrogance lies a worried bunch of
people who were seeing another potless season looming. Sir Alex
certainly seemed in a perkier mood as his fans chanted 'Where's your
treble gone' at us, hop, skip, and jumping his way along the touchline
with a grin bigger than his ego (and that is a very, very big grin) and
saying he thought we'd lose to Chelsea at home despite having the
away goal advantage. Wenger sighed when informed of this claim. 'I
am not intelligent enough to understand that, I'm afraid.'

**Arsenal:** Jens Lehmann (yellow card), Kolo Touré (yellow card), Gael Clichy, Sol Campbell, Robert Pires (yellow card), Thierry Henry 57, Patrick Vieira, Fredrik Ljungberg, Edu, Nwankwo Kanu 76, Lauren (yellow card), Jeremie Aliadiere, José Reyes 57, Dennis Bergkamp. Subs not used: Graham Stack, Martin Keown

**Manchester United:** Roy Carroll, Mikael Silvestre, John O'Shea, Gary Neville, Wes Brown, Paul Scholes (yellow card), Ryan Giggs, Roy Keane, Darren Fletcher, Cristiano Ronaldo, David Bellion 84, Ole Solskjaer, Philip Neville 75. Subs not used: Tim Howard, Nicky Butt, Eric Djemba-Djemba
**Paul Scholes 32**

## Chelsea
### CHAMPIONS LEAGUE, HIGHBURY
### RESULT: 1-2 LOST
My location: at game

As usual, I took my oldest journalist friend Rob McGibbon, who has sat and suffered next to me for almost every one of the eighteen long miserable games that Chelsea have failed to win against us. I expected him to be downbeat about their prospects as usual, abjectly resigned to failure, and yet he was strangely chipper. This worried me. But the way we played in the first 25 minutes dashed all those fears. We were sensational, Henry leading from the front with two scorching early runs and shots. It was fast, furious, and ferocious in midfield, where Parker and Lampard matched up powerfully to Vieira and Gilberto. Ranieri's Chelsea are tight at the back, sniffing for that break so loved by Italian sides. But just before half-time, Lauren crossed from the right, Henry headed it back and Reyes nipped past Terry to knock it through Ambrosio's legs. Cue utter delirium. There is no better time to score, and Chelsea slope off like beaten men. I spent half-time telling my sons on the phone that we are all going to the Bernabeu for our semi-final with Madrid. This sparked a furious response from Rob, who screeched: 'Oi, oi, it's not over yet, sunshine. Bit premature, isn't it, Christ Almighty. Even by Gooner standards this is disgusting.' I stood frozen in time for a second and realised he was right. It *was* disgusting, and very premature.

Gronkjaer came on in the second half and we were suddenly under tremendous pressure which resulted in Lampard swooping on a Lehmann parry from Makalele to equalise. Game on, and we all realised suddenly that if they scored again we'd have to score twice to win under the away goals rule. Terrifyingly, rather than rise to this challenge we started to fall away. Henry, in particular, faded spectacularly from view, a pitiful shadow of his first-half

performance. He's done this before in massive games, from our FA
Cup finals to European crunch games against the likes of Valencia
and Deportivo. Does he bottle it? Maybe, or perhaps he is just such
a thoroughbred athlete that too many games in too short a time and
his legs run out of steam. I think he chokes a bit, that he is not so
great when the heat is really on – and Chelsea were turning up the
gas in a brilliant way, no question. I also think he's not enjoying
seeing all the attention he is used to receiving going to young Reyes.
The chemistry is poor between them, and I reckon Thierry's just the
tiniest bit jealous. Which from a man who prides himself on being
Mr Team is not good to see. His mediocrity was so obvious that
Wenger eventually substituted him in the 80th minute for
Bergkamp, an almost unheard of event. Henry looked momentarily
stunned, standing there like a king who has just been told to
abdicate by a knave. On TV, Ron Atkinson apparently said it was
Wenger's biggest ever gamble as a manager. But none of us in the
crowd thought that. Most of us just thought how ironic that our
weakest player on the night was the one given the FA Cup semi-
final off so he could put his feet up and rest.

As Chelsea grew stronger, we grew weaker. Lampard was *The
Boss* by the end, so strong in the tackle and constantly charging
forward to create attacking chances. He is a great player and just
seemed to have a bigger heart and engine than our big stars on the
night. As they came after us more and more, we retreated into our
own penalty area like lambs to the slaughter until, in the 87th
minute, Bridge steamed in to do a quick-fire one-two with
Gudjohnsen to fire low and hard into the far corner. It was over.

Rob, biting his entire face next to me, went into what I can only
describe as some weird sort of contortional fit, writhing his hands
and feet into a slow break-dance of joy masquerading as misery to
avoid getting a thoroughly deserved beating from my upper East
Stand colleagues. Bizarrely, I was pleased for him, genuinely. My
God he's earned something from this fixture. But my charitable

thoughts didn't extend to the rest of the Chelsea fans still inside the stadium 15 minutes after the end chanting 'Champions League ... you're having a laugh' over and over. A chant that works on two levels, one a straight acknowledgement that they can't believe their luck, and the second that we're not going to win it after all. Over dinner later I shook Rob's hand and told him how happy I was for him. He laughed, and with a shocking lack of grace grabbed my mobile and posed for a photo of himself giving The Bird. That's the trouble with Chelsea fans, no class. I saw Abramovich on the box later, with a smile as wide as the Volga. His side walked to the plate tonight and played like champions, no question. If I was Ranieri, I'd be straight round to ask for a new contract. But he's too nice to do that. He may be a tinkerman, but his bringing on of Gronkjaer to tease and torment Cole down the right wing was masterly.

**Arsenal:** Jens Lehmann, Sol Campbell, Ashley Cole, Patrick Vieira, Fredrik Ljungberg, Lauren (yellow card), Robert Pires, Kolo Touré, Edu, José Reyes, Thierry Henry, Dennis Bergkamp 81. Subs not used: Graham Stack, Martin Keown, Gael Clichy, Gilberto, Sylvain Wiltord, Nwankwo Kanu

**Chelsea:** Marco Ambrosio, Mario Melchiot, John Terry, Wayne Bridge, William Gallas (yellow card), Claude Makelele, Frank Lampard, Scott Parker, Jesper Gronkjaer 46, Damien Duff, Joe Cole 82, Eidur Gudjohnsen, Jimmy Floyd Hasselbaink (yellow card), Hernan Crespo 82. Subs not used: Neil Sullivan, Robert Huth, Geremi, Adrian Mutu

**José Reyes 45, Frank Lampard 51, Wayne Bridge 87**

## 8th April 2004

There are days as a football fan, even an Arsenal fan, when you just want to stay in bed, turn the mobile off, don't go near a computer or TV and hope you die before having too many nightmares about what has just happened to your team. And this was most definitely one of those days. Dumped out of the Cup by those grim-faced, mean-spirited Mancunians on Saturday, and now dumped out of the Champions League by Chelsea – who obliterated those eighteen consecutive failures to win, by winning the big one when it *really, really* mattered.

Unfortunately, staying in bed all day incommunicado is not the natural preserve of a daily tabloid editor, and I was woken at 6.45 a.m. by the first of sixteen text messages from Chelsea fans.

The sheer scale of gloating is quite revolting, but I can only imagine the mounting intensity all those disappointments must have created in the poor lambs, so I can almost laugh at their impudence. I am less tolerant of those I actually employ though. They are in for a slightly rougher ride if they continue this line of communication with the editor all day.

By the time I got to work, my e-mail system was jammed too. All with the same message. An entirely predictable, and under any other circumstances reasonably amusing, Patty Rice Car Boot Sale. It reads as follows: For Sale: One Arsenal dartboard. Has no doubles or trebles. For Sale: Arsenal Treble Winners 2004 T-shirts, hats and scarves – never worn. For Sale: Two metres of trophy cabinet carpet, slightly dusty. Oh ho, ho, ho, bloody ho. The first person to send it was, naturally, Sir Alan Sugar – barely able to contain his glee. Amazing these Spurs fans, literally the only joy they get these days comes when we lose the very occasional game and they can taunt us that we are not completely perfect. The Arsenal websites are a cyber-morgue.

What's unbelievable is that Madrid and Milan have also crashed out after comfortable first-leg leads. Wenger seems very twitchy about the effect this double blow might have on our Premiership hopes. 'When you are on such a long unbeaten run it's a big blow to lose,' he said. 'It's strange. Once you hit the wall it's hard to recover. Football is cruel. It's like that – difficult to accept.' The league is far from won. The most difficult thing is in front of us; it's a big weekend.' Of the game itself, he said: 'We were very good in the first half but we dropped too deep, ran too much with the ball in the second. We were not compact enough.' Neither were Henry's hamstrings. He is injured, allegedly, and may be out for a few games. Call me cynical but he seemed to trot off quite happily yesterday. It seems rather convenient that his poor performance has now been commuted down to a bad hamstring.

## Liverpool
### PREMIERSHIP, HIGHBURY
### RESULT: 4-2 WIN

My location: at game

A nightmare start. We looked dead and buried, a pale and insipid mockery of the team that has torched the Premiership all season. The atmosphere was sobre and fearful on and off the pitch. It was as if we all knew, players and fans,that we'd blown everything in a few disastrous days. Liverpool seized on our collective despair by scoring early, Gerrard heading down a corner for Hyypia to bang it in from two yards. Unwisely they then put defence before attack when they'd have been better off pulverising us when we were down. Against all expectations Pires found Henry on the half-hour and he shot instantly, diagonally inside the far post. But our relief was short-lived when Owen pounced on a Gerrard through ball, and Lehmann stood there like a big useless Frankfurter as the small but lethal England striker raced on to score from less than ten yards. 2-1 down at half-time and nobody gave us a prayer. Our season was over, crushed, cremated. I've never known Highbury so miserable. Just the quiet shuffling of a crowd that couldn't bear to attend the inevitable funeral to come.

But something miraculous then occurred. Wenger must have delivered something almost Churchillian in the interval because we came out like a different team, tearing into them as if the very security of our nation depended on it. Pires slickly fired in the equaliser from a Ljungberg pass and then Henry completed a breathtaking, wondrous hat-trick. As if he'd been injected with neat adrenalin, he waltzed past Hamman, dummied Carragher in hideously embarrassing fashion and side-footed it past a flailing Dudek. Then, minutes later he ran on to a long ball from Bergkamp and shot hard, scoring from the rebound. Henry sprinted dementedly round the ground like a gazelle with a spear in his back, growling and flapping. This was his way of telling us it was all going to be OK. We'll still win the League at a canter, let's stop crying, guys. Wenger smiled afterwards: 'Thierry was very doubtful but we gave him a warm-up, and I thought he played quite well, didn't you!' The manager was obviously relieved our week hadn't ended how he must have feared it might at half-time. 'When you get knocked in the face you want to respond, and when this team's backs are to the wall, they produce.' Gerard Houllier concurred: 'I feared Arsenal would react like a wounded animal and they did. They're the best team in the country when they play like that.'

**Arsenal:** Jens Lehmann, Sol Campbell, Ashley Cole (yellow card), Lauren (yellow card), Fredrik Ljungberg, Robert Pires, Edu 72, Patrick Vieira (yellow card), Martin Keown 90, Kolo Touré, Gilberto, Dennis Bergkamp, Thierry Henry. Subs not used: Rami Shaaban, Gael Clichy, José Reyes

**Liverpool:** Jerzy Dudek, Sami Hyypia, Jamie Carragher, Dietmar Hamann, Harry Kewell, Steven Gerrard, John Riise, Igor Biscan, El Diouf (yellow card), Danny Murphy 85, Emile Heskey, Milan Baros 66, Michael Owen. Subs not used: Patrice Luzi Bernardi, Stephane Henchoz
**Thierry Henry 31, 50, 78, Robert Pires 49, Hyypia (5), Owen (42)**

## 8th April 2004

A rather fetching young lady called Rebecca Loos has sold her story of an affair with David Beckham to the *News of the World*. This is obviously a fantastic story, but the edge is slightly taken off it for me when I am informed by an excitable cousin that Rebecca and I are related. Admittedly in a rather tenuous way, but definitely related. It comes to something when members of your own family sell their story to a rival paper ...

SUNDAY
**11**
APRIL

# Newcastle United
**PREMIERSHIP, HIGHBURY**
**RESULT: 0-0 DRAW**
My location: watching TV at home

After the Lord Mayor's Show, definitely, but an important draw nevertheless. Newcastle are desperately chasing that last European place, and were always going to be up for it tonight. Lehmann and

Vieira kept them at bay, though, with superb performances at the back. The German was responsible for two of the goals that sent us out of the Champions League, but he has been very consistent this season and in the Premiership has conceded a goal every twelve shots, compared to Seaman's final average of a goal every eight shots.

Shearer was his usual bustling, aggressive self, and gave his usual totally non-committal reply to the regular cries of 'Shearer is a w***er' which is a familiar term of endearment he has now had to endure at every ground in the country for about fifteen years. I love the guy though. Strong as an ox, always trying, a natural goal-scorer, and clever enough to quit international football before it quit him, and concentrate on extending one of the greatest Premiership careers ever. It was a tight game, nobody got a really good chance, though Henry did round Given to hit the post late on and Reyes hit Given from six yards from a Henry cross. But that is four points from six in two massive games after we were ditched from two competitions. And dog-tired though we look, there is a steely glint in the lads' eyes that says we are not going to throw away the one that matters most.

**Arsenal:** Jens Lehmann, Sol Campbell, Ashley Cole, Gael Clichy 90, Patrick Vieira (yellow card), Lauren, Kolo Touré, Gilberto, Edu, José Reyes, Dennis Bergkamp 79, Thierry Henry, Sylvain Wiltord, Robert Pires 79. Subs not used: Rami Shaaban, Martin Keown

**Newcastle United:** Shay Given, Andy O'Brien, Jonathan Woodgate, Aaron Hughes, Olivier Bernard, Laurent Robert, Hugo Viana 79, Jermaine Jenas, Darren Ambrose, Lee Bowyer 78, Gary Speed, Craig Bellamy, Alan Shearer. Subs not used: Steve Harper, Titus Bramble, Shola Ameobi

**FRIDAY**
**16**
**APRIL**

## Leeds United
**PREMIERSHIP, HIGHBURY**
**RESULT: 5-0 WIN**
My location: at game

OK, Thierry, we get the message, mate. When you play like this the entire Roman army would struggle to stop you. This was just utterly sensational, the kind of one-man show that would run for ten years on Broadway if you could capture it in words or music. Wenger has built this team around Henry, and when it clicks like today you see why.

The carnage started after six minutes with five first-time passes at breakneck speed before Pires raced onto his eighteenth goal of the season, amazing for a midfielder in this league. I really worried after the home Inter Milan game that Pires might never recover from that broken leg, but his pace and technique tonight showed he is better than ever. It's always Henry, Henry, Henry. But nobody should doubt how brilliant Pires can be when he's in the mood. And all this with two of the flattest feet seen since I won the non-finalists' race at school. Henry smashed in two goals from Gilberto passes, a penalty when Duberry handled a Bergkamp flick, then brought the stadium to its rafters with a dazzling slalom into the box ending in a superb jab as he was felled by Kelly. 'Boring boring Arsenal' sang the Clock End gleefully.

Leeds were horrific, apart from Smith as ever. Their tactic of trying to defend with a back four pushing well up the pitch was like watching a load of lemmings edging to the side of a cliff. It seemed like a good idea at the time, until they started falling off. Henry just skimmed through them like a samurai through a plate of sushi. After the game, Leeds manager Eddie Gray summed up the unilateral onslaught succinctly: 'The only way to stop Henry is to knock him out.' Wenger said simply that Henry was 'the best striker in the world', and who would argue? Occasionally infuriating, yes.

A bit of a choker in the big games, maybe. But week in, week out, he is the top dog – no question. 'It's difficult to find each time new words for Thierry,' Wenger said. 'Rather than talking about him, it's better watching him. When the team is on the same wavelength, with his power and pace and skills, it's a joy to watch. We have many players who can put him through.' His finishing gets better and I think in recent games he's come back to a more central position again. For a while he went systematically out wide left. With a more central position he's more dangerous.' He now has 150 Arsenal goals and is closing in on Ian Wright's record of 185. Like the championship, that will surely not be long in coming.

**Arsenal:** Jens Lehmann, Gael Clichy, Sol Campbell, Robert Pires, Ray Parlour 72, Patrick Vieira, Kolo Touré, Gilberto, Edu 69, Lauren, Dennis Bergkamp, José Reyes 72, Thierry Henry, Sylvain Wiltord. Subs not used: Graham Stack, Martin Keown

**Leeds United:** Paul Robinson, Dominic Matteo, Gary Kelly, Lucas Radebe, Nick Barmby 72, Ian Harte, Michael Duberry, Stephen Caldwell, James Milner, Jermaine Pennant, Mark Viduka, Simon Johnson 84, Alan Smith. Subs not used: Scott Carson, Matthew Kilgallon, Aaron Lennon

**Robert Pires 6, Thierry Henry 27, 33 (pen), 50, 67**

**SUNDAY**
# 25
**APRIL**

## Tottenham Hotspur
### PREMIERSHIP, WHITE HART LANE
### RESULT: 2-2 DRAW
My location: at game

There are great things to enjoy in life, like hiring a gondola in Venice, riding camels around the Pyramids, or watching the Australians lose at anything, anywhere. But for Arsenal fans the prospect of actually winning the League at the home of our most bitter sworn enemies was too gloriously exciting to even contemplate. And yet, here we were, and it was now a distinct possibility. If we didn't lose and Chelsea didn't win then we would win it here at White Hart Lane. The last time that happened was in 1971, when Frank McClintock's great Double-winning side were on fire.

I was a guest of Sir Alan Sugar, a *Mirror* columnist and a very amusing hard-nosed tycoon who loves a bit of vile banter and a wind-up or ten. I spent most of lunch in the Spurs boardroom teaching his grandchildren Arsenal chants and generally irritating him with requests for a pass to go onto the pitch should we win the title that afternoon, and so on. Most Spurs fans feared the worst anyway, and their mood was sullen. I would imagine that is how the poor souls are most of the time at the moment. It's bad enough being as bad as they are without Arsenal playing out of their skins at the same time. The sullenness turned to abject horror when news came in that Newcastle had beaten Chelsea. I actually saw some Spurs fans *leave* the ground at that point, clearly unable to take the risk of being there if it happened. They've always had a lively crowd here, but you can sense the dejection at their total lack of competitiveness any more. For a team that always boasted a superstar, be it Lineker or Gascoigne, Villa or Ardiles, or Klinsmann, Spurs walked tall with big, big players. But today there was nobody, just a bunch of pedestrian second-rate journeymen who most kids would never have heard of. The whole set-up stinks of mid-table ennui, and the cynicism is tangible and nasty. These are bitter people, bitter at the way their club has been mishandled for decades now, and genuinely wondering if it will ever change. Although the rival fans will still clump seven bells out of each other, the truth is that the professional rivalry is non-exsistent. Frankly, the gulf is so big that it doesn't matter any more what Spurs do. And it's that fact that hurts them most. I don't like it, to be honest. I'd rather they were a massive club again so the rivalry really meant something. My dad watched them every week for eleven years and to hear him talking wistfully of the days when Danny Blanchflower strode White Hart Lane like a colossus is sad. That was forty years ago.

The game started frantically, as it always does, but we looked completely in control this time. And after just three minutes Henry scooped up the ball from a Spurs corner, hared upfield and passed it to a flying Bergkamp who crossed it to a rampant Vieira. Our skipper nearly missed it but somehow got one of his giant feet to the ball and prodded it home. It was a fast, furious, brilliant goal and knocked any stuffing Spurs may have had out of their tormented hearts. In the 35th minute it was two, Bergkamp again finding Vieira who cut it back for Pires to side-foot in. This was all too easy. As the players went in for half-time, Arsenal fans began chanting ''71, we'll do it again, '71, we'll do it again.' The party was in full swing.

But Spurs have a habit of ruining our best-laid plans, and sure enough they came back at us in the second half – playing with twice the passion they had mustered in the first. With half an hour to go Redknapp scorched in a 25-yarder and it really livened up, Pires hitting the bar, Redknapp and then Henry going close. Then, just as the three minutes of injury time started, the nightmare happened. Spurs got a corner, and Lehmann stupidly held Robbie Keane in the goalmouth. Keane got up to score the penalty and their fans went absolutely potty.

It was a weird atmosphere at the end. We'd won the League, but Spurs had definitely put a dampener on things. It just all felt a bit flat, with even the Arsenal directors looking rather miserable. Then we went inside, got the champagne out, remembered what we'd just actually achieved and enjoyed ourselves. Outside, I could hear the Arsenal players partying with the 3,000 Arsenal fans left in the deserted Spurs stadium. This was as sweet as it gets, and no last-minute equaliser is going to ruin this historic moment. Unbeaten champions ... at Tottenham. Life truly cannot get any better than this, surely. I was in the boardroom afterwards having a drink with my father – a long-suffering Tottenham supporter. It was 8 p.m., getting dark, and nearly everyone had gone – though outside the ground police were still coping with rioting fans. The door then opened and in walked Arsène Wenger, alone. He strolled to the bar and asked for a glass of red wine, then stood smiling to himself. Barely believing my luck, I went over and asked if we could join him for a celebratory drink. 'Of course,' he said, radiating that charm which is as genuine away from the TV cameras as you hope it might be. For half an hour he then held court about the amazing season we had enjoyed – 'I never thought it would be possible for any team to go a whole season unbeaten, it's just fantastic', on his amazing players – 'Thierry is the fastest I have ever seen, he is just unbelievable'; and on next season, 'I want to keep winning, we have the team now.' As I rather embarrassingly got him to pose for a picture with me on my mobile phone, I mentioned that I'd sat next to Michael Owen at the *Mirror*'s Pride of Britain awards and tried to persuade him to sign for us. Wenger laughed, 'He wants to come, I know that. They all do.' And who can blame them? What player in the world would not want to be managed by Arsène Wenger, and run out alongside Thierry Henry? And what fan in the world wouldn't want to be where I will be come August, watching it all from the upper East Stand at Highbury.

**Arsenal:** Jens Lehmann (yellow card), Sol Campbell, Ashley Cole, Robert Pires, Ray Parlour, Edu 67, Patrick Vieira, Lauren, Kolo Touré, Gilberto, Dennis Bergkamp, José Reyes 80, Thierry Henry. Subs not used: Graham Stack, Gael Clichy, Martin Keown

**Tottenham Hotspur:** Kasey Keller, Stephen Kelly, Gustavo Poyet 79, Anthony Gardner, Mauricio Taricco, Goran Bunjevcevic 90, Ledley King, Simon Davies, Jamie Redknapp (yellow card), Michael Brown, Johnnie Jackson, Jermain Defoe 45, Fredi Kanoute, Robbie Keane. Subs not used: Lars Hirschfeld, Rohan Ricketts

Patrick Vieira 3, Robert Pires 35, **Jamie Redknapp 62, Robbie Keane 90 (pen)**

## 26th April 2004

The post mortem rages across Britain – just how good is this Arsenal side? Better than the Double side of '71? Certainly. Up there with Blanchflower's Spurs and the Treble-winning United team? Definitely. But can we really lay claim yet to be as good as the great Liverpool side of the eighties that won four European Cups? Or even Cloughie's Forest team that won it twice? I don't think so. Great sides win great tournaments. We are a very good side who play great football, but we haven't won the big European prize yet and until we do, that must be the benchmark. The players, though, understand the significance of winning the Premiership at

Spurs. Henry said: 'Although it was quite important for us to win the title here, it was more for the fans.' You don't win the title every day. It happened that it was at Tottenham and that's more special but we would have done it everywhere. We know that it's special for the fans so you can't just leave and go home. They deserved it.' But Wenger's concentrating on that unbeaten season. Now *that* achievement could propel us to the official level of 'Great', definitely. 'That's my biggest target, to keep the players focused,' Wenger said. 'Do we switch off or not? That will show how much we want it. To lose a game or two because we are champions and switch off would not be ideal. We are so close I would love to keep it going.'

## 27th April 2004

The rumour mill has gone into overdrive about our transfer targets. The *Sun* reckon we've got Gerrard and Terry sewn up in a £35 million double swoop. Yeah, right. The *Mirror* says Owen might come for £12 million, which seems rather more likely given my little chats with him and Wenger. And everyone seems agreed that Lehmann's going to get the chop, though I don't see why. He's had an excellent season. The best gossip, though, concerns van Nistelrooy, who is being linked with Real Madrid all over the place. Now that really would put the icing on the cake.

## 30th April 2004

Lehmann's going nowhere, says Wenger. 'He is my number one, 100 per cent. He has had an outstanding championship. I am not looking for another goalkeeper. Jens has shown remarkable consistency and I cannot think of any mistakes he has made in Premiership games. He doesn't get the credit he deserves.' High praise indeed. And I agree with him. He's barking but brilliant. Unfortunately Wenger fails to confirm Cygan's departure. We can but hope and wait.

# MAY

'Arsenal are quite simply the
most fluid, devastating team
that the British Isles
has seen'

ALAN HANSEN

## Birmingham City
### PREMIERSHIP, HIGHBURY
### RESULT: 0-0 DRAW
My location: at game

I was a guest today of Karren Brady, the dynamic female boss of Birmingham. Blonde, ballsy, and great fun, Karren was fatalistic about her team's chances: 'Look, we're not going to win this in a million years but since I'm an Arsenal fan, although I keep that quiet obviously, I am going to love every minute of today.'

The Arsenal boardroom is everything you hope it will be: dark, austere, reeking in tradition. The contrast between City's board members and ours is amusing. They, led by porn barons David Gold and David Sullivan, are all flash checked suits, lots of gold, with peroxide blondes on their arms. Arsenal's chiefs are sobre-suited, tasteful, classy. They all seem to get on pretty well though. John Motson cuts a bit of a sad figure, sat in a corner in his sheepskin coat. He's a lovely guy, and a brilliant commentator, but most people aren't that excited to see him – an indicator that his time may be nearly up. I have a chat with Peter Hill-Wood, the wonderful chairman of Arsenal and a senior member of the family that has effectively owned the club for decades. Avuncular, impeccably attired, and very open even to journalists, he is an impressive character in a world of sharks and cowboys. He's also great for quotes, especially after a 'long lunch'. Most football reporters short of a juicy story on a quiet news day float a call into Hill-Wood on the off chance he might be up for a bit of banter. I remember when Vieira was playing his usual contract games. Hill-Wood let it go on for a bit, then popped up to make a thunderous statement about loyalty, greed, the honour of playing for Arsenal. Vieira signed pretty quickly after that. He was very funny about Abramovich: 'He says he doesn't speak a word of English, but when he came here with all his armed bodyguards everywhere I reckoned he understood everything I was saying. It just suits him to play dumb.' Another source in the boardroom, who shall remain anonymous because I want another invite obviously, later confides that the Russian made a firm bid of £50 million for Henry almost as soon as he bought Chelsea. And then tried to get Wenger for £10 million, an offer that Wenger apparently seriously considered for a long weekend. Very, long if you are on the Arsenal board. It is gratifying to learn that money can't buy everything, and very reassuring that even with the pressures of financing a new stadium, our board realise when they have irreplaceable jewels in the crown. As one director put it, what's the point in having a fabulous new ground if you don't have the best players to fill it or the best manager to run the side?

The League won, it was time for a bit of fun. 'What the f***ing hell was that' chanted the Clock End when Henry fluffed one early on, to general hilarity including a huge knowing grin from the great man. That was about the most exciting moment of a crashingly dull game. The biggest cheer of the day came when Keown replaced Bergkamp with a few minutes to go. The crowd know all about his need to get on the pitch to earn his medal, he knows it, Wenger knows it – and when he finally trotted out in that gladiatorial way the place went mad. Keown's a very popular player here. Mainly because he's got the Arsenal spirit carved onto his heart. You just know he'd die for the cause if he had to.

**Arsenal:** Jens Lehmann, Sol Campbell, Ashley Cole, Patrick Vieira, Fredrik Ljungberg, Robert Pires 69, Lauren, Kolo Touré, Gilberto, José Reyes, Jeremie Aladiere 79, Dennis Bergkamp, Martin Keown 90, Thierry Henry. Subs not used: Rami Shaaban, Ray Parlour

**Birmingham City:** Ian Bennett, Jamie Clapham, Kenny Cunningham, Olivier Tebily, Matthew Upson, Robbie Savage (yellow card), Stephen Clemence, Stan Lazaridis, Damien Johnson (yellow card), David Dunn, Bryan Hughes 76, Clinton Morrison, Stern John 72. Subs not used: Colin Doyle, Aliou Cisse, Martin Taylor

# Portsmouth
## PREMIERSHIP, FRATTON PARK
## RESULT: 1-1 DRAW

My location: watching TV in London

Portsmouth, emboldened by their terrific achievement in staying up for another season of Premiership football against all the odds, came at us like electric eels. Yakubu stole the ball off Cole to force a Lehmann save, then LuaLua dispossessed Campbell but hit it just wide. It was frantic, exciting stuff and Portsmouth fully deserved their goal in the 30th minute when Yakubu chased Taylor's long punt, saw it bounce off Touré's head back to him and squeezed it inside the near post. We equalised four minutes into the second half when Reyes latched onto an Henry corner. And after that it looked like both sides were quite happy to take the draw. What was amazing was that adulation shown to one of our team. I've seen some bizarre sights in my football-watching time, but the extraordinary love-in between Thierry Henry and the Portsmouth fans today was something else. They spent most of the last quarter chanting 'We're gonna buy Henry', 'You're the best player in the world' and so on. Just one long orgy of love for a guy playing for the other team. 'They were singing my name for the last 25 minutes of the game, something I've never had in my whole life, and it was as if we were at Highbury,' he said afterwards. 'That's why I love the game in England – the people are so passionate. I've seen it at Highbury, too. When one team is better than the other they can get a standing ovation, even from the opposing supporters.'

**Arsenal:** Jens Lehmann, Sol Campbell (yellow card), Ashley Cole, Ray Parlour (yellow card), Patrick Vieira, Fredrik Ljungberg, Jeremie Aliadiere 90, Lauren, Kolo Touré, David Bentley, Nwankwo Kanu 61, José Reyes, Martin Keown 90, Thierry Henry. Subs not used: Rami Shaaban, Gael Clichy

**Portsmouth:** Shaka Hislop, John Curtis, Matthew Taylor, Arjan De Zeeuw, Dejan Stefanovic, Amdy Faye, Richard Hughes, Nigel Quashie, Steve Stone, Tresor Lua Lua, Yakubu Aiyegbeni, Ivica Mornar 80. Subs not used: Harald Wapenaar, Richard Duffy, Kevin Harper, Teddy Sheringham

José Reyes 50, **Yakubu Aiyegbeni 30**

# Fulham
## PREMIERSHIP, LOFTUS ROAD
## RESULT: 0-1 WIN

My location: family christening in Wiltshire; listening on car radio

This was always going to be a threat to our unbeaten record. Fulham have played consistently well under new manager Chris Coleman and are hunting hard for that sixth place, and Europe. But this was our 15th clean sheet of the season, our eighth away from home. An amazing record from an increasingly solid, dependable back four.

Our goal came thanks to a terrible blunder from Van der Sar, who was so outstanding at Highbury. For some inexplicable reason he tried to dribble a back pass from Goma past Reyes, who has the quickest feet in the hemisphere. The Spaniard nicked it off him with ease and strolled it into the net. Nine minutes in, and 1-0. Pressure off. Fulham tried everything to unsettle us, changing their midfield formation five times. But nothing really worked. The dodgy pitch was littered with useless lumps, and I'm not just talking about Boa Morte. Some of our boys appeared to have been celebrating a little too keenly. Pires, especially, appeared to be viewing the day as a good walk spoiled. But we did the job required, and the record now looms as a reality.

**Arsenal:** Jens Lehmann, Sol Campbell, Ashley Cole, Ray Parlour (yellow card), Patrick Vieira (yellow card), Fredrik Ljungberg, Martin Keown 87, Robert Pires, Gael Clichy 78, Lauren, Kolo Touré, José Reyes, Jeremie Aliadiere 71, Thierry Henry (yellow card). Subs not used: Graham Stack, Dennis Bergkamp

**Fulham:** Edwin Van der Sar, Alain Goma, Ian Pearce, Martin Djetou, Collins John 58, Moritz Volz, Carlos Bocanegra, Junichi Inamoto, Brian McBride 58, Steed Malbranque, Sean Davis (yellow card), Sylvain Legwinski, Luis Boa Morte. Subs not used: Mark Crossley, Mark Hudson, Bobby Petta

**José Reyes 9**

## 10th May 2004

Andy Gray's picked his team of the season. Lauren gets in, to my surprise – 'consistent high quality, defends well, recovery good, strong, uncompromising and likes to get forward.' Could apply to most of our players, to be honest. Sol's there, and that is no surprise. What a fantastic player he is. No fuss, no hysteria, very few mistakes. As Gray says: 'A lot of people would be fazed by following in the footsteps of Tony Adams but Campbell's been perfect. He shares that hunger, experience, hates losing and is an unbelievable competitor.' Vieira's in the middle, of course – 'Graeme Souness said to me recently, if you see Patrick tell him from me he is the top man', and if Graeme thinks he's the best then he is. Pires is next to him – 'Nineteen goals this season, if you're looking for a wide player to create and score then he's the best in the business.' Up front Henry, obviously. 'He's a phenomenon.' And next to him, Shearer. Now that I would love to see.

## 11th May 2004

Thierry Henry has been voted the Football Writers' Player of the Year. This comes a few days after he won the Players' Player of the Year award. And he so deserves all the honours being heaped upon him now.

## 14th May 2004

I've been fired as editor of the *Mirror*. But still, worry about that next week. There's a massive game tomorrow.

**SATURDAY**

**15**

**MAY**

# Leicester City
**PREMIERSHIP, HIGHBURY**
**RESULT: 2-1 WIN**
My location: at game

The script was straightforward. Turn up, beat hopeless team about
7-0 and have a party. As usual, we tore up the script and went behind
in the 26th minute to a piece of freakish genius from Frank Sinclair
(yes, I know, not the most natural bedfellows, Frank and genius)
who strolled towards us from the halfway line than casually planted
a sensational cross straight onto Dickov's head and into the net.
'Invincible my arse' came the cry from the ecstatic Leicester fans,
who suddenly saw a tiny glimmer of a chance of celebrating something
in their miserable little season: wrecking our bid for history.

We looked tired and worryingly nervous as the minutes dragged
by, and Leicester's increasingly irritating fans even started Olé-ing
as their team started passing it around like AC Milan in the Gullit
days. I would love to have been a fly on the wall of our dressing
room at half-time. Wenger must have flipped his lid completely
because we came out like rabid bears. Later, Wenger said the
atmosphere during his pep talk had been one of open 'revolt' with
players queuing up to shout at each other. Anyway, Bergkamp
quickly lobbed the ball to a marauding Cole who was tripped by
Sinclair, now playing his usual role of bumbling fool, and won a
penalty. Henry thumped in his thirtieth goal of the Premiership,
comfortably winning the Golden Boot. He also has the most assists,
something van Nistelrooy wouldn't know how to spell. An amazing
pair of statistics from an amazing player.

Re-energised by the goal, we began to attack. Bergkamp led most
of it, playing the best football we've seen from him in three years.
Leicester retreated to their own half, barely moving except to lob
the occasional hopeless pass to the lone Dickov. The second goal was
just brilliant, Bergkamp again delicately slicing apart Leicester's

defence to meet a charging Vieira who never broke his run as he
steamed into the ball and crashed it past Walker. The win was in
the bag, the record guaranteed.

But there was still one hugely important moment: Martin
Keown's vital tenth cameo role of the season, which would earn him
a title medal. He prowled the touchline like an excited hyena, as
Wenger played hilarious mind games with him, first ushering him
up, then sending him back with a laugh. We all knew the game, and
we all knew Keown would eventually get on, which he did with a
minute to go – to the biggest roar you've ever heard. A perfect end
to a perfect day, and a perfect season. Played thirty-eight, won
twenty-six, drawn twelve, lost none. Incredible. Wenger seemed
almost overcome by it all. 'I am shocked,' he said. 'My dream was
always to go through a whole season unbeaten. It's beyond belief.
Not many managers can say they did that.' He can say that again.
The last in this country, Preston's Major William Sudell, is long
dead. The 1,060,444 fortunate souls who have clicked through the
Highbury turnstiles this season have watched history unfurl. And
they have watched it happen in sensational, wonderful style.

**Arsenal:** Jens Lehmann, Sol Campbell, Ashley Cole, Patrick Vieira, Fredrik Ljungberg, Martin Keown 87, Robert Pires, Edu 70, Lauren, Kolo Touré, Gilberto, Dennis Bergkamp, José Reyes 82, Thierry Henry. Subs not used: Graham Stack, Ray Parlour

**Leicester City:** Ian Walker, Danny Coyne 78, Nikos Dabizas, Matthew Heath, Frank Sinclair (yellow card), Billy McKinlay, Lilian Nalis, Jordan Stewart, Steffen Freund, Paul Brooker 76, James Scowcroft, Paul Dickov, Trevor Benjamin 85, Marcus Bent. Subs not used: Keith Gillespie, Steve Guppy

Thierry Henry 47 (pen), Patrick Vieira 66, **Paul Dickov 26**

## 16th May 2004

The tributes are cascading in, from the great, the good, the showbiz,
the political – everyone, it seems, wants to get in on the Arsenal act.
Philippe Auclair, a respected commentator for *France Football*, says
we are the 'Harlem Globetrotters of the world right now, playing
poetry, absolute poetry'. He goes on to drool that we're better than
Real Madrid, and right up there with 'the great Ajax, the great
Milan side of Gullit. They are just beautiful.' Brian Glanville of the

*Sunday Times* urges a little caution: 'I rank Herbert Chapman's 1930–31 Arsenal champions better than this team, because they at least had some hard competition.' What a load of garbage. How could we have more ferocious competition than United and Chelsea, the two richest clubs in world football history? Alan Smith, still reviled by Gooners for his trashing of the team after the Battle of Old Trafford, says this is the 'best team Highbury's ever seen', in a belated effort to redeem himself. Spurs fan and author Hunter Davies is typically churlish, hilariously claiming that 'Carlisle have been just as good as Arsenal in the last two months'. Hunter, go and have a lie down, mate. Dale Winton, that well-known connoisseur of world football, is less reserved, cooing in a slightly unsavoury way before the Leicester match, 'I am keeping every moveable part of my anatomy crossed for good luck'. Barry McGuigan, another Spurs fan, admits 'through gritted teeth' that it's all down to Arsenal's fitness levels. And he's right there, they really are supreme athletes. My favourite two quotes, though, come from Alan Hansen, whose opinion I really do respect given the fabulous success he enjoyed as a player: 'Arsenal are quite simply the most fluid, devastating team that the British Isles has seen', and, from Mr Johnny Rotten, who when asked for his opinion replied: 'They've been a disappointment to me this year.'

# England XI
## KEOWN TESTIMONIAL, HIGHBURY
## RESULT: 6-0 WIN
My location: at game

I've spent the last few years lying awake at night wondering what it would have been like to see Thierry Henry and Ian Wright play up front together, and now it has finally happened. Some 38,000 people paid good money to see Keown's Arsenal XI play an England XI. It was cracking fun, and a fantastic way for Keown to bow out. But despite all the fuss about Beckham playing – in the end he could only kick off because Real Madrid banned him at the last minute – there was only one gig in town and that was the amazing sight of the two greatest Arsenal strikers ever, running out together, wearing each other's shirts. It genuinely sent a tingle down my spine, and the mutual respect between them was marvellous to see. Wrighty hobbled off after ten minutes, leaving Reyes to score a dazzling hat-trick – and Keown to bid an emotional farewell. That's the end of George Graham's fabulous defence now, and what magnificent servants they were. As I leave the ground, a steward shouts out to me: 'Hey Piers, almost worth getting sacked for, mate, isn't it, watching us this season?' Almost? Definitely, mate.

**Arsenal:** Graham Stack, Lee Dixon, Ashley Cole, Patrick Vieira, Martin Keown, Ian Wright, José Antonio Reyes, Thierry Henry, Edu, Sol Campbell, Freddie Ljungberg, Dennis Bergkamp, Jeremie Aliadiere, Marc Overmars, Lauren, Pascal Cygan, Gilberto, Philippe Senderos, Gael Clichy, Kolo Touré, Sebastian Svard,

**England XI:** Robert Green, Jlloyd Samuel, Chris Powell, Matthew Upson, John Terry, David Beckham, Jermain Defoe, Andy Cole, Jason Euell, Ray Parlour, John Salako, David Beckham, Joe Cole, Ledley King, Ian Wright, Robbie Fowler, Paul Gascoigne, Shaun Wright-Phillips, Mark Howard, Justin Hoyte, David Bentley

Ashley Cole 17, Jeremie Aliadiere 23, 77, José Antonio Reyes 53, 58, 66

# STOP PRESS:

As I write this, Kanu's been sold to West Brom, Martin
Keown's gone to Leicester, Sylvain Wiltord's transfer to
Marseille has collapsed but he's still likely to leave, and we've
signed Spanish keeper Manuel Almunia and Dutch striker
Robin Van Persie. It seems virtually certain now that Patrick
Vieira is going to Madrid for around £23 million. Francis
Jeffers is still here, so that goes to show what I know about
football, doesn't it, and Ray Parlour, an outstanding servant,
has taken a pay cut to go to Middlesborough, presumably just
to irritate his wife. Tragically, Pascal Cygan was leaving, but
Lille refused at the last minute to buy out the last two years
of his contract. Christ, I'd pay it myself if it meant he was
definitely going ...

# Any Street A

## W. G. Graham

### Acknowledgments

Thanks to Charles Blyth, Gary and Moira Galbraith without whose assistance this novel could not have been completed. And to Ross Matheson for the cover illustration.

### Disclaimer

All events and characters in this novel are entirely fictitious. Any resemblance to any character living or dead is purely coincidental. The football passage is in no way intended to be a reflection on our present National Football Team.

**ISBN 978-0-9576818-2-8**
Published by MDPD
(enquiries@mdpd.co.uk)

the room for Doddie, contemplating telling him what he thought had occurred. Neither he nor Sadie were there. Therefore, he concluded that he had dreamed the whole thing after all.

How long had he slept, if slept was the right word, he wondered? The cold morning air hit Colin as he staggered up the garden path, feeling only a slight pang of guilt at throwing up in the flower bed and giggling at telling the flowery recipients they were a lucky bunch as it was all good vitamins he was endowing on them.

Colin was in a silent world as he made his way home, the estate ghostlike in the early morning summer air. Somewhere a dog barked and had its protest taken up by its pals further along the street. All those dogs who saw him were probably discussing this apology on two feet they were seeing and lamenting the demise of the present generation of teenagers. How many times had one seen a canine in such a condition they would be barking in their own doggy language?

The drunken boy chuckled, halting to draw in a lung full of air in the hope of staving off another gut wrenching vomit. Never again he promised himself. However, it had been a good celebration. After all, how many races had he won in his short career since joining the senior ranks? None! He had been a pretty good junior though it was now tougher in the senior ranks where you were up against maturity and experience. Colin smiled. It had indeed been a good celebration. He looked up at the sky and inhaled again to clear his lungs, pleased at the way he had teased Doddie about his win, his smile quickly vanishing at the distance he still had to cover to reach his home. Now he wished he had his bike right now, this walking would take ages. Most probably he would be in the veteran ranks before he glimpsed his house.

It sounded like dishes being thrown against corrugated sheeting; knives and forks dropped from a great height on to hollow enamel bowls, the sounds rushing all the way from the kitchen to echo around his bedroom. Colin pulled the bedcovers over his head to drown out the noise and that of his mother outside his door calling to him that his breakfast was ready. He drew himself into the foetal position and ran a dry tongue over even drier lips, pushing the cover down a little to let himself breathe, as well as away from the smells underneath. All the while inside his head, a Jamaican steel band played at full pitch, and not all on the same tune.

"Come on ye drunken bum." Colin had not heard the bedroom door open and his young brother come in. "This place is mingin." Fifteen year old Peter turned up his nose in disgust and took a tentative step into their shared bedroom. "Are you no getting up? Mammy has yer breakfast ready." At the mention of food, Colin gave a deep moan, clutched his stomach and slid even further under the bedclothes.

"Get lost ye wee toad," the invalid mumbled from under the clothes, "Tell mammy I won't be wanting any breakfast."

"Ye mean the day or no ever?" Peter taunted the inebriated bike rider. He gave a shrug of resignation and turned for the door. "It's a good job you don't win races every week. Then again, if that was the case there would be nae chance o' you ever becoming an alcoholic. How did ye manage tae win anyway?" he asked, addressing the bedcovers whilst contemplating tugging them off the silent corpse. "Were ye the only yin that turned up?" Peter beat a hasty retreat before the corpse came to life.

Later, much later that July afternoon, Colin decided to go for a ride. It always helped to take a gentle ride out in the fresh air after a heavy bout of drinking as it let more oxygen into the system. He took a large water bottle, or a bidon as it was known in racing circles, as he still had a thirst. His mother had discreetly ignored him as he made for the back door and *he*

4

in turn had pretended not see his mother, all the while his fingers busy as Piranhas, texting his girl.

Once on the coast road, the rider headed for North Berwick, the wind as usual behind him, which would make the return journey harder. Here, in the summer, a ride to the coastal town was a 'doddle', but in winter with the wind and rain in your face it could be a nightmare, especially if this was the last leg of the journey when you had been as far afield as the Borders.

Colin screwed up his eyes behind his sunglasses, vowing never again to indulge - not until the next time - he grinned. It was then the silver Honda Civic passed him from the opposite direction, going so fast that he had scarcely time to notice the driver. It was this that jerked his memory back to the party, for the driver was none other than Max Duffy, or 'bare arse' as he had called him. Not one of his favourite people, Max ran about in his car with a druggie called Gil Robertson. Colin wished the car had not brought back the memory of last night. Now, it would appear, he had not been dreaming after all. Or, then again had he? Dreams could always appear to be real, especially if they made sense. Should Duffy have done something unrealistic then he would have known for sure that he had been dreaming. What Duffy had done was anything but unrealistic - immoral perhaps - but how to prove it? After all, he had been drunk and had not told anyone of his fears.

Colin negotiated the bend at Longniddry, toying with the idea of having a word with Doddie tomorrow, should he come upon him whilst out training. What to say and how to say it was the problem. After all, what if he was wrong? Then again, would Sadie herself not have known afterwards if she had been violated? True, she had been unconscious at the time, but even so .... The rider shook his head. It could wait until tomorrow. Perhaps if Sadie had confided in Doddie, he in turn would discuss it with him. However, had she done so, Duffy would not be driving past him today, not if he knew his pal Doddie. Colin pedalled faster, as if by doing so he could leave his dilemma behind. Perhaps Sadie had been unable to tell her boyfriend what had happened … at least not just yet. Colin sighed and reached for his bidon.

*******

"Whit are we sitting here fur?" Gil Robertson asked.

Max took an impatient look at his watch this Monday evening after the party as they sat parked on the hill looking down towards the crossroads in the direction of Pencaitland.

"Can ye no jist enjoy a summer's night?" Max asked, closing the window against the various insects that were also enjoying the summer evening.

"Yer no becoming a nature lover are ye?" Gil giggled, clearing his throat of phlegm. "At least no this kind o' nature." Gil was aware of his pal's reputation with the girls. How they admired the nineteen year old's good looks, although he could not see the attraction himself. Max was a little above average height, a couple of inches taller than himself, dark curly hair, with a complexion one could only describe as weather beaten. The short nose was slightly bent - the result of many an altercation - over which at this precise moment he could not recall. Max threw him a look that had him turn to stare out the window. To prevent himself from feeling the fool that Max had always taken him to be, Gil pointed to the sky.

"Dae ye think there's anybody up there?"

"Aye, how else wid ye get back frae Majorca?" Max clicked his teeth in contempt.

"No in planes, I mean outer space. Dae ye think there is life in other planets?"

"I suppose so," Max sighed, already bored by the subject. Why, he thought, did he put up with Gil's company?

He glanced at him sitting there, his brown tousled hair, Jeans that had seen better days, a complexion that left no one in any doubt as to his being a drug addict. It was also difficult to realise that Gil was only a couple of years older than himself, the drugs having taken their toll. Max knew why he knocked around with him. It was because Gil's presence made him feel and look better. Impatiently he shifted his gaze to the crossroads at the foot of the hill.

"They say there has been a lot of alien sightings aroon Bonnybridge, through the West," his pal was saying. Max wished he would shut up, the longer he waited the more nervous he was becoming.

"Is that a fact? There are a lot o' Westies wi their heids in the air. Maistly fitba supporters," Max said sarcastically.

Gil felt annoyed that his in-depth conversation was not being taken seriously by his pal, who had always considered him as being a 'thickie.' He was not to be put off.

"They say there are far mair sightings on a Tuesday night."

"Why a Tuesday?" Max hit out with the back of his hand at a stray fly on his windscreen, cursing as it flew away buzzing.

"Maybe because there's Bingo on a Tuesday," Gil chuckled.

"Oh aye, some aliens away oot there somewhere, sayin where will we go the night? Fancy Jupiter or Pluto? And another yin sayin, naw, fancy goin tae Bonnybridge, it's Tuesday and there's aye Bingo on?" Max sneered.

Gil laughed at the notion. "Well there are some good snowballs tae be won so they tell me."

Max shook his head in disbelief. "Ah can just imagine it, sittin there at Bingo wi two heids and four arms and legs."

"Och the aliens will have seen worse!" Gil guffawed, swiping at the same fly that had lost its way.

Already bored by his pal's uncharacteristic inactivity, Gil chewed his gum and peered up at the heavens. "Whit dae ye think wid happen if we got hit by a big haemorrhoid frae ooter space, Max," he asked emitting a bubble of gum.

Max was too nervous to be bothered by such stupid questions.

"Wid be a bummer, ah wid think pal, especially if there were piles o' them." He watched for any sign of Gil having realised that he had made a couple of puns and when his pal had not, turned away in disgust, too worked up to enlighten him about his play on words.

Max took another look at his watch. He had missed his chance yesterday as he was sure that it had been Colin Lamont that he had passed on the coast road. Had he seen Lamont sooner he could have stopped and under the pretence of asking if he had enjoyed Saturday's party would have seen his reaction. He could of course have turned around and caught up with him, but that, he felt, would have been suspicious and out of character as neither of them liked one another. In fact, Lamont detested him, even more so, his moron of a pal sitting beside him.

"Ye're no sniffing are ye? Max asked his friend. "I mean the noo, and ye've got nothin wi ye, ah hope?"

Gil slid a new piece of gum into his mouth. "Naw, ye asked me that afore we left. Why is it important all of a sudden?" He pointed to droplets of rain on the windscreen. "That was a short summer," he laughed. Max thought he appeared even more stupid a character when he laughed. In reply Max started up the engine, his heart pounding.

"Ye better no be lying, Robertson or we are baith in the shit."

The car had reached third gear when Gil saw the figure on the bike through the hedges downhill to his right, heading towards the crossroads. Max steadily raised his speed until the car was in top gear.

8

Colin Lamont was at the junction, ready to turn right when he saw the car, and slammed on his brakes as he made the turn, horrified that the car had covered the intervening distance between them in so short a time. When he had last looked he had ample time to cross over. The car hit his front wheel, and he fell, sliding along the road, metal tearing and pushing into his flesh, the grass verge coming up to meet him. Strangely, the only thought flashing through his mind, was, that these injuries were likely to put him out for the rest of the racing season. Then everything went black.

"Ye could have slowed doon, Max!" Gil exclaimed in horror, punching the dashboard and staring out of the window although there was nothing to see of the rider.

Max threw the door open, calling out to his friend as he quickly got out of the car. "Get on tae 999. Get an ambulance and the polis." He hurried to the front of the car and looked down to where Colin Lamont's head stuck out a little beyond the front wheel and the twisted frame of his bike; more than blood sticking to the car tyres. Max bent down and gently raised the boy's head. He felt for a pulse on Colin's throat with two fingers and carefully lowered the head back on to the grass verge. Still kneeling, he took off his hooded top, folded it and put it under the injured rider's head.

"I got the polis," Max heard Gil call out at the same time as a car drew to a hasty halt.

Max got up. "Noo mind and tell them he didnae stop when he came oot the junction there," he cautioned his pal.

Gil's face was chalk white, his lips twitched nervously, and he looked close to being sick. "Ye could have slowed doon?" he choked.

"Did ye no see me swerve tae miss him?" Max didn't wait for an answer as he turned to face the driver of the car that had just drawn up. Then, as if from nowhere there were more cars on this recently deserted country road.

"He didnae look where he was goin... came oot o' nowhere like a bat oot o' hell." Max walked towards the newcomers, spreading out his arms in a gesture of despair.

One man trotted past Max, anxious to be of help and knelt down beside the injured boy. "Have ye phoned for help?" he asked without looking up, as another dropped on to his knees beside the questioner.

The newcomer wriggled on to his side looking under the car to where Colin's lower body was entangled in his cycle. Almost immediately he was on his feet again, spewing vomit on to the wet grass at his feet.

"I cannae feel a pulse," the first helper shouted up to them over his shoulder.

Max stood looking down at the men huddled around the injured boy, then around him where more cars had come to a halt. Christ what hiv ah done, he thought? If Colin Lamont was to live, he could still tell what had happened at the party. He bunched his fists. He should have waited to see if Lamont *would have* told his pal Doddie or if the lassie herself would say anything. And even if she had been aware of what had happened to her, was she likely to say so, or just hide her shame?

Pushing back a strand of wet hair, Gil left one of the curious bystanders and stood beside Max. "The polis will no be long 'till they're here. Whit am I tae tell them Max?"

Max's eyes were still on the men huddled around the injured boy, a few, unable to bear what they had seen, walked slowly away, horror etched on each face. Max answered his pal quietly. "The truth, pal, the truth. Tell them he came oot the side road there, without lookin, and that I tried tae swerve tae avoid him."

"But, Max..." Gil stammered, staring at his pal in disbelief.

Max turned quickly to confront him, his eyes blazing. "That's whit ye'll tell them if ye ken whits good for ye. That's why ah had ye along as a witness ….a good witness. Yin that kens how tae say the right thing and no hiv the law stickin their big noses in tae oor business, especially yours, Gil." The reference to his friend's drug dealing not lost on the other, amid the sound of the siren of the approaching ambulance and police car.

*******

The rain had ceased, and although the evening was cooling from the earlier heat of the day, the house felt cold, as if in sympathy with their loss.

"Put the kettle on would you pet?" Jean asked of her daughter, her voice scarcely audible. The young woman turned for the kitchen. Peter switched on the TV and sat looking blankly at the screen.

"What happens now?" Jean asked her husband, sitting down on the settee in a way that suggested that she had reached her limit of endurance.

"Don't worry, plenty o' time tae get things done," Harry answered his eyes on the flashing images on the wide screen.

Jean's eyes stared out of the window and tears came to her red rimmed eyes. Was it only a few short hours ago that Colin had put away his mobile and given her a wave and a smile as he pushed his bike past that same window? Her son, happy with the prospect of doing well in his next race this weekend, never knowing that not only would he miss it but that he would not be alive. She cursed the driver of the car, whether or not he had been at fault, hoping he was feeling as much pain as she herself. How could he? Only mothers and wives could ever experience such pain. To have seen her son grow up to be the young man he had turned out to be; to have

11

his life snuffed out....

"Here Mammy, it's the way you like it." Jenny held out the cup of tea to her. "Do you want a biscuit? Or a sandwich or something?" she asked in a tone that might entice her mother to have something to eat.

Jean shook her head. "No pet this will do fine." As she leaned back in her seat she could see auld Moffat across the street watering his flowers, raising the hose to send a stream of water across the lawn. Did he know about Colin she wondered? God she thought, I hope not, I don't want him at my door offering his sympathy, or, come to think of it any of her neighbours. She just was not ready, not yet. Although it would be unfeeling not to let Nellie and Wullie their next door neighbours know what had happened.

Jean's son in law, Glen Meikle, seemed to have read her thoughts. "I telt the Wilsons next door what has happened tae Colin. They said they will no bother ye the noo but if there is anything ye want, just tae let them ken."

Jean nodded. She had not heard Glen go out. Tell Jean if there is anything she wants, she repeated silently to herself; only one thing - her son.

For a while the grieving family sat silent in the semi-darkness of the summer evening, each alone with their thoughts of Colin and trying to remember the last time they had spoken to him, of his replies, his gestures.

Feeling awkward at the family's silence, Glen signed discreetly to his wife that they should leave. Jenny nodded that she understood and stood up.

"Well, we best be away and see to wee Drew, Grandpa will be wondering where we have got to."

"Och I forgot about the auld soul looking after wee Drew!" Jean put a hand to her mouth in alarm as she stood up.

"Did anybody think tae tell him aboot Colin?" Harry asked looking around him guiltily.

"Naw. It wid no have been right tae gie the auld soul the news ower the phone frae the hospital, even though he would want tae know as soon as possible," Glen said. "If ye like, we can break it gently tae him when we get hame: much better than ower the phone, dae ye no think?"

"Aye, yer right son," Jean sighed. "It will break the auld yins heart, for he fair loved the laddie." Her voice trembling, she took a step away from the settee. "Whit are ye watching on that thing?" she asked sharply of Peter sitting playing with the remote control, and unaware of what he was doing. Startled the boy was jerked back to his surroundings.

"Ye better get yer things ready for school tomorrow," his mother suggested. This time her voice was gentle as if ashamed at having snapped at the boy: something she must not do, for he was now her only son.

"Dae I hiv tae go tae school the morn?"

"Best thing for ye son," his father suggested, firmly. "Noo away and get ready."

Reluctantly the boy rose and walked slowly towards the bedroom which he and Colin had shared. Suddenly it was too much for the fifteen year old, and he spun on his heel.
"Can I no stay at Glen and Jennie's place...just for the night?" he asked, his eyes pleading.

Now understanding his son's reluctance to enter the bedroom, Harry looked first at his wife then to Jenny and Glen.

"Aye Daddy he can come with us for the night," Jenny replied. What else could she say? She could not have her wee brother spending the night all alone in the room next to an empty bed.

Gathering his school uniform and books together, Peter was back out of the bedroom in a flash, the relief showing on his face. "See ye the morn Mammy," he said, already heading for the door where Glen stood.

"Aye, see you tomorrow son." Jean gave the boy a brief

13

smile, adding firmly, "After school that is."


"He's trying no to show it, but he's taken it bad." Harry stared at the door of the bedroom through which his father-in-law had just disappeared. The room had been Jenny's before she had married and when her grandmother died, grandfather had moved into their house and her room.

Jean heaved another sigh in the growing darkness; neither had wished to switch on the light, as if by doing so they would see each other's grief.

"I'll have to tell my work that I'll no be in the morn." Harry got up. "Want a cuppa?" Jean shook her head. "Ye will have tae eat something… keep yer strength up."

"For what, Harry?"

"Tae keep on livin. Ye have another son ye ken and he needs ye mair noo than ever."

"What's all to be done, Harry?" Jean ignored the question of food.

"Plenty o' time for that first try something tae eat."

"I'll have to phone in early in the morning, there's that much to do in my department."

"Well, they'll just have tae manage. So come on, try a bite tae eat."

*******


The cortège of three cars drove slowly through the main street of Tranent. Only a few passers-by it appeared to Jean gave a second glance as they drove passed. An old man halted and removed his cap. She gave him a little smile of appreciation, forgiving the uncaring world for not sharing her grief. They moved further down the main street of the town, passed the chemist, hairdressers, bookmakers, butcher shop and

14

the wee shop that sells everything until the pedestrian lights at red stopped them for a few seconds or so outside a baker's shop, the pavement littered with paper bags, courtesy of a few inconsiderate youngsters and others who should have known better.

It was an obsession of her father's, this constant littering of the streets and he would often reminisce on how in his day as a schoolboy he would never have thought of not taking his rubbish home and had it come to the attention of his headmaster, his hands would have nipped for days. Here her father had sighed. If they were to try this today the civil rights would be down on you before you could say injustice or something similar. As if he and sight impaired people had no civil rights and could fall their full length on a bag of greasy chips without redress.

Despite the severity of the occasion, it still made Jean smile. She also remembered when he had reported the polluted pavements to one of the rare police officers actually walking in the street, the officer had asked him if he ever felt menaced by such people. He had answered, 'Naw, I jist dress masel up as a litter bin and naebody comes near me.'

The cortege moved on past the War Memorial and turned right, down Church Street, heading for the church. Jean felt guilty as so many other folk did at only making use of the church for weddings and funerals. The minister had been nice when he had called at their home to offer his comfort and condolences, telling the family it had been God's will. God's will she had thought angrily! How could God be so cold hearted as to take away her son? A son who had not yet reached his prime of life - to be denied enjoying life, to marry, have children. No, only a cruel God could do this.

They had reached the church yard where a few mourners waited outside, some of whom she did not know. Perhaps they worked beside Colin. Harry took her hand as

15

they walked side by side into the church, her family behind her, walking down the main passageway to the front pew of the church.

Harry's thoughts were not on the sermon. He had gone through the hymns that they had selected beforehand and now was scarcely able to sing a note. How was it some words never seemed to fit into the tune and you were left hanging on to a word until it came to the right moment to stop. He had insisted that not all of the verses of the hymns be sung as he was sure that, as did the congregation, they would find the singing of solemn hymns an ordeal.

The first hymn over, the minister was telling them how God had taken Colin to him. If only he could believe that, Alex thought, sitting next to Peter. Suddenly the old man was afraid, not for himself and that his own time could be near, but for Peter. Could a God as unpredictable as this, also take an innocent boy such as Peter? The old man shuddered, surely not.

The congregation was on their feet again, singing Amazing Grace. There was always someone, Jenny smiled, who enjoyed showing off their vocal skills at the top of their voice, probably Auntie Margaret, who had always fancied herself as a singer. Colin would have got a kick out of that. Her eyes strayed to the coffin and suddenly the tears came for her wee brother lying there, so near but now an impossible distance away.

Peter listened to every word Doddie had to say about his pal Colin as he gave the eulogy, making them laugh at some of the funny things Colin and he had done together. Then it was the last hymn. Glen glanced around him as the minister spoke, and wondered how many believed in what he was telling them, on how they would all meet Colin again when their time came. How many here had their thoughts on what the preacher was saying? How many minds were on what they

16

would do when they got home, or what was worth watching on the telly that night? This and a hundred different things that made life go on. Only those who knew and loved Colin would find the rest of the day an endurance and the night even worse.

Although this was not the place to think of revenge, Glen's mind pictured Max Duffy happily going about his life while someone, whose shoes he was not fit to polish, lay in a coffin not so very far away from where he stood.

The service over, the bereaved family stood at the entrance of the church shaking hands with everyone and in return receiving whispered condolences from each as they filed past, some, unknown to the family until they introduced themselves as workmates or cycling friends of Colin.

Jean and the women stood back from the graveside as Colin was lowered into his last resting place. Harry at the head of the coffin, Peter engulfed in huge sobs, not caring who saw him. Alex, her father, head bowed, mumbling his last farewells to a grandson he adored, Glen his face red with anger, Colin's only uncle, Uncle Jimmy and finally Doddie, let the cords slowly slide through their fingers. And then it was all over.

Jean turned away from the graveyard, the sound of traffic on the bypass a testimony to everyday life going on. It was not too far from where they lived to the cemetery. She would try and visit Colin every week so that he would know he had not been forgotten. He was with his Granny now and Jean wondered what her father was thinking of at this time. Now the old soul had two to mourn over when he paid his visits. Jean turned one last time before walking to the waiting taxis.

"Goodbye son. God keep you." And she vehemently hoped that there *was* indeed a God, and that this was not really the end.

"Nice spread ye have here, Jean," Margaret her sister-in-law applauded, "and an awfy nice service too." The overweight lady sat down, her eyes on those helping

17

themselves to sausage rolls and freshly cut sandwiches. "They have really done ye proud Jean," Margaret said, referring to the catering done at the inn.

"Thanks, Margaret."

Jean's eyes strayed around the gathering to where Doddie stood with a few gathered around him, some in cycling attire. She heard them laugh, a sound which somehow did not seem out of place. Peter stood beside Doddie, looking up at the taller man, an admiring smile on his face at the things he was saying. It was good to see the wee soul smile. He was all that she had left. No, that was untrue. She still had Jenny and wee Drew, besides Harry and Faither. She sighed, knowing what she really meant: she had only one son left, though to be truthful, Glen was also like a son to her. Jenny had made a good choice there.

A few folk came to say their farewells, leaving with a promise 'that she knew where they lived and if there was anything she needed done, just for her to say the word'. Promises she herself had made on similar occasions but seldom fulfilled.

Jean rose, "do you want anything, Margaret? I'm just having another cup o tea."

" Naw, Jean, thanks aw the same. I think Jimmy would like tae get across the bridge afore the rush comes on," Margaret answered in reference to her husband and the traffic on the Forth Road Bridge.

"Aye, whenever ye are ready hen, and thanks for comin."

"Nae bother pet. Ah only wish it had no been for this. How is it," she said sadly "we seem only tae meet at funerals or weddings?"

"Aye, yer right there." Jean walked to one of the tables where a chrome urn stood. She turned the little black handle sideways, her eyes on the hot liquid flowing into her cup, added milk and sugar and turned to stare around at those still there.

"So this day I was oot training wi Colin," Jean heard Doddie's voice above the other little groups in the big room. "Colin says tae me, Doddie ye train very hard. Oh I says, I train harder when I'm on my own. Oh, says Colin I wouldna like tae be with you when your on your own."

Jean smiled at her son's sense of humour, as the rest let out peals of laughter.

*******

# CHAPTER 2

Six weeks had passed since Colin's funeral. Prompted by his daughter, Grandpa Alex Henderson found himself at his granddaughter's back door. He turned the handle and stepped inside, instantly alert for the expected attack from wee Drew, the youngest delinquent in the business.

How was it he thought, that Jenny's own strict upbringing had not lent itself to Damien Two, as he was wont to call his great-grandchild?

"Hello, anyone at home?" Alex called out, making his way into the living room, where he threw a furtive glance around him while endeavouring to predict the direction wee Batman would strike.

Jenny suddenly appeared out of the bedroom. "Hello, Grandpa, I didn't hear ye come in. We were just going out."

"I'll no stop ye then hen. It's just that yer mammy thought I should pay ye a visit since it's a wee while since I last ca'ed," the old man explained as Glen entered the room.

"Hello there, Grandpa. How's it goin?" the young man asked cheerfully, "Still playin fast and loose?" He laughed giving the old man a wink.

"Oh aye, the only thing that is fast and loose aboot me noo a days is ma bowels. Ye cheeky sod," Alex laughed back.

Alex gave a quick glance around the room. "I brought these for wee Drew, but seein as he's no in, I'll just eat them mysel." Alex held out the tube of Smarties to Jenny, knowing that this was the quickest and surest way of flushing out his 'wee cherub'. The old man's deductions quickly proved correct, as if out of nowhere the child appeared, his toy sword held out at the ready, his free hand outstretched for the Smarties.

"Say hello tae yer Grandpa," Jenny told the child: great-grandpa being a bit of a mouthful she had always thought.

20

His eyes on the sweets, Drew muttered a greeting at the same time as he grabbed the tube, ripping the top off.

"Did ye say thanks to your Grandpa?" Jenny asked her sweet devouring off-spring. "Ye'll not be able for your tea. And are you not going to give your Grandpa one?"

Reluctantly Drew placed a solitary sweet into his Grandpa's hand.

"Ye're no leaving yersel short by any chance?" Alex asked, eyeing the round sweet in his hand, and for answer saw it disappear into an eager multi coloured mouth. "Serves me right," the old man smiled with a shake of his head.

"Now that you are here, Grandpa, could you do Glen and me a favour?" Jenny asked as if she had just thought of the idea. "Could you take the bairn to the park, and let us go shopping by ourselves?" she asked, though not expecting a refusal. "He could take his ball, it will keep him happy 'till we get back."

Although Alex had agreed, he did not relish watching Damien for too long. He did not have the energy to look after him in such a wide open space as Polson Park. But now that he was here he would have to do his best.

Dropping his football, Drew kicked it along the grass. It's a pity, Alex thought that there was not a pond in the park and Drew could have brought his yacht and perhaps re-enact the juvenile version of the Titanic and go down with his ship.

Alex sat down on a bench nearby, his eyes on his charge. He wasn't a bad wee lad…well, now and again, he chuckled.

A man about his own age of around seventy sat at the other end of the bench. He lowered his paper and pointed with his pipe to where Drew was kicking the ball against the bandstand. "Yours?" the man asked.

"Naw, the ba belongs tae ma grandson." The man smiled at Alex's joke. "He's my granddaughter's wee boy,"

Alex said by way of apology.

"What age? And I don't mean yer granddaughter," the stranger warned with a smile.

"Three, goin on thirty."

"I ken what ye mean," the man nodded. "They grow up a lot faster than we did. I wonder though, if they are no missing the fun we used tae have. But things have changed, and no for the better. And the way some kids talk tae ye, they think they are the untouchables. I ken what I wid gie them," the man finished sadly.

"Bring back the belt that's whit I aye said," Alex said, happy to find someone who sympathised with his way of thinking.

The other shook his head. "Bringing back the belt would no help."

"Dae ye no think so?"

"Naw. But maybe replacing it wi a machine gun or two might." They both laughed.

"Aye. I think the only two things they teach them in schools are, keep away frae strangers and litter bins. In some o' thae streets ye would have tae get the 'Time Team' in tae find the pavement, and when they did find it, it would be covered in chewing gum."

Alex laughed. "Well, chewing gum cannae be that bad, especially if ye want tae become a fitba manager!"

They both chuckled.

The old men were silent for a moment or two, watching Drew play with the ball.

"I'm Davie Ingram by the way." The stranger introduced himself, his eyes still on the small football player.

"Please tae meet ye Davie. I'm Alex Henderson." The other nodded and drew on his pipe.

"It's quite warm for this time o' year," Alex said as a way of beginning a conversation. It was nice to leave some of his worries behind. It was not altogether a happy household at home at present. Already he could see a change in Jean, therefore any contact out-with the sadness of the household was a welcome distraction.

"Aye it is," Davie replied. "It will no be long tae winter again. How the time goes in. It seems nae time since Christmas."

Alex agreed. "Then, when the cauld weather comes we will have tae sit at hame and watch the telly," he said sadly.

"Aye, and how that cheers ye up. Nothin but cookery programmes on."

Alex laughed. "Ma opinion exactly."

"It woudnae be sae bad, but aw thae mothers sitting there, too busy watching folk cooking that they don't have time tae cook a decent meal themsels. In fact Ironside gets aff his backside mair often than thae dae."

"Yer right there, Davie. Then when yer ready tae watch the afternoon film, on comes some eejit tellin ye if ye'r ower fifty ye better start savin for yer funeral. Cheery ah must say."

Davie concurred with a nod. "No tae mention the other eejits tryin tae sell ye car insurance. How can ye trust a company that has tae rely on a dog or a parrot for advice? Anyway, ah will have tae go, Alex, the wife is no happy if ah don't come hame in time… mair unhappy if a dae."

Alex watched his new found friend give wee Drew a friendly smile as he passed and give the ball a kick. Alex hoped they would meet again, as it had helped to cheer him up.

*******

It was after midnight. The September chill did little to cool Peter's excitement. Max Duffy's silver Honda stood in the driveway of his house. Crouching, he ran stealthily to the car, under the cover of the moon disappearing behind a dark cloud. He was almost there, the Stanley knife in his hand when he heard a car approach. He turned, swithering in that moment whether or not he had time to slash the tyres before the car drew too near. The car speeded up, the car radio blaring full blast, irrespective of the lateness of the hour, and Peter recognised the driver as Gil Roberstson.

Peter dropped the Stanley knife and took to his heels, the sound of running feet not so far behind, intermingled with swear words and threats. Now he *was* afraid. He did not want to be caught by someone as vicious as Max Duffy, or his nutter of a pal.

He should not have tried to do it. If he were to be caught, his mother would kill him. Wrong choice of words he thought under the circumstances. Peter vaulted a fence, landed lightly on the other side, and ran through some one's back garden. The sound of oaths filling the semi darkness as his pursuers clambered over the fence behind him. Panicking, the youngster grabbed at the side gate, angered and frustrated at finding it locked. The two men were at the other end of the lawn, close enough for them to recognise him. Peter stuck a rubber trainer on to the spar of the wooden frame and levered himself up, one leg over the top of the gate as Max Duffy threw out a hand to catch his trailing foot. Peter snatched his foot away, and dropped down on the other side, and ran for the safety of his temporary home.

Peter was almost there. The youngster halted to draw breath, and took a quick look behind him. No one there, but he knew he had been recognised. He swore, and began to run, rounding the last corner to his home, and almost bumped into Gil Robertson coming the other way.

Before he knew it, the older boy had him by the throat, a smile of triumph on his face.

"Thought we dinnae ken that ye lived here wee man, eh?" Gil's grip tightened as he spoke.

24

"Well, well, who dae we have here?"

Although unable to look round, Peter knew who it was by the sound of the voice. It was Max, the man whose car tyres he had almost succeeded in slashing. Now he felt even more afraid. The man was a well known bammer, besides being the person who had murdered his brother; for to Peter it was nothing less.

Gil took his hand away from the boy's throat, and for a brief second Peter was tempted to take a chance to run. His captor must have read his thoughts and with a shake of his head, said quietly, "don't even think aboot it," as Max came to confront the frightened boy.

"So ye thought ye would have a wee bit fun wi my car did ye?" Max grabbed the front of Peter's T-shirt. "Dae ye ken what that car cost?"

Peter lowered his eyes and murmured something about not knowing. The T-shirt was grabbed tighter, and twisted, and he saw the glint of a knife in the others hand. "I might let ye aff this time seeing as ye are still upset aboot yer brother, or I would gie ye this." Max held the knife close to the trembling boy's face. Peter swallowed, fear momentarily replaced by relief that the bammer was not going to use it, at least not on this occasion. Instead, Max took a slight step back and slashed the shirt above where he still held it, pieces of fabric coming away in his hand. "Next time ye'll no have a shirt tae protect you." He laughed at the frightened boy, letting drop what material still remained in his hand. "Noo away hame and change yer boxers."

As Peter disappeared out of sight, Gil turned to his friend with an astonished look on his face. "Ye let him go? That's no like you, Max. Efter aw, look whit wid have happened tae yer car if we had been that wee bit late o' comin hame."

Max gave a shrug. "Yon family has enough worries

25

without me giein them mair." Although his real reason was that he did not want to get involved with the Law, especially with a knife in his pocket.

Almost at his temporary home, Peter still did not know what to say as regards his tattered T-shirt should his mother ask, as she still did his washing. He had been caught. His heart thumped at the thought. But why had Max Duffy let him go? He sighed. What a fanny Duffy was, and his pal was even worse. Well, there was always the next time, only next time he would not get himself caught.

*******

It was the hill where Colin had made his winning break, which sadly was to be his last race; the hill just outside Bolton.

Doddie looked around him at what was left of the original riders, 'the bunch' as it was known in cycling parlance. For a second he thought of trying to emulate his pal, even if only to remind him of Colin, and how he had loved his sport.

A rider made a break and Doddie could not bring himself to react. It just was not there. He had lost interest in the race, and wondered why the hell he had bothered entering in the first place. The reason for his dismal performance was simple; it was the absence of his best friend.

They had reached the junction at the top of the hill, turning left for the finish just outside of Gifford. The race was over, 'three riders up the road' and he just sitting in at the back of the other four riders, the chance of finishing in a minor place if he won the sprint, the last thing on his mind. Now all he wanted was to see the race over, ride back to the changing room, or 'the strip' and drive home.

Usually he would have enjoyed the post race analysis and banter as riders changed themselves in the main hall, oblivious, or in some cases 'too knackered' to bother about the women; mostly wives or girlfriends of the host club dishing out tea or hot soup to hungry riders who were not too tired from their efforts to force down a bite. In contrast to an hour or so later, when, stomachs settled, they would have eaten the women serving, as well as the last remnants of food, edible or otherwise.

That he had not done well in the race did not surprise him, as he had not really trained since losing his pal. And when he had, his heart had not been in it.

He missed Colin and his sense of humour. It had been good to train together. Sometimes they would meet up with another group of riders, generally known as 'the chain gang' on the coast road, which would give them some added protection from boy racers, and those old enough to have known better

How many times he wondered, had he seen or heard of near misses by the usual inconsiderate motorist coming out of a side street. Who if they had not intentionally looked away as if hoping you would miraculously disappear (and not fall beneath their wheels) would look one way and drive out the other. Or look through you as if to say 'you can't hurt me' as you came to an abrupt halt. It was then you had to control yourself, or murder would be done when your adrenaline reached its limit, having realised what could have happened to you. For, as a cyclist you were not a respected sportsperson as you would be on the continent, rather a nuisance to be treated as if your life was only one up from a rabbit's.

Even when road racing, irate motorists would not respect your sport should it hold them up for a few seconds or minutes although these same inconsiderate individuals would still have time to contact the police, or hurl abuse at you as they drove passed, polishing your cycle shoes with their metal doors on the way.

He remembered Colin quip's about the examiner asking the learner when he knew he was in a built up area. "That's easy," says the learner, "I'm knocking down more cyclists now."

Yet for all its trials and tribulations he still loved the sport. The sense of having achieved something when returning from a hard training sessions, or a leisurely run over the Granites, or Paddy Slacks to St Marys Loch, and all the beauty of his own country, something which no motorist could ever imagine or achieve. With this, and feeling a little better, Doddie reached home.

"Hello, Sadie you fancy goin oot the night? Maybe get a Chinese or something?" Doddie asked of his partner, as he dropped his racing kit on to the floor.

Curled up on the sofa, Sadie gave a shrug without taking her eyes off the TV. She pointed at the flat screen, her eyes wide in astonishment." She's eaten aw they grubs!"

"That's nothing. Ye should see whit we cyclists eat when we get hunger knock on the bike." Doddie gave a sniff of his nose.

He took a look at the screen. "Whit's aw this rubbish? Don't tell me it's 'I'm a greedy eejit get me oot o' here?" he tut tutted.

Sadie gave him a glower. "Could ye eat aw thae creepy crawly things, smart bum?"

"Depends where ye go. Some o'they fast food places, ye never know. That's why they call it fast food - in wan end and oot the ither afore ye can say diarrhoea."

Sadie's attention swung to the TV again. "What's up with your face? Come in last again did ye?"

Doddie picked up his holdall. "Well if ye must know, there were two ahint me." He pretended to sound annoyed.

"Whit happened tae them? Did they puncture?" Sadie chuckled

"Well, if ye must know." Doddie threw his head in the air in preparation of leaving the room. "Only yin punctured.

28

The ither yin was riding side saddle."

The meal had put Doddie in the mood to drink. Sadie would have much preferred to have returned home, even though there was nothing on the TV worth watching this Saturday night. However, as Doddie had declared his intention of visiting the nearest night club with, or without her, she had agreed.

She knew Doddie only too well when he was in one of his moods, how he could become that little bit argumentative, not to say aggressive, so she had agreed to go along, with the express purpose of keeping her big man out of trouble.

"Let's go in here, and have a quiet drink before we go tae the disco," Doddie suggested, pushing the door open of the small pub and not waiting for Sadie to answer.

It was as he looked around him for a secluded place to sit, that he remembered Scotland had been playing at Hampden earlier that day, and by the mood of the residents, their National team had again finished second. Only to have his deduction confirmed by the fact that one patriot was attempting to strangle the life out of a lesser patriot with the National flag draped around his neck.

"Two nothing, and as the man says, lucky tae get the nothin," a mourner said with a shake of his head, as Doddie edged his way to the bar.

"At least we won the toss," another wit joked.

"A crowd o' tossers if ye ask me."

"We thought we were bad enough when we had yon German guy Thirty Volts as manager... but yon the day," he sighed again as he downed his Grouse, which had Doddie thinking was a good choice of name in the circumstances.

"And they expected us tae sing Flower of Scotland tae. Mair like We've Got a Lovely Bunch o' Coconuts."

Drinks in his hands and unable to suppress a grin, Doddie made his way back through 'the wake 'to where Sadie had found two seats in a corner of the mortuary.

"Is it the game they are on about?" Sadie asked with the usual ignorance most women have for the 'beautiful game'.

Doddie nodded, listening to one pundit analysing what had gone wrong. "We were doin no bad until that bawheid o' a goalie came oot tae take that high ba' and tripped ower his guide dug."

His pal gave a sombre nod of understanding. "Yer right there Sandy. And the ref wisnae much better either. I think his rule book was written in Braille by the looks o' it."

Doddie turned to Sadie with a smile, and she laughed.

"Ma wee nephew's studying foreign languages at school," one drinking supporter was saying. "I said tae him, are ye goin tae be a teacher when ye grow up then? Naw, he says, a want tae play for Celtic."

His companions gave a laugh. "He's aboot right tae. Some o' oor teams are mair like the Foreign Legion…and I don't Beau Gest," he laughed.

Another sitting at the table gave a slight burp. "And wi oor luck," he began, "when we sit doon tae the telly the night, the announcer will say 'now for tonight's film, Braveheart, except for viewers in Scotland, who will have another chance to see the 1966 World Cup Final."

This was followed by a roar of laughter, the quip spreading around the bar to those who wanted to know what all the jollity was about on such a sober occasion.

Half an hour later the cyclist and his partner decided to leave - a wise choice as the TV sports reporter was about to announce the result of the recent international, and Doddie had just closed the door behind him, when from within, the lights had grown dimmer as the TV suffered the same fate as their belated football team.

"We'll go in here, Sadie. Aw right wi you?"

"Aye, I suppose so," Sadie answered, already having to

shout above the music blaring out through the open door as the bouncer stood back to let them enter.

Doddie swung a glance around the room filled with gyrating bodies and flashing lights, looking vainly for a place to sit.

"Up there," Sadie shouted, pointing to the balcony running the length of the dance floor.

Doddie nodded and took her hand, guiding her up the few steps to an empty table overlooking the crowded dance floor. "I'll get us a drink."

Sadie watched Doddie wind his way through the dancers, often having to stop until an entwined couple separated in order to show off their masterly footwork which in no way would have worried Patrick Swayze or even Patrick Swayze's dog.

Sadie saw her partner reach the bar and lean forward to attract busy bartenders' attention as they hurried past as if anxious to serve drinks before the supply ran out. She looked away, her attention drawn to a few newcomers being greeted cheerfully by a group of earlier gyrators, all shouting to be heard above the ever increasing volume of music.

"Here, I got ye a double, I don't fancy fighting my way through that mob for a while. My toes must be black and blue," Doddie moaned, setting down the two glasses of Vodka on the table and sitting down to observe the crowded floor below.

Sadie lifted her glass. "Cheers. It's a good job we're getting a taxi hame." She pointed to Doddie's glass of beer beside his Vodka.

Doddie gave a shrug. "I need it tae quench ma thirst after the race the day."

Why, by saying this did it remind him of Colin that night of the party...Colin's last party. He sat silent for a moment willing himself back to the present, not wishing to

31

dwell on what had happened. It was scary; Colin had been the most cautious of riders. Therefore, what had happened to his pal, could just as easily happen to him. But he had never really been fully convinced that his pal was to blame. Somehow, God knew why, that shit, Max Duffy had got away with it.

"A penny for yer thoughts." Sadie interrupted his reverie.

"As my auld granny would say, they're no worth tuppence," Doddie replied with a grin.

Sadie thought for a moment before giving a laugh.

"That was a pre decimal joke was it no?"

Doddie smiled back. "Wid ye care for tae partake of a shot aroon the flair?" he asked in mock seriousness, and his intentional phraseology.

"Naw," Sadie relied in the same parlance," I wid jist be pleased tae keep sitting ma bum on ma chair if ye don't mind kind sir." Both lifted their glasses and laughed.

It was quite revealing how different the disco, or for that part, any social occasion appeared to the sober, with people shouting to make themselves heard above the blare of music. Contrasting to, when inebriated out of your tiny skull, it was just great and the only place to be at that time. The entire floor filled with, what could well be described as, some wild tribe doing their war dance before going into battle. Tattoos, studs through the nose, earrings as worn by some ancient tribe, Sadie thought, looking down at the gyrating mass. Now all they needed were spears, and back to darkest Africa to say hello tae mammy and daddie.

Later, Sadie's eyes followed Doddie to the bar, his empty glasses held high before setting them down on the bar counter. The young woman's heart fluttered a little at the prospect of what was to come when they got home. Doddie's love making was always at its best after a hard race.

That's how they had come to make love in an upstairs

room in the house of the party the night Colin had won his race. It really was not like them to have done so. Yet it had happened all of a sudden, with Doddie being unable to curb his desire. Of course they both had had too much to drink. She could not really remember coming back downstairs, only that later she had come to on a settee, feeling uncomfortable and had gone to the bathroom to rearrange her clothing, besides feeling a little ashamed of what she and Doddie had done in someone else's home.

Involuntary Sadie's eyes followed three men snaking through the dancers to the bar. She let out a gasp, realising that on their present course they would come in contact with Doddie, for one was none other than Max Duffy, and if her assumption was correct, one of the others was his wee ' yes man' Gil Robertson.

Doddie saw the three men at the same time as had Sadie. For a moment the man decided to ignore his pal's murderer. He stepped back from the bar, his drinks order forgotten. Yet, he could not let this opportunity pass. Doddie felt the alcohol rise within him, and sidled closer to Duffy. His target saw him, and gave a nod of recognition before turning his attention back to the bar.

"Pity ye had no done that when ye were in yer car yon day." Doddie walked round a man standing between them.

Max pretended to be engrossed in studying the row of bottles behind the bar. Doddie gripped his arm. "I was talking tae you pal."

Max turned slowly round, leaning his back against the counter to confront his antagonist. "Whit dae ye mean?"

Doddie gave a smirk. "I mean, had ye turned away frae ma pal Colin, instead of *in* tae him yon day, he wid still be alive."

"It was his ain fault. Was it no Gil? Ye were there."

Gil Robertson felt uncomfortable. He knew it would

33

come to this someday. Whatever reason Max had given for his actions on that fateful day, he had never fully discussed it with him. "Aye, yer right Max, ye couldnae have done anything tae avoid the bloke, he wasnae watching where he was goin," he lied.

"Colin Lamont would no have come oot yon road withoot lookin. I can tell ye that right now. It could only have been some eejit goin, Christ knows how fast, that knocked him doon."

"Are ye tryin tae say I was speedin? Well no according tae the polis and aw.'" Max emphasised his conviction with a sharp downward thrust of his hand. "The polis breathalysed me, and took statements and nae charges were laid afore me. So don't try and say am an eejit. OK?"

Doddie drew back as if better to focus on his adversary.

"I would never think that o' you Duffy, it takes brains tae be an eejit."

"Maybe ye would like tae back that up." Max levered himself off the bar, his face twisted in an angry leer.

The man beside Doddie, sensing trouble drew out of the way as best he could in the crowded bar. A bartender having spotted the confrontation leaned over to where Max stood facing his adversary. "Take it outside guys," he advised, "unless you want security up yer arses."

Max turned his head slightly to the speaker. "Aye, aw right pal. Aw right wi you Shaw?" he asked turning back to where Doddie stood, fists clenched by his side.

Doddie nodded. "Let's go."

It was just what he needed to rid himself of the tension that had been building up since driving back from the race, and if he was to be truthful with himself, ever since Colin had died. Now he had a chance to avenge his pal by giving this piece of shit a right doin, which he had no doubt he could do.

Max was the first to come out of the side door leading

34

into an alleyway, winking at Gil and another young man he knew from his home town, while awaiting Doddie to emerge.

"Cannae dae it on yer own, I see." Doddie's eyes travelled to the two Tranent Belters standing a little way behind Max.

"Merely spectators," Max sneered, as he took a few steps forward as Doddie descended the steps to the alleyway, and as he reached the last step Max threw a punch. Doddie dodged the intended blow, countering with a punch of his own that had Max rapidly stepping back. Now they were in the centre of the dark alley trading blows, Doddie's height coming to his advantage, but wary of the two onlookers a little ways at his back.

"Stop it, the baith o' ye!" Doddie heard the shriek behind him. Then again, this time as he moved a little to his right to avoid his foe, he glimpsed Sadie at the top of the stairs.

"Better ca it a night, Max, here comes the law," Doddie heard one of Max's friends shout out.

Max held up his hands in a gesture of a truce, and snapped a quick look up the alleyway where to two dark blue uniforms were approaching at a determined pace.

"And what's going on here?" the taller of the officers wanted to know.

"Jist showing this big man how tae box, jist in case he needs tae defend himsel sometime." Max gave a short laugh, looking at the men in blue.

"Aye, that's right PC World," one of Max's henchman laughed, coming to his friend's aid.

"Don't get smart with me pal," the taller officer warned, turning a hostile eye upon the would- be joker, who in turn shrugged and found his shoes to be more than interesting at that precise moment.

"I would advise all of you to be on your way. And you two," the shorter officer pointed a finger at Max and Doddie, "I would suggest that you confine your boxing lessons to a gymnasium in future."

For a moment the adversaries glared at one another, both reluctant to be the first to do as the policeman had suggested, for fear that their action could be seen as a sign of giving up the fight. Then with a shrug, Max moved towards the steps of the disco, Sadie flattening herself against the railings to let him past, and for a moment their eyes met, Max searching the woman's face for the briefest of signs that would tell him that she knew what he had done to her. And to his relief he saw none.

In the alleyway Doddie's eyes followed Max and his pals until the door closed behind them, his decision as to whether to re-enter the disco or not made for him by Sadie descending the steps to him.

"I think I have had enough Disco for one night Doddie, let's go hame." She put a hand out and turned his head towards what little light there was in the alley, and tenderly touched his cheek. "You'll have some keeker the morn mister," she assured him.

"You should have seen the other guy," Doddie grinned, then winced at the pain.

*******

Max stared through the windscreen as he drove down the Bridges, cursing at some drunkards tempting providence by trying to cross in front of him in the busy street. He wound down the window and shouted a few obscenities at them, releasing the tension of the events of the evening.

At the foot of the Bridges he turned right at the lights, and headed for Milton Road and the bypass, gripping the wheel tighter and inwardly cursing himself for being such a fool. Sadie Muir had not known that it was he who had done that to her that night of the party, for if so Doddie Shaw would have come after him by this time. Nor had he seen it in the girl's eyes when they met on the stairs back at the club. Even had she known, and had not wished her shame to be known, he would still have seen that sign of revulsion. No, he was in the clear, there had been no need for Colin Lamont to have died. Max's mind raced back, seeing again Colin Lamont standing there watching him having his way with Sadie Muir. Max Duffy cursed again. He should have waited, waited to see if Lamont would have said anything.

Max drew up at the traffic lights at Meadowbank, scarcely aware of having done so. Lamont could not have been aware of what he, Max was doing for surely had he known he would have done something about it, and, if not by himself, would have gone in search of his pal Doddie Shaw. No, there was no need in his killing the cyclist, a boy who had never done him any harm.

In the passenger seat Gil sat silent, waiting for his pal to say something about the fight. At length, by the time they had reached Bailliefield and still Max had remained silent, Gil broke the tension. "Dae ye think ye could have taken him, if the polis hadnae come?" he asked staring out of the window.

"Whit?" Max swung the wheel to his right.

Gil repeated the question, now wishing he had not done so.

"Probably. But, ye'll find oot the next time I see him."

The car had reached the slip road to Tranent before Max spoke again. "Dae ye want me tae take ye straight hame, or are ye comin in for a drink? I could go wan masel after the night." Max heaved a sigh.

Gil nodded, not about to differ with his sullen friend. Besides, there were a few questions that need answering.

Max drew to a halt in his cul-de-sac. Opened the car door, and stepped into the cool September evening, waiting for his pal, before turning for his home.

Gil had always been surprised how clean and tidy the house was, although he suspected it was the work of Max's older brother Cameron; Cammie, as he was known, was entirely the opposite of his brother, honest and hard working, unlike his layabout brother who, Gil knew, could never keep a job. This he knew for certain, as Max had worked beside him as a plumber, until being dismissed for having too many Mondays off work.

"Cammie no in?" Gil asked as a way of conversation, though it was blatantly obvious that there was no one there but themselves.

Ignoring the senseless question, Max handed Gil a large Vodka, and sat down on the settee knocking back most of his own drink in one swallow.

"Yon Doddie was looking for a fight the night, Max. He must still hate ye for knocking doon his pal." Gil sipped his drink, his eyes watchful for his friend's response.

"Why should he be? It was an accident. You were there." Max's eyes bore into the man sitting across from him.

Gil gave a twist of his lip. "Well, if ye don't mind me sayin so, pal, it looked tae me as if ye were sitting on yon hill waitin for the boy tae come along."

Max's cheeks coloured and Gil retreated a little into his chair. "Whit dae ye mean waited? Were we no just enjoying the scenery until the rain came on? Then when it did, did ah no start for hame as there was nae use hanging aroon any more wi the rain on. Was there?"

Gil gave a nod of understanding and took a nervous swallow of his drink, thankful that his walk home was not so very far.

Max's eyes burrowed into his friends face. "There was nae reason for me tae knock the boy doon. He should have looked where he was goin. It was just yin o' these things."

38

"Aw the same," Gil started.

Max cut him short. "As I said afore, ye were there. And ye gave evidence tae that affect tae the polis, did ye no." Max rose and walked to the kitchen.

Gil watched him go. It would not do to push his pal further. But to him there were too many unanswered questions. Why, for instance had Max insisted that there be no trace of drugs on him on that particular occasion? Although Max never dealt, or used drugs himself, it had never worried him before. And why had, he chosen to sit on that stretch of road and at that particular time? He had never known Max to be an ardent lover of local scenery or otherwise. While he had been thinking this, his fingers had been busy texting, and he quickly put his mobile back into his pocket at the sound of Max returning.

Max came back with two bottles of cold beer from the fridge and handed one to his guest. "Get that doon ye, and nae mair aboot me running doon Colin Lamont. OK?" Max's tone sounded almost like a threat.

Gil nodded and took a sip of his beer. Now all he wanted was to get out of the house before his pal became that wee bit obnoxious when his dander was up, especially after he had had a few.

Max sat for a while talking about the recent confrontation with Doddie Shaw, exaggerating what he would have done to the car salesman, big as he was, if the Law had not appeared. Gil let him rant on, and with his drink finished rose to leave.

"I think I'll be on my way then, Max. See ye the morn?."

Max got up to see his friend to the door. "Aye, ah will text ye and tell ye what ah am doin."

They reached the door. Gil turned the door handle to let himself out and Max followed him out to the front lawn.

"Might rain," he said looking up at the night sky.

Agreeing with his friend's weather forecast, Gil walked to where Max had parked his car. "Christ Max!" he let out, pointing to one of the rear wheels. "Ye've got a puncture!"

Angrily Max walked sharply to where Gil stood. "Puncture, my arse!" he seethed, pointing to the flat tyre on the nearside front wheel. "It's that wee bugger Lamont! Baith tyres have been slashed. "This time ah will no let him aff."

"Better make sure it was him Max, afore ye dae anything," Gil cautioned his friend.

"Who else could it be? Have ye forgotten ah caught him that last time?" Max gave an angry kick at the deflated tyre. "And me skint and aw and if ah make a claim through my insurance it will cost me a fortune. The wee bugger," he said again. "If it had only been wan tyre ah could have used the spare.

"Nae worries there pal, ah ken someone who will sell you them cheap. We can use my car. Ah owe you for giein me as many lifts. As for the money, ah can lend you some until ye're flush again."

Max gave his pal a look of gratitude, his earlier anger at his friend forgotten. "Ye're a pal Gil, and ah appreciate it. I'll no forget it in a hurry."

Gil watched his pal close the front door before turning to make his way home. Around the next corner, the figure of a young teenager appeared from behind a hedgerow. The boy was small for his age, and not too clean. A mop of black hair almost hid his face.

"Ye did well." Gil did not smile, as he fished out a ten pound note and held it out to the boy.

"When dae ye want it done again?" the youngster asked.

"I'll text ye. Aw right?" Gil said earnestly to his young accomplice.

40

"If it's this late I'll want double, ah had tae run like the clappers tae get here, ye ken." The boy gave a sniff and drew a finger across the bottom of his nose.

Gil made a face at such crassness. "Ye'll take a tenner and like it. Only next time make it three tyres." The youngster opened his mouth to protest, and Gil jabbed him in the ribs with a finger, "or I'll get somebody else dae it for me. OK?"

And with this, pocketing the money, the youngster gave a shrug of his shoulders and disappeared into the night.

Gil whistled softly all the way home. He almost had Max Duffy where he wanted him and by tomorrow he would be sure when he bought the replacement tyres for him.

He knew Max's only income was from Unemployment Benefit, this and one or two labouring jobs he would manage to do from time to time and which he was apt to forget to mention to that same organisation.

Gil's whistle rose an octave or two at the thought of the prospect of his pal losing his Honda Civic, his pride and joy. Max could of course put in an insurance claim, which in turn would lose him his 'no claim bonus,' and if he, Gil, played his cards right - or to put it another way, if his young criminal friend did his job correctly - it would cost Max a fortune in renewing his tyres, unless his pal found another place to park his precious vehicle, and knowing Max, he would not want to walk too far.

Gil reached his front gate, bathing in happiness at the thought of his pal's humiliation before his fellow boy racers should he come to lose his precious car. Max had always played the big man, treating him as nothing more than his 'yes man', although Gil knew he not only earned much more than him through his job as a plumber, but much more in his drug dealing. Therefore, with his drug dealing in mind it suited him to act the 'daft laddie' around Max and his pals while keeping a relatively low profile. Although his pals knew he took drugs, none were aware that he also dealt in them. Nor could they ever have guessed what amount of money he had put aside because of this. Gil gave a chuckle. He could afford to buy Max's car, or any model like it three or four times over, had he a mind to. No, his aim was to build up enough capital, then quietly disappear down south, where no one knew him. Moreover, should things go right he would start his own plumbing business and forget the past.

******

# CHAPTER 3

Jean Lamont hurried through the concourse, waving to Betty seated at one of the tables. The place was busy, with queues at each of the several kiosks serving food.

"I got you a coffee, and a ham sandwich," the girl said as Jean drew up a seat.

"Thanks pet." Jean looked around at the line of people waiting patiently to be served at the kiosk whose speciality was baked potatoes. The aroma made her hungry. "I don't have time to stand in a queue." She tore open the cellophane wrapper of her sandwiches. "How is it, Betty, that every time I'm ready to leave for my break somebody is sure to arrive at the counter? Usually one that doesn't know what she wants."
Betty smiled, gave a nod of understanding and emptied some sugar into Jean's coffee for her. "I think I might be in trouble if that last customer reports me." Jean bit hurriedly into her sandwich.

"Why, was she one of those awkward ones?" Betty asked.

"Awkward? In more ways than one! I think she must have tried on every skirt in the shop. Then she says as bold as brass, 'Have you got anything larger that would fit me?'
Well, Betty by this time I had had it. It was almost lunch time, and I still had to put away all those skirts she had tried on. No, I says, tents are in the camping section."

Betty choked on her cup of coffee. "You never did, Mrs Lamont?"

Jean nodded, though she realised that it really was no laughing matter. Since Colin's accident - she couldn't bring herself to say death, or murder as she still saw it - she had been making mistakes and had been uncharacteristically short with some of her customers, a fact that had not gone unnoticed by her supervisor. Any day now she expected to be taken into the

43

manager's office. But what the hang? Although she did not relish losing her job, not only for the loss of money but how difficult it would be to obtain another position as well paid as the one she had, and she really did enjoy the work, it was just ..

"It was nice that you could make the time to see me Mrs Lamont," Jean heard Betty say. "I should have called in to the house more often, but..." The girl drew silent, looking, down into her coffee cup, seeing, yet not seeing anything in particular.

Jean patted her hand. "No need to apologise pet. I quite understand."

"No, I should have called, or phoned to see how you were ... all were getting on."

Jean took another bite of her sandwich. "It will take a wee while to get over what happened to Colin. Every morning I get up in the hope it was only a dream." She gave a shrug of resignation and sipped her coffee. "How much do I owe you for this Betty?" Jean referred to the coffee and sandwich, as if by doing so the girl would find it easier to say what was on her mind.

"My treat Mrs Lamont."

"Do you not think you might call me Jean?" she said cheerfully.

Tears came to Betty's eyes. "I thought someday I might call you mother."

"Or some words to that affect." Jean tried to make a joke of it.

Betty stirred her coffee. "It's just every time I see that no use, Belter, Max Duffy driving down the street at home; I wish it was him that had been knocked down. I'll never believe it was Colin's fault, never in a hundred years Mrs Lamont...never." The girl's tear-filled eyes blazed as she looked at the older woman. "Wasted my life he did...and yours too."

Jean set her cup firmly down on the table. "Look Betty, I know what you are going through, but you're young. You will have to learn to get over it."

Betty drew back as if she had been hit. "You are asking me to forget Colin, after all we meant to each other?" That this should come from Colin's mother she could scarcely believe.

Jean understood the look. "We cannot bring Colin back, Betty, God that we could, but he is gone. Don't ruin your young life by dwelling on what happened to my son. Don't let bitterness get you down. Max Duffy will get his comeuppance, don't you worry." She gave her watch a quick glance. "I better get back Betty. Now, do as I say, start a new life."

She lifted her handbag off the table and put her hand on the young woman's shoulder. "I'll not think any less of you if you find someone else. And I'm sure, if Colin is watching, he would want that too." Jean slid her chair under the table. "Don't be a stranger, our door is always open to you Betty. I always liked you and I always will. Cheery for now."
The busy woman left the youngster to her own thoughts.

It was later on in the day when Jean received the phone call from Peter's school, informing her that the head teacher wished to see her and could she call when she finished work. Saying that she could and not a little concerned, she made her way to the school where that teacher was waiting for her.

"I hope I have not kept you from going home," Jean apologised as Mr Smith; a middle aged man offered her a chair.

"Not in the least Mrs...I may call you Mrs?" he asked, sitting at his own desk and giving her a smile, which lit up his homely countenance. Not a bit like her own teachers, who had never been known to melt, not even in a heat wave, who stared at you from granite faces which failed to crack under the most hilarious of situations.

"Aye, old fashioned Mrs will do fine Mr Smith." Jane returned the smile, hiding her apprehension of what was to come.

"Well, Mrs Lamont, I thought that I should have a word with you concerning Peter's behaviour ...or to put it more bluntly his misbehaviour." He saw the shocked look on the parent's face and hastened to soften the blow. "I am well aware of the loss of your other son. A very good student here, not so very long ago, I might add. And for a time Peter followed in his brother's footsteps so to speak, except lately, according to his teachers, he has become a disrupting influence on his classmates. So much so, that it has come to the point where Peter's suspension is a very likely possibility."

Jean felt her face burn a bright red, never having had to deal with trouble either from Jenny or Colin, within or without school.

"His homework is poor...that is when he condescends to do any. You may have noticed this yourself when he is at home?" Mr Smith cocked a bushy eyebrow. He pushed a sheet of paper across the desk to her. Jean read it, her face even brighter red when she had finished.

"That's the trouble Mr Smith, Peter does not live at home, he stays with my daughter and her husband. She hurried on before the man leaped to the wrong conclusion. "Peter has trouble accepting his,"- she made to say his brother's death but had trouble with the phrase- so said instead, "trouble with Colin's passing. They shared a room you see. "

Mr Smith did see, for he gave a nod of his almost bald head. "I can very well understand the boy's feelings, but even so, it is no excuse for his behaviour, though I can understand that it is his way of relieving his grief, his way of dealing with his loss." The teacher gave a sigh and put a second sheet of paper back into the folder on his desk, which Jean guessed, was her son's school report. "If you can find time to have a word or two with your husband, perhaps you could discuss it with Peter. If in turn Peter promises to behave himself in class, I believe

46

that I may be able to convince his teachers to give him another chance, considering the circumstances." The teacher spread his hands out. "However, if Peter does not make amends…"

Jean understood very well what Mr Smith meant. "I'm sure we can make Peter see what he is doing is wrong and how hurtful it is to all concerned. And I'm also sure he will apologise for all the inconvenience he has caused."

"Excellent." Mr Smith stood up. "Thank you for coming, Mrs Lamont. I am sure we can work something out." Then, as if wanting the meeting to end on a cordial note, he added, "Peter is a good boy at heart and when this little episode has sorted itself out he will once again be back to his old self again, I am sure."

"Hopefully," Jean said with a parting shake of the head teacher's hand. "Hopefully."

Hopefully, Jean said to herself as she made her way out of the school gates. Harry would have to wait for his tea. Then she remembered it was Thursday, Faither would have bought fish and they would have fish and chips. Well, they could put hers in the oven, for she was going to pay her little angel of a son a visit. It was time he was home again. He had been at his sister's far too long.

Jean found her daughter preparing her own meal.

"Sorry Jenny, I'll not keep you from your tea, I just want a word with his lordship. Is he here?"

Jenny stirred a pot on the cooker. "No, Mammy, but he'll be here in time for his tea. That laddie can smell the cooking a mile away."

"Aye, you have been good to him Jenny. He should not have been here so long. It's not fair on you and Glen. That's why I want a word with the wee bugger… if you will excuse my French."

"What's he been up to now?" Jenny asked with a sigh of resignation, letting the ladle rest on the side of the pot.

47

"He's been playing up at school, not doing his homework. Mr Smith the heedie had a word with me, that's where I have just come from."

"Hello Mammy." Neither woman had heard Peter come in, now he stood looking at them from the kitchen doorway.

Jean swung round. "I'll gie you, hello Mammy, my lad," she threw at him angrily. "What's this I have been hearing about you at school? And don't give me that all innocent look either," she reproached her son as he took on an air of innocence.

"Whit dae ye mean?"

"Whit dae ye mean?" Jean mimicked. "You have been annoying everyone in your class including the teacher. I have just finished speaking to Mr Smith your heedie."

Peter laughed at the description of his head teacher.

"It's nothing to laugh at my boy."

"I was only laughing at ye callin oor head teacher, 'heedie'"

Jean turned to her daughter, her face livid. "You ken, Jenny, the teacher showed me his homework. He was supposed to write a two thousand word essay on what would you do if you saw a spaceman. And what do you think my darling son wrote?" Jenny waited patiently fearing the worst. "He wrote if I saw a space man, I'd park my car on it man!"Jean exploded. Whilst Jenny turned away pretending to look for the salt in the cupboard to hide her smile.

"Right, you are back home…and now," Jean pointed a stern finger at her son. "So get your things together."

"The night?" Peter exclaimed in horror.

"Can he no bide until next week Mammy? Have you forgotten we are booked for the weekend in Newcastle? We can't let Sarah down."

Jean made a face. She had forgotten all about the shopping weekend, which Jenny and her pal Sarah had arranged for her as a way of cheering her up and to help her forget Colin for a wee while, though she did not think she would. "Aye. OK but you have to do your homework my boy," she warned her son. "Or you know what will happen to you, and I don't mean from your teachers."

At the prospect of not having to return home, at least not for a week, Peter's face lit up. "Aw right mammy I will dae my homework," he promised as he moved into the kitchen to see what was in the cooking pot.

"Right then, I'm off. I'll no hold you back from your tea." Jean turned for the door. "Cheery, Jenny. See you on Friday if not before."

*******

Jean did in fact enjoy the weekend break from home and although Colin was never very far from her thoughts, she had not let it show; at least she thought she hadn't.

Jenny drew the car up outside her mother's door. "Have you got everything Mammy?"she asked her as she got out of the car.

Jean looked a little mystified. "Are you both not coming in for a cuppa?"

"No Mammy, it's getting on a bit. I texted Glen when we stopped at Berwick and said we would be back in an hour or so, and to have the tea ready. Besides, he'll want a break from that laddie o' mine." She gave a laugh, though happy at the prospect of seeing Drew again and his reaction to the presents she had brought him.

"Aye aw right," Jean agreed. "I'll keep his presents 'till I see him myself. So, if you two are no coming in I'll say cheerio for now." Jean ducked her head down to speak to Sarah in the passenger seat. "And I'll see ye again Sarah. And thanks for your company, you really cheered me up."

49

Sarah, a plump girl of about Jenny's own age waved a hand. "It was a pleasure Mrs Lamont...eh I mean Jean." She gave a titter, remembering that Jean had insisted on calling her by her first name.

Jean closed the car boot and waved as the vehicle sped off.

"Did ye have a nice time Mammy?" Peter rushed out of the house to help her with her packages.

"Ye can take that smile off your face wee man, there's nothing in there for you," she teased him.

"Och it wasnae that," Peter beamed at her. "It's the surprise we've got for *you.*

Furrowing her brows and wondering what was in store for her, Jean followed her son into the house. "Smells like paint," she sniffed, drawing up in the hallway. "Don't tell me you have decided to paint the kitchen after all this time?"

"Better than that." Harry appeared out of the kitchen and relieved her of the parcels she had been carrying. Turning her round he pointed her in the direction of what was now Peter's room, and threw the door wide open.

At first Jean was startled by the transformation of the room. Where Colin's bed had stood, there was now an empty space- Peter's bed a little to the right of it now closer to the window - new wallpaper adorned the walls - a new carpet on the floor- Peter's computer and desk snug in the corner.

"Well, what dae ye think o' it?" Harry asked the pride in his voice only too obvious.

Jean stepped into the room, turning first one way then another to inspect the alterations. When she turned again her face was like thunder. "How dare you! How dare you all, without first asking me!" she roared at them, so much so, that Peter standing just inside the room reeled back in alarm. The look on his mother's face as it had been when he or Colin in her parental opinion had done something terrible, only this time

50

it was darker, frightening him that his mother could show such anger.

"Ye cannae have Peter sleeping in a room that would aye remind him o' Colin." Harry was angry at his wife's ingratitude for the work he and the family had done to the bedroom.

"Oh aye, mind yer precious son." Jean's face was now a deep red, and veins stood out on her forehead. She stepped to the centre of the room, pointing to the wall above where Colin had slept. "Where are Colin's posters?" She swung round. "And where is his set o' drawers with all his trophies on top? Do you mean to forget our Colin all together?" She was roaring now and knew it, but she could not stop herself at what she saw as nothing other than a betrayal to her son's memory.

Alex came up the hallway drying his hands on a towel, halting at the open bedroom door. He had been busy putting the final touches to the evening meal, which he hoped would be ready for his daughter's arrival and could scarcely believe what he was hearing.

"That's enough oor Jean." The old man's voice was sharp. "The laddies worked hard tae have this ready afore ye came back. Glen came straight frae work at night tae help. Have ye thought, wumman, as yer man has said, whit it would be like for wee Peter here tae be in this room without his brother? For heavens sake wumman have a heart. Naebody has forgotten Colin, and never will... with, or without posters or trophies."

Jean knew her father was right but the hurt was still there. Without another word she pushed past Peter, thinking as she strode up the hall to her own bedroom, that she should never have gone on that holiday trip.

After the episode of the decorated bedroom, Alex Henderson, as did young Peter, spent more time in Jenny and Glen's home, treating this as a sanctuary, away from the prevailing silence of their own home. His daughter, it would appear to Alex, had retreated into her own world. And when she did speak, it was usually short and curt, young Peter bearing the brunt of it. He had tried to reason with her, tried to make her see how she was destroying the family, pushing them away, but it was to no avail. To her they had desecrated Colin's memory.

"Oh it's you Grandpa," Jenny welcomed the old man cheerily.

"Aye, hen, I thought I might take the wee yin a walk in the park, if that's aw right wi you?"

"Aye, Grandpa, that's if you can find him." She gave Alex a wink. "But seeing as he's no here, you will just have to go to the park without him."

Jenny's words had the desired effect to flush out her off-spring from behind the curtain.

"Me an Indian," Drew proudly announced, pointing to his headdress of feathers.

"Very good, wee man," Alex replied as politely as he could, while tentatively awaiting the hurled tomahawk. And should it strike this white man, Little Running Daft would rapidly become the last of the Mohicans. "And do you know where Indians come from, Drew?" Alex asked, determined to remain as polite as possible. A shake of the little chief's feathers signified that he did not. "Well, they come from North America. Do you know where that is?" Again a shake of feathers. "Well Drew, you go out the front door, turn left and ask the first long distance lorry driver...."

"Grandpa!" Jenny feigned annoyance. "Don't put ideas into the bairn's head, there's enough rubbish there already, with the things you tell him."

"Och, ye ken I'm only joking wi him." Alex looked down at his great grandson with affection. "He's the only thing that gies me a bit happiness noo adays."

52

"Is it that bad at home, Grandpa?" Jenny asked, referring to her mother's attitude since the rearranging of Peter's room.

The old man nodded. "I've tried reasoning wi her. Tried to make her see the harm she is doin tae her family." He shook his head sadly. "It doesnae seem to matter. I wonder whit she is like at work. She has tae serve customers aw day, that's her job and if she means tae keep it, she will have tae be polite."

"I can't see mother not being polite, Grandpa. She is sensible enough to know that. It could be that her work is her only relief. Maybe, it's only when she comes home and realises that Colin is not there, that she acts the way she does, although it's not fair on the rest of you."

"Ye could be right pet. I had thought o' takin a wee peek in tae the store just tae see for mysel," Alex shrugged. "Then I thought if she was tae see me she wid think that I was spyin on her."

"Which would be right." Jenny made a face.

Alex sighed. "Well ah better take oor nibs here ower tae the park." He looked to where the child was sitting on the settee playing with his tomahawk. His mother had dressed him in a red T-shirt and blue jeans, which for once were stain free. "Are ye takin yer ball wi ye tae the park, Drew?" he asked.

The wee boy shook his head. "Taking my plane."

"Right. Get yer plane and we're away then."

Alex wished that he had not agreed to take little Drew to the park, it was too cold for his old bones on this day in early October. However, he met his newly acquired friend Davie, sitting on his usual bench by the bandstand.

"How's it goin then, Davie?" he asked sitting down with a shiver beside him.

"Doesnae seem tae feel the cauld," old Davie commented with a nod as Drew, his plane held high, ran over the grass towards the football field.

"Just what I was thinking," Alex agreed, his eyes on his charge. "Should we no get in tae a heated argument aboot something, tae keep oorsels warm, dae ye think?"

Davie gave a smile. "I've had aw the arguments I want for yin day. I nearly got knocked doon in the supermarket this morning."

"In the car park?"

"Naw, by a trolley near the cooked meat section. Yon supermarket should have traffic lights up and speed limit signs."

Alex chuckled and had a look to see where his junior Biggles had got to, as his friend went on. "How is it, that I always get stuck ahint some women who have mair bairns than Barnados? Or some other wife that has that much on her trolley ye would think she is starting a country of her ain. Then, when it's my turn at the check oot, the lassie there asks, 'do ye want a wee bag' so I says, naw hen, I'm merit tae wan. No a flicker o' a smile. See friendly service ... it's deid."

Alex could not help himself from chuckling at the other's deadpan expression.

Davie took a look at the sky as if contemplating rain or even snow. "Then they get a taxi! A taxi wid ye believe! In oor day, taxis were only for weddings and funerals, no for goin the messages."

"I ken Davie, but times have changed."

"Yer right there. See the working class noo, bigger snobs than ever the rich folk were, with their so called designer labels and their personal number plates on their cars. I'm glad I don't have a car. What pleasure is it in getting stuck in some big toon, where signs say 'no right turn, no left turn and no straight ahead, reversing only, or something tae that affect."

Alex's laughter at Davie's theory turned to one of pain as the toy plane Kamikazied into the back of his head.

Davie stood up, his eyes twinkling. "A head on collision I'd say," as Alex rubbed the back of his head, and looked for little Drew San with the intention of sending him to meet his ancestors.

******

Despite the raw coldness of that early October day, Doddie sweated underneath the latest of bike gear. Except, that was, for his extremities, which never appeared to get warm despite special gloves and a woollen hat stuck under his crash helmet or 'bash hat.' He had climbed over the hill to Haddington from Ballencrief Crossroads known to cyclists as the 'Yak' having resisted the temptation to halt for a plate of soup in that market town before journeying on. His reluctance to stop was not because of the price of the soup but the thought of climbing back on to his bike after leaving the warmth of the café. The climb had made him sweat more but now on the comparatively level roads he began to feel the cold, despite pedalling furiously in the direction of Dunbar. His training bike, complete with mudguards, felt heavy and did not respond to his efforts. Now the wind was in his face and he relished the prospect of its assistance on his return journey, that was if it did not change direction and hit him full blast on his front on his way home to Edinburgh.

Away to his right The Lammermoor hills stood silent in a gray and darkening sky. All of a sudden Doddie felt a loneliness he had not felt before when out training by himself. Perhaps it was the weather? Then again, perhaps not. A sheep bounded across the road in front of him and he touched his brakes to arrest his speed, following the animal's flight as it sped down the banking into a field.

"Daft sheep, do ye no ken yer highway code?" he shouted out loud after the retreating hindquarters. His dark mood darkening as he came to understand why he felt the way he did. He had no one with whom to share his humour.

Doddie felt angry at himself. Would he never stop missing his pal? Every time he mounted his bike, Colin came into his thoughts. How they had trained hard and laughed together, sprinting to beat one another to road signs on the country roads and weather permitting, halt for a spell to take a sip from their bidons and admire the scenery. Scenery which had never ceased to excite his pal, which in turn would have him talking about his cycle trips to his beloved Highlands and his sense of achievement at having ridden all the way to Inverness, then across the Kyles to Skye.

A lump came to the rider's throat. Poor Colin, he would never see his Highlands again.

Doddie was angry now, angry at Max Duffy. No matter whether the boy was innocent or not, he had killed his pal.

It was unfortunate that the car should have come hurtling round the corner behind Doddie at that precise time. Instantly aware that the car was behind him, Doddie made for the grass verge as the driver screeched to a halt.

The anger at what had happened to Colin still fresh in his mind; Doddie dropped his bike on its side and strode angrily towards the car.

"Can ye no watch where ye are goin ye bammer?" The cyclist's rage mounted as the thirty year old driver threw open his door to confront, what was to him, nothing other than an antiquated nuisance on the road.

"Serves you right. Get into the twenty first century and stop trying to balance on two wheels. You lot should be in a circus," he raged at Doddie.

"Aye, ye are right there pal. Maybe we should and we could learn something aboot road courtesy frae *clowns* like you." Doddie was now close to the others face.

How the confrontation would have ended, neither party was to know, for at that moment, another car flew round the same corner, failing to halt as he took Doddie's antagonist's open car door with him.

Doddie swivelled round to see where the door had landed and with a broad smile said. "Yours I believe. Try and no litter the countryside." Adding as he strode back to his cycle. "There's a good chap."

It kept the rider in good spirits as he chuckled and pedalled his way towards Athelstaneford, where, from his left, a dozen or more cyclists appeared, all heading in the same direction.

"Look who it is!" one sang out cheerfully at the sight of the lone rider.

"Well if it's no Big Doddie," another hailed him.

Feeling much better at the prospect of company, not to mention shelter in the 'bunch,' Doddie fitted into the travelling cyclists, the pace already much faster, now that everyone took their share of the pace against the wind when they hit the front.

As they travelled along Doddie told them of his recent incident with the motorist and how that irate man had come to lose his door to a passing fellow motorist. Their laughter Doddie thought, could be heard as far away as the coast road.

It was when riding along the dual carriage way - the first of its kind in Scotland he had been led to believe - that he suddenly, and against his better judgement decided to leave the safety of his travelling companions and head to see Colin's folks. He had not visited them since Colin's accident and now he felt guilty for not having done so. Therefore, with the last "cheerio" ringing in his ears, Doddie headed for Tranent.

When Doddie arrived at the Lamonts, the door was opened to Doddie by young Peter, who, with a howl of delight called over his shoulder who it was that had come to see them. Doddie had his hand shaken first by Harry, then Alex and was ushered into the dining room.

"I thought it was aboot time I paid you a visit," Doddie

apologised.

"I'm glad you did son," Harry said, happy to see Colin's pal again. "Put the kettle on Peter," he ordered the boy.

Jean had heard the voices from where she sat in the bedroom. She was annoyed that she would have to go and say hello. It was not that she did not like Doddie, it was only that to see him again would deepen the hurt that her own son was not with him.

"Hello Doddie," Jean greeted her visitor. "Some day to be out on yer bike. Looks like rain ... snow even."

"Hello Mrs Lamont. How are you?"

"Fine thanks." Jean tried vainly to smile. "I'll get you something to eat." She made to turn.

"Don't bother Mrs Lamont, ah cannae stay long. Ah would like tae be hame before it gets dark."

Jean swung back to face her visitor. "Fine then, Peter will get you a biscuit. You will have to excuse me Doddie, I have quite a lot to do."

Doddie watched her leave, mystified by her behaviour. When he had called before with Colin the woman could not have made him more welcome. Now she was withdrawn, curt even and where her face had once shone bright with pride and happiness for herself and her family, now they were deep lines. Her hair too, was not as tidy as it had once been.

His wife's abrupt departure had left Harry more than embarrassed. This would have to stop. To snub Colin's best friend was just not good enough. Every day she was becoming more morose, more distant. How she held on to her job he did not know, not if her attitude was the same as it was here at home.

"Ye'll have tae excuse Jean, son, she is a wee bit under the weather."

Doddie nodded. He knew Harry was lying, but it was not his place to pry. Obviously, the woman had still not got over Colin's death.

Alex returned to the room carrying a plate full of cakes and scones. "Get this intae ye before ye leave." He set the plate down on a coffee table and without turning, shouted over his shoulder to Peter to hurry with the tea.

"How's the job goin then, Doddie?" Harry asked, sitting down in his favourite chair and turning up the gas fire.

"No bad, Mr Lamont, though some days I never sell a car."

Peter set down the teapot. "Whit does ye're boss say tae that, Doddie?" he asked eagerly, as he had visions of becoming a car salesman himself.

"No too pleased, Peter. Take last Friday for instance. He comes in tae the yard and says'Doddie, 'I don't think you're pushing my cars hard enough.' "Well, ah says, if they had an engine in them ah widnae have tae."

Peter laughed, his eyes gleaming in admiration. "Whit did he say tae that Doddie?" the boy urged.

"No very pleased ah can tell ye. He looks at this people carrier we've got - real keen tae git rid o' it. He's got this card on it that says, 'only one careful owner.' Doesnae mention the four ither careless wans!"

Alex poured out a cup of tea, pushing the plate of cakes and scones across to Doddie inviting him to help himself. It was nice to hear laughter in the house once more, although it would have been better had Jean joined in.

"Can ye no sell the people carrier, Doddie?" Peter asked.

"It's the fuel it goes through that does it Peter, the big engine guzzles it up. It was funny, yesterday, a wee wumman had come in tae take a look aroon. When she had left, auld misery guts the boss says, 'I saw that old lady looking at the 4X4. Could you not have interested her in it?' Have a heart ah says, that wee wumman would need a Stannah Stairlift just tae reach the driver's seat. So the boss says,' Why? Don't I pay you good commission? Oh aye, ah says, ye do, but that sale was commission impossible!"

Amid the laughter, Doddie glanced out of the window. He had stayed longer that intended, having enjoyed the company and was now reluctant to leave the warmth of the room.

Harry followed Doddie's gaze. "It will be dark afore ye get hame. A bit risky noo a days."

"I'll be aw right, Mr Lamont, thanks."

Harry shook his head. "I'll run ye hame."

"There's nae need for that. Besides it's a long way intae the toon and back."

Harry rose. "Nay bother. I'll get the keys."

Peter stood up, "Can I come tae Faither?" he asked, having enjoyed Doddie's company. It had been a long time since the house had heard so much laughter and he shot a quick look at his mother's room wondering if she had heard it and hoping that if so, it would have cheered her up. Maybe then, she would ease up on him, as in her eyes he never seemed to do anything right.

Harry nodded. "Aye, it will be company on the way back."

On the way into town, sitting beside the driver Doddie was aware of Harry starting to ask him a question then halt. For a little while Harry sat silently concentrating on his driving, then, as if having summoned up enough courage, started again and Doddie sensed that whatever the question was, it appeared to be too difficult for the man to ask.

"Is there something on yer mind, Mr Lamont," Doddie asked quietly, his eyes on the road ahead.

"Well there is son. I have some o' Colin's cycle clothes in a bag in the boot, and there's also a pair o' cycling shoes practically new they are," the man explained. "Cost the laddie ower a hundred quid. I never kent bike stuff was that dear. No that ah want anything for them," Harry went on. "It's just that as things are the noo, wi the wife an aw, it would be best if they were oot the way and she didnae come across them when she was cleaning oot. I dinnae ken if any o' it will be any use tae you or no. If they are, ye are welcome to them, if no, maybe somebody else could make use o them."

"I'll see whit ah can dae, Mr Lamont, but Colin's feet werna onything the size o' mine. I mind him lookin at ma new shoes and sayin, 'so shipbuilding on the Clyde is no deid yet!' All three laughed. "I'm sure somebody in the club will buy them, and if so, I'll see ye get the money, though ah dinnae ken how much," Doddie promised.

Harry swung the car around a corner. "Dinnae worry aboot the money. If ye dae manage tae sell them, gie the money tae yer club."

"That would be nice, Mr Lamont. It's funny you should mention the club, for we had a meeting, and we would like tae haud a race in Colin's memory. Dae ye think, Mrs Lamont would object tae it if we did? It would be later on in the season next year, so that we can get it organised, and get it added tae the racing calendar. "

"Ah would think the wife would like that son and that the club would dae this in his memory. Ah will hae a word wi her when ah think the time is right."

Peter leaned forward in his seat in the back. "If ye dae haud that race Doddie, it would be nice if you won it," he said earnestly, his eyes shining.

Doddie laughed. "Nice tae win it? Not only nice, it would be a flaming miracle!"

It was not until Doddie was in the hot shower that he recalled his day. He always had a quick temper, but now it had become even quicker. Earlier that day when the driver had

61

almost knocked him down, he would have loved nothing better than to have picked a fight with him. It had been the same that night of the disco when he had confronted Max Duffy, as he firmly believed that man to be the cause of it all. Duffy was changing him, which he had also done to the Lamont family, and who else, he did not know. Colin's death had affected all their lives, but Duffy strutting around was affecting them more. No doubt his own grief would end in time or until Max Duffy had met his own fate.

*****

Jenny had thought it would be nice to hold Christmas away from home, so she had booked a well known restaurant in Edinburgh. She would have gone for one in her own Tranent, but was afraid that perhaps they might encounter too many locals enjoying the festivities if she had: too many people wishing to express their condolences or asking after their health in relation to Colin's death. This, she believed would be too much for her mother to bear: bring it all back… as if it had never left her, Jenny thought. This was the problem, her mother was becoming more despondent each day, and poor Peter bore the brunt of it all.

Jenny gave a little sigh, her thoughts turning to earlier in the day and the ordeal of having to call at her mother's house. Peter had run to her as she stepped through the door, as if meeting a rescuer, greeting her with 'a Merry Christmas' and the most affectionate hug she had ever known her brother to have given her. The look of what she could only describe as desperation on his young face. Her Father and Grandpa had shown equal delight at her, Glen's and wee Drew's presence.

Presents had been exchanged. Their laughter exaggerated at not so very funny jokes. Her mother had taken her and Glen's gift, staring at it and running her fingers over the small package before opening it. A quiet thank you and a smile was all that she had offered.

Now here in the restaurant, Jenny watched her mother who sat at the opposite end of the table. She had asked her mother's next door neighbours, the Wilson's, to the Christmas dinner in the hope that the more the merrier would help to cheer up her mother. They had declined however, with the excuse of being invited elsewhere. So too, had Betty, though the girl's reason had been on the grounds that her presence was more than likely to upset Colin's mother. She was right of course, as she looked across at Jean's pale face.

What too, was worrying was that she had heard that her mother had been reprimanded at work for her mistakes through absent mindedness. Should she lose her job, it would be the end of her, as Jenny knew that without work she would remain at home and mope even more. She shuddered to think what affect it would have on the rest of the household, more so Peter.

There was a sudden burst of loud laughter from the opposite table, and Jean stared at those sitting there, as if to say 'how can you all sit there enjoying yourself when my son is lying cold in his grave.' It was that plain on the woman's face. Perhaps, Jenny thought, this was a bad idea after all as she could see the signs of the strain etched on every face around the table, each searching for something to say, something that would draw her mother into the conversation and away from her eerie scary world in which she now lived. Jenny gave a little shudder at the thought that New Year was going to be an even greater ordeal.

*******

"Will you never learn laddie? Look at the crumbs you've made, all over the carpet that I have just swept. Do you think I'm worked with electricity that I can do a full day's work, then come home and run after you?" Jean was shouting at her offspring.

Grandpa made a face of sympathy at the boy behind his daughter's back, then a little move of his head indicating that Peter should make himself scarce before his mother continued with her tirade. He had tried talking to Jean, but she would not listen: always comparing Colin to Peter. So much so that he had given up, for fear of making things worse.

As these thoughts ran through Alex's mind, Harry had just got out of his car in the driveway.

"Hello, Wullie," Harry greeted his next door neighbour. "Will ye and the misses be ower to First Fit us at New Year as usual? We will be expecting you baith."

Wullie Wilson shook his head. "Naw, ah don't think so son. Oor Mary has asked us tae her place. We didnae think you would want tae be bothered this year seein…"

"Ah understand. Well have a good time. And we'll see ye baith next year, if no before." He gave the old man a wave as he made for the front door.

This would have to stop; they were losing all their friends. No one wanted to call anymore, either by phone or in person. And the only reason for this was Jean. Nobody wanted to make a visit that turned out to be nothing other than a wake. But with only five days of the old year left, he thought he would have to leave it in the meantime, and hope that Jean would eventually see what she was doing to all around her.

"Hello son, had a hard day?" Alex greeted his son-in-law.

"No bad, Faither," Harry answered, joining the old man in the kitchen. "What's for dinner?"

"Mince and tatties, I'm afraid. I forgot tae go tae the butcher's." Alex lifted the pot off the ring. It will no be long."

Harry nodded and made his way into the empty living room. He sat down and took off his shoes. "Where's Peter,

Faither?" he called out to the old man.

"In the shower, I think," came the reply.

Harry didn't bother to ask about his wife's whereabouts, she would be in her room as always, and would only emerge at meal times to pick at what had been put down to by her father.

Harry leaned forward and turned on the TV. He was late, so had missed most of the news. 'Now for to-nights sport' he heard the announcer say.

"You mean fitba," Harry heard from the kitchen. "It'll be Rangers and Celtic the night again. Ye would think there was nae other sport. Ye would think that havin a World Champion in yer ain toun would go for something. But naw, because it wasnae won wi a roon ba it disnae count."

Harry chuckled to himself. Alex was on his high horse. It would not surprise him if the old man did not follow up his nightly tirade by saying that it was about time the TV folk mentioned some of the youngsters who were a credit to their country and were not out knifing, drinking or obese as the media were wont to imply. He was right of course, the nation expected these same athletes to do well for their country, and when they did, would not be heard of again, or for another four years, while football got all the nightly coverage, even when the season was at an end. The reason was money of course, and the lack of enthusiasm by so called reporters to seek out the news other than football. And money talked, as it did every evening on the national news channels.

Alex came into the living room carrying a steaming plate of mince and potatoes. "Here son, ye can get started while ah gie Jean a shout," he declared, setting down the dish on the already set out table.

Harry rose. "Gie, Peter a shout as ye pass, Faither, he should be oot the shower by noo. He cannae be in there aw this time. He cannae be that dirty."

Alex returned to the room. "Ah gave baith o' them a

shout. Jean says she's no that hungry…as usual." The old man turned his eyes up to the ceiling. "She'll fade away tae nothing and gie herself something she doesnae want," he prophesised, glumly.

A little later as both men sat at the table, Alex gave a grunt of disgust. "Yin comes oot, like a moose oot its hole, and takes its dinner intae its room, wi hardly a 'thanks Faither, or kiss ma bum, and the ither is still sulkin in the shower."

"Whit's happened this time?" Harry sighed.
Briefly Alex told him what had transpired between mother and son before he had arrived.

"Poor laddie, Harry, ah can see him leaving tae bide wi his sister if this keeps up."

"Ah should think she would have had Peter long enough last time. They have a right to have their home to themselves." Harry gave Alex a look, asking for his concurrence.

"Yer right Harry." Alex rose and pushed back his chair. He put the two dirty plates together, placing the knives and forks on top. "I'll gie the bathroom door a dunt, and see if that wee scunner is aboot ready tae come oot. His dinner will no be worth eatin if he doesnae get a move on."

Harry too rose and sat down on the sofa as was his custom before helping with the washing up. Sometimes, however, Jean made an appearance from her room to share in the washing and drying up of the dishes. He switched TV channels and heard Alex shout to Peter to get out the bathroom and had he used all the hot water? He heard him thump on the door, this time in anger and frustration at the occupant.

"Peter!" Harry shouted rising, although he didn't expect him to hear him from the dining room.

"He's no answering, Harry." Alex looked anxiously at the other. "Dae ye think that something has happened tae him?"

Although he too was worried, Harry did not want to alarm the old man unnecessarily.

"Fell asleep maist likely." He took his fist and hammered angrily at the bathroom door. "If yer no oot this second, I'll break the door doon and ye'll hiv tae pay for it oot yer pocket money."

"Ah think something's happened tae him Harry." Alex's face twitched nervously. "He's never been that long in there before." Already he was thinking all sorts of things and none of them were good.

Harry took a step back, lifted his foot and gave the door a kick with all the force that the narrow hallway would allow him to. The door split with a shudder just under the lock, engulfing the men in steam.

Alex was the first to enter, waving aside the steam that filled the entire room as if swimming, reaching the glass cubicle that housed the shower, and the faint outline of the hunched figure of Peter sitting in the corner, blood mingling with the hot shower water flowing into the drain.

"My God!" Alex exploded.

Harry shoved the old man out of the way, turning off the shower and bending over the unconscious figure of his son, clad only in his boxer shorts, all in one swift movement.

He heard Alex at his back. "Poor daft wee soul." It was almost a sob.

"Quick, Faither, dial for an ambulance." Harry was looking wildly around him for something in which to bind the slashed wrists. He grabbed some hand towels, shouting out to tell Jean what had happened to her son, the venom in his voice clearly stating who it was that was responsible.

Jean and Harry waited in the 'sanctuary', a room provided for families waiting to hear news of someone critically ill. They had not been allowed to see their son, he was still unconscious. Touch and go was the general prognosis.

Jean walked to the window, staring out into the black night, at the street lights and moving cars. She didn't move as Harry came up and stood beside her.

"We've lost yin laddie, Jean, and if we lose another it will be aw yer fault." Harry's face was twisted in contempt for his wife of twenty two years. "Aw ye could think of was yer precious Colin, as if he had been a saint instead of an ordinary laddie with the same faults as any other. Ye couldnae see that could ye? And ye took it oot on that wee soul in there." Harry jerked his head in the direction of the theatre. "Whit dae ye think went through oor wee son's mind tae take a Stanley knife tae his wrists, cut through the skin and veins and sit waiting for it aw tae end, aw because his mother wished it was him that was dead instead of his brother. Well, Jean ye might get yer wish."

Harry had been intentionally cruel, reasoning that if Peter was to live, this was the time for Jean to make amends. He did not really believe what he had said about his wife wishing Peter dead instead of Colin, that was extra cruel, but he wanted to shake the woman back to what she had been: a good and caring mother, before all of this sad business.

The woman did not turn, only a quiver of her shoulders told that she had heard what her husband had said.

There was the sound of footsteps on the hard corridor floor and Jenny and Glen appeared.

The girl rushed forward and put her arms around her mother.

"Déjà vu," Glen said quietly to Harry, comparing the scene to when they had last been here when Colin had died.

Harry nodded. "Let's hope it's no the same result," he choked.

Jenny stood talking to her mother in whispered tones.

Jean still had not moved.

"Mr and Mrs Lamont you can see your son now. He's conscious but do not tire him by staying too long," the white coated doctor advised.

Jean had turned from the window at the sound of the doctor's voice. As she drew level with Harry, she put a hand on his arm. "Let me see wee Peter first, Harry, I've something to say to him."

Harry gave his wife a brief smile of understanding.

As the doctor had advised, Jean did not stay long alone with her son. When Harry came into the room, he knew by the look on the faces of both mother and son that the rift had been healed. He never asked, then, or later what had transpired between them, but what he did know was that it was for the better.

\*\*\*\*\*\*\*

## CHAPTER 4

"Don't go any further, we'll no get oot for yonks if we dae," Gil shouted in Max's ear.

Max could scarcely hear his friend above the music from the bands down in Princes Street Gardens. Mostly they were drowned out by the exuberance of thousands upon thousands of New Year revellers who yelled and sang, or just shouted for the sheer hell of it-all happy to be part of the greatest Hogmanay party on earth.

It was almost midnight. The noise intensified by the closeness of the hour. Gill gave Max a wink before being pushed forward by a sudden surge in the crowd. Somewhere below, the bands raised their music. Then just as quickly a hush fell over that long line of revellers that stretched from the West End of that famous street to the Scott Monument.

The clock struck midnight. Fireworks lit up the sky; bells pealed; ships horns blared from the Forth. Somewhere in amongst the hubbub a piper played. Everyone was happy, every stranger a friend.

"Where are we for?" Max shouted to his pal as they were jostled towards the Bridges. Some boisterous revellers stopped to shake their hands and wish them 'aw the best for the New Year,' before singing and pushing their way towards wherever they thought they were going.

A youngster, no more than fifteen, stared glassy eyed at Max, as if trying to remember where he had last seen him, before spewing up on to Gil's shoes.

"Ye f... wee arsehole!" Gil gave him a push which had the domino effect of sending already unsteady bodies reeling down the crowded side of the street.

Max punched the air with his fists, laughing, and took hold of his friend's shoulder. "Let's get oot o' here."
Gil nodded, and found a quieter spot in which to examine the

vomit on his highly polished black shoes.

"Ye look aw dolled up as if ye were goin somewhere, Gil. I didnae ken ye had such cool gear." Max gave his friend the full benefit of his examination; his dark blue suit white shirt and smart silk tie. Until now he had never seen his friend wear anything other than jeans and tank top, or hooded jacket when it was cold.

Max caught sight of his friend's wrist watch and his eyes popped in amazement. "That's no a Rolex is it? How the hell can ye afford something like that?"

Gil beamed at his friend, elated that he had impressed the very person who took pleasure in showing him up as nothing other than an eejit. However, he did not want Max to alter his opinion of him, it was better that he still looked upon him as an eejit. Therefore, to allay any suspicions his pal might have had, said tongue in cheek. "The street put the gither tae buy me it - it's whit ye might call the neighbourhood watch."

Max let out a howl of laughter. "Good yin Gil." Though he still would have liked to have known how his moron of a pal had come to possess an expensive watch such as a Rolex. "Ye smell nice tae pal."

"It's the soap ah use. It suits ma personality don't ye think?" Gil beamed with pride.

Max was not to be outdone. "It suits yer personality aw right. Whit is it, Simple Soap?" Max gave his pal a wink, and turned to looked down the street at a small band of revellers, then back to Gil. "Ye hiv a place aw lined up then?"

Gil cleaned the offending shoe with a handy piece of chip paper. "Aye, follow me. Hiv ye yer Ner'day bottle wi ye?"

Max patted his leather jacket. "Safe for noo."

Gil led the way up the Bridges, the flood of revellers gradually reducing to a trickle as they neared Nicholson Street

71

and Newington.

"How much further Gil, ma feet are killing me?" Max protested, drawing to a halt.

"No much further pal. It will be worth it, I can assure ye." Gil gave his friend an encouraging smile.

"It better be," Max growled, limping after this well dressed companion of his.

Eventually they reached their destination. Max had almost emptied his bottle of good cheer, as he stumbled up the pathway to the large house, where the sound of loud music and equally loud laughter assailed them through bay windows already steamed with perspiring bodies, or bodies just expiring.

No one asked who, or why they were here as they pushed past people wrapped up in each other in the hallway. A few halted in their work to wish whoever they were a Happy New Year before eagerly returning to their labour of love, in the hope of finding that little bit extra overtime.

They reached the first open door, which led into a large, high, white-ceilinged lounge, and Gil raised a hand above the crush of revellers, indicating that Max should follow him. Max took a step around a hugging couple and felt a hand on his shoulder turning him around, a kiss planted on his unexpected lips, before his well wisher moved on.

Gil saw what had happened and waited until his pal had caught up with him. "I telt ye I kent where there was a guid party, did I no?" He gave Max a wink and started deeper in to the crowded room, and was instantly swallowed up by gyrating bodies, all of whom appeared to be enjoying themselves in a way that only alcohol can do.

Eventually both pals emerged on the opposite side of the room. "Try in there," Gil shouted above the clamour, pointing to the large kitchen.

Here, a table in the centre groaned under the weight of various bottles of alcohol, both full or empty that covered its entire length. Max lifted one and after examining its contents returned it to its rightful position, having decided to imbibe from his own bottle of what was left of Grants best. Emptying the whisky into a seemingly clean glass, Max downed it in one swallow, squeezing the empty bottle in amongst the rest on the table when he had finished.

"That bottle is empty. What good is that?" a male voice asked him from behind.

Max shuffled round to face the speaker. "It's for non alcoholic drinkers, pal," he answered, with a turned up lip.

For a moment Max's bearded antagonist stared at him through thick lens glasses, then, as if the confrontation was not worth the effort; or in this case the risk, moved on, hiccupping into someone's unsuspecting back.

Gil, Max discovered, had not followed him into the kitchen. He turned back to the table and lifted a bottle to examine the contents, then having decided to sample the unknown spirit poured a large measure into his glass. Tentatively he sipped a little, swirling it around his mouth savouring the strange flavour, pursing his lips together as a sign of approval and took another sip, then a gulp, to finish what was left in his glass. The effect was not as other drinks which crept up on you gradually to dim your senses and blur your vision. This, in contrast, galloped and hit you full blast in the back of the head.

Max belched and drove through the press of laughing people to lean his back against an empty space on the kitchen wall.

Now it seemed to Max there were twice as many loud mouthed revellers in the kitchen, many of whom were twins. He shook his head; a little afraid it might fall off, and took a deep breath.

"You all right?" a voice asked. Max nodded at the voice. "You don't look too good to me," the owner of the voice suggested.

Max's vision began to clear to the small bespectacled man before him. "You're no Brad Pitt yersel pal." His own voice reverberated inside his head.

"Only trying to be helpful. I'm studying to be a doctor you know. I have learned to recognise the first signs of alcoholism." Max was sure his diminutive adviser would have rocked back and forth on his heels, had there been room, while saying this.

"Too late pal, I'm a life member of the AA. And I don't mean the car yins either." Max had leaned a little forward as he spoke intentionally steaming up Doctor Know All's glasses.

Believing this ruffian to be a hopeless case, the little medical student moved on.

Max took an unsteady step forward and lifted a bottle from the table. This, he decided was something he knew about: Peach Schnapps. This would hold him for a wee while.

He moved through the kitchen throng, leaning his back against the wall just inside the lounge, sweeping the room for Gil.

It was then he saw her, the fair haired girl in the centre of the floor, her hands on the shoulders of the boy she was dancing with. Max swallowed. He had never seen anyone as lovely as this. She had everything a boy could desire - a flawless skin, peaches and cream complexion, slim figure - Max willed her to turn in his direction, already guessing her eyes to be blue. She was about his own age, around nineteen, he guessed. To his disappointment she leaned forward and kissed her partner on the cheek. Max fumed, already disliking this boy who was kissing his girl, for in his mind this is what she was, or to be more precise, would be. Now to Max the party was over, the floor empty, only the blonde girl existed. He wanted another drink to steady his nerves, but he was afraid to lose sight of this vision of loveliness.

"Want to dance?" a young woman asked. Max had been unaware of the girl whom he judged to be in her early thirties standing a little to his side. Annoyed, he swung to her. She wasn't a bad looker and at any other time he would have enjoyed her company. She smiled at him, her long black eyelashes fluttering as if in an attempt to seduce him, at the same time drawing forward to grip him in the crotch. "Well hello big boy!" she let out throwing her head back in laughter.

Max tore the offending hand away. "How would ye like tae breathe through the yin nostril hen?" he stormed at her, angry, not at the offence, but at her interruption to his studying of his blonde.

The woman turned sharply away, and Max, his eyes back on the blonde, heard her say. "Gay, if ever there was one."

"Enjoying yersel I see."

Max had not seen his friend standing next to him. "Mm," he muttered. "Where have you been?" he asked blandly, his eyes having never left the dancing couple.

"Upstairs," Gil answered, raising his glass in a gesture of salute to someone in the whirling crowd of dancers.

"Lucky bugger," Max answered, but not really caring where his friend had been or what he had been doing.

"Strictly business." Gil let out a sigh.

"Aye, dirty business."

"In a way," Gil laughed.

"Who's that bird there?" Max asked his friend, nodding in the direction of the blonde.

"Whit yin?" Gil sounded irritable.

"Whit yin? There is only the yin, ye bammer, the blonde walking tae the settee."

Gil turned up his lip. "Dinnae ken. Want me tae find oot?"

"Could ye pal? I widnae mind a piece o' that."

75

Gil turned to stare at his friend. "Ye're no goin tae say yer for her, are ye?"

"Whit dae ye think? She is the loveliest bit stuff I've ever clapped eyes on."

"Ye say that every time ye have had a bucket fu. Whit was it this time, Vodka?"

"Naw." Max was angry now. All he wanted from his friend was for him to find out as much as he could about this vision of loveliness across the room.

"Ok, I'll see whit I can dae."

A man, a little older than the others, spotted Max, and pushing a shoulder or two here and there made his way to Max's side. "Bit of a shambles would you not say?" He faced Max as if seeking concurrence.

Max gave a shrug. "Depends whit yer after pal, and if it is whit I think it is, ye best get on yer bike." The man moved off.

"Whit did ye say tae him?" Gil was at his side again.

"Nothin. Whit did ye find oot aboot her, then." Max was aware of the excitement in his voice.

"She's well oot o' yer league pal. Yon bird's faither comes frae Haddington…has a construction business. And her nibs there," Gil gave a nod in the blond's direction, "goes tae the Uni."

"Whit's her name?" Max asked impatiently.

"Alison Jeffries."

Max rolled the name around his tongue, repeating it over and over again to himself as if afraid to forget it. "And the bloke she was dancing wi? What aboot him?" Max already hated the young man though he had never met him. It was enough that he had the unbelievable good fortune to be dancing, touching, kissing the girl that he Max had fallen head over heels for.

"Works in the toon: no sure where. Naebody seems tae

know much aboot him, goes by the name o' Alan Hunter, ah understand."

Max slid back into the kitchen. A body lay on the floor close to the door, those wishing to disappear into the garden stepping over him, or in some case stepping on him. The human doorstep in no way resenting what was happening to his anatomy, though he was certain to do so come morning...or as it was, later in the day.

Max found a kitchen chair and sat down. The room was emptier now, a few having left, either physically or mentally, or in other words had passed out, and lay at various intervals along the floor. He was distraught. Every time that he looked at his blond; for in the young man's mind she surely was, he felt an anger which in his drunken state he found hard to explain.

His anger was mounting. Once, when the blond was dancing, she had turned in his direction and for a brief moment their eyes had met, until she looked away, as if he had never existed, which had made him feel even worse. No love at first sight for her, he thought angrily.

"Haddington", Max murmured, emptying the dregs of a bottle of he did not know what into his glass. So, he had every chance o' seeing her again, such as a Saturday morning for instance.

Max gulped down what remained of the unknown drink, gave a large burp, unfortunately catching a passer bye.

"Do you mind!" the young student said indignantly, his eyes blazing at what he saw as nothing other than an uncouth youth.

Still angry at the blond, Max's stare bore into his antagonist. "Whit are ye on aboot? Lucky for you it came oot that end, or ye wid be drinking broon ale wi lumps in it ye bammer," he said haughtily. "Noo bugger aff."

Much to Max dismay, his vision of loveliness was ready

to leave. A well built man of medium height with the rugged appearance of an outdoor worker, stood just inside the doorway of the room, and Max had no doubt that this was Alison Jeffries' father.

Alison gave him a hug and a kiss and together with her young man whom she had been dancing with for most of the night all three left, the father with a protective arm around his daughter.

Now was his chance. Max started across the room bent on begging a lift home, after all, they could pass through where he lived in Tranent. His mind raced. To be sitting near her in the same car... beside her! His breathing came in great gulps, his stomach in knots.

An arm came out of nowhere swinging him round, a voice singing in his ears to join in the dance as he reached the centre of the floor. By the time he had pushed his would be partner away, the departing party was gone.

For a moment Max believing that he had missed his opportunity of a lift, was in two minds of turning upon the person responsible for inhibiting his progress across the room, and in his drunken phraseology 'give him a right doin'. Then again, perhaps he wasn't too late after all?

Max staggered down the hallway towards the open outside door, the walls on either side advancing and retreating upon him, until he was almost sick. Only his obsession of finding himself in the car kept him going. He stumbled, cursed and hauled himself to his feet and had almost reached the end of the hall when the front door closed. Frantically, Max wrenched at the handle, throwing the door open in time to see the car speed off.

Max stood there, using all of the four letter words in his vocabulary as the car disappeared out of sight. Then, as he turned to go back indoors, he saw his would be rival stagger down the street in the opposite direction from which the car had taken.

Max fought the fuzziness in his head and the sickness in his stomach. So, her boyfriend had not gone with her, and as daddy had not given the young man a lift, he could not live so very far away.

Max was never quite sure afterwards what had decided him to follow the young man. He only knew it was because this man had kissed his girl. Max's anger was reaching boiling point; closer, when conjuring up what else there might be in their relationship.

The young man had disappeared through an open gate to a house. Max increased his step to a staggering run. This could well be where he lived and the reason for his not having taken a lift. He would have to hurry, perhaps catch him as he fumbled for his latch key. It was as he reached the gate that he heard the sound of retching, Max drew up, and cautiously took a look. There, his head in a hedge was the person he most hated in the world, vomiting his wee heart out. Max chuckled at his choice of words. The figure was almost doubled up, his head buried in the hedge row.

In an instant Max was behind him, his hand jerking the startled man's head back, his knife slashing at the face from eye to chin. Even as he heard the shriek of fear and pain, the attacker was across the road and out of sight, leaving his victim holding his face and screaming for help.

"Maybe ye have had yer last kiss frae ma bird, wee man." And he let out a howl of laughter as he staggered in the direction of the Bridges.

Holding his hand up to his face, Alan Hunter staggered to the pavement, screaming for someone…anyone to help him. Vaguely aware of where he was headed, he made his way back to the party. Now when he most needed his mobile he had left it at home. Blood soaked his hand. The excruciating pain in his right eye added to his fear and panic, and he pressed his hand against his eye and cheek.

Alan reached the house and ran up the path, party music and laughter mocking his scream, as he staggered through the door.

"I'm blind, somebody attacked me!" He pushed past startled revellers, heading for the main room. "Get me an ambulance! I've lost an eye!" He crumpled to his knees on to the floor, screams from women further frightening him.

A few stood back in horror as if he had suddenly become a monster. He hated them standing there. Why were they not doing something to help him? "Get an ambulance!" he shouted hysterically at one girl in particular who stood helplessly, a hand at her throat, her eyes wide in horror.

Blood ran down his shirt front on to his trousers, dripping on to the polished wooden floor.

Someone came and tried to lift him to his feet. A girl endeavoured to pull his hand away from his eye in order to see the damage, as she tried to calm him. He held his hand tighter as afraid that if he let go, he would lose his eye. Someone in the semi circle around him threw up. More screams, more panic. Others pushed their way out of the room, the party forgotten. This was not what New Year parties were all about. They did not want to know. Alan was sobbing now. The pain was worse. After an eternity the ambulance arrived.

*******

It was Saturday, a week after the party, Max sat in his car a little way up the street from the Jeffries residence in Haddington. 'Lockwood' stood in its own grounds at the end of a gravel driveway. Max let out a low whistle. "No lackin a bob or two there," he reasoned, though it was not the house that he had come to admire.

Although it was not yet quite 9 o'clock in the morning,

he had sat in his car since before seven in the off chance that Alison might leave on some early errand or other. So far there had been no sign of life from the house.

Max sat bolt upright as the thought stuck him. What if she was not here at all? Perhaps, as she attended Uni, she lived in the Halls of Residence in the town? If so, it would be more difficult to make her acquaintance there. Damn, he had already worked out his story line should the opportunity arise that he could speak to her here in Haddington.

It was as his mind mulled over these points that he became aware of someone at one of the double garage doors. From where he sat in his car, he was unable to see the front door, and had not been aware of someone coming out. Max held his breath. The figure opening the up-and-over door was female, and slim, and in his mind he had no doubt that the figure was no other than, Alison Jeffries. *His* girl.

Max watched as the car slid down the driveway, and turned right in the direction of the town. A few seconds later, Max followed. The car, a bright red sports model was not difficult to follow as it turned up Newtonport passed the old library, and drove into the supermarket car park.

The young man gripped the steering wheel tighter.

"Yes!' he exclaimed, drawing into the vacant space next to the sports car. "Couldnae have been better."

Max got out as the girl locked her car, and as he reached the rear of his own car looked in the girl's direction. He gave her a brief nod and walked on. Suddenly he halted and turned to face, Alison, a look of practised surprise on his face. "Sorry, but dae ah no ken ye frae somewhere?"

Alison's look told him that she thought this nothing other than a chat-up line, no doubt having had heard so many before.

Max snapped his fingers as if suddenly remembering. "The New Year doo, in Newington…you were there! Ah kent it was you. Tae tell the truth ah couldnae keep my eyes aff ye."

The girl gave him a little shy smile. "Thanks. And you are correct, I was at that party you mentioned... The Lairds to be precise."

Max felt himself tremble. She had spoken to him!

"Well, I didnae ken whose place it was, seein as ah went there wi ma pal," the besotted young man explained.

Alison started to walk past him. "Perhaps we might meet again next year, when you can again admire me from afar."

Max did not know whether she was mocking him or not, the way it was said. Uni types were always difficult to fathom in the real world amongst real people, he thought.

"A long while tae wait, ma eyesight could fail afore then. So hows aboot noo in the the café there?" Max indicated the supermarket.

Alison laughed at the way this stranger had expressed himself, her eyes twinkling with amusement. She had never met anyone like this rough-looking being before; at least not to speak to. Oh, there had been many who had tried to get to know her, a few, when she had visited some new construction site, but Daddy had kept them all well away. She gave a hurried glance at her watch. "All right, but just for a coffee," she gave him a brief smile, as if already having regretted it.

Max found it difficult to breathe. Now that he had broken the ice so to speak, he felt a sudden surge of panic as he escorted her to a corner table that looked out into the parking lot.

"Coffee, ok?" he asked, and heard a little tremor in his voice. He had never felt less at ease with a girl. At least not one he cared for as much as this one.

Alison was aware of how this young man's eyes never left her face, except to roam over her body. "Do you like what you see, or do you want a photo?" her smile teasing, as she lifted the cup to her lips.

"Whit? Oh, sorry, was I staring?"

"Yes you were… mister…eh?" She put down her coffee cup.

"Sorry," he apologised again. "I'm ca'ed Max…Max Duffy tae be exact."

"And I'm Alison Jeffries." She held out her hand to him. "Please to meet you Max Duffy."

Max took the hand and instantly his body was on fire as he tightened his grip on the slim fingers. His mind flashed back to the party and how he would have risked everything to have done this that night. "I ken, somebody telt me at the party. Was that yer faither that picked you up yon night, when ye left wi yer boyfriend?"

"Boy friend?" Alison wrinkled her brows.

"Aye, the yin I saw ye dancing wi for maist o' the night."

"Oh, that boy!" Alison gave a little laugh. "Well I suppose one could have made that assumption. Alan Hunter, is my second cousin on my mother's side. I had not seen him in ages. Then, all of a sudden, he was there at the same party. We used to play a lot together when we were kids." She stared into space for a moment as if seeing those happy days again. "It was so nice bumping into him."

Max did not know whether to be elated or downright sad at what the girl had just told him. He had done it again, jumped to the wrong conclusion as he had done with Colin Lamont.

"It was so sad what happened to him afterwards. I saw him in hospital." Alison gave a shudder. "I think he has lost the sight of his right eye. Whoever did that terrible thing to him should be put away for life."

Max saw the hatred for this unknown attacker and felt an inner revulsion at himself. The drink had helped that night of course, but this in itself was no excuse, jealousy had been the real reason, jealousy for this sweet innocent creature across the table. And should things turn out as he hoped, it was something which he would have to conceal from her for evermore, besides having to live with what he had done to an innocent young man.

"What happened tae him, that he lost his eye?" He asked, hoping she did not see the guilt in his eyes or the tremor in his voice.

Alison raised her eyebrows in surprise. "You don't know? You did not read about it in the papers?"

Max gave a shrug. "Ah must have missed that yin. So what did happen tae him?" Just in time he prevented himself from saying, 'when he left you outside.' Had he done so, she would have known instantly he had seen them separate and that his victim had made his own way home.

"Daddy offered to drive him home, but Alan said the cold air would clear his head as he was sure he would have a hangover come morning. Oh, how I wish he had taken Daddy's offer."

"Sorry, ah didnae ken that," Max lied.

"I intend on seeing him in hospital after his operation. I really hope it is successful. I cannot imagine what it must be like for him. His entire life altered, if not ruined, by some insensitive moron." Again the girl gave a little shudder.

This is not what he had in mind when he had proposed a coffee, Max thought. Then again it was all of his own making.

"When are ye goin tae pay him a visit? Maybe I could come wi ye,…. just tae see how he's getting on?" he asked hopefully. Not that he cared too much about his victim, although it would be interesting to see what damage he had needlessly inflicted on the poor guy. No, his offer was only in order to see this lovely creature again.

Alison thought for a little while. "That would be nice

of you. Yet, somehow I have the feeling that you are more interested in seeing me rather than the patient." She cocked her head a little to one side and Max's heart beat faster at the movement.

The young man seized the chance before she thought of changing her mind. "Good. When are ye thinking o' seein him and I'll be there?" Perhaps he had said this too eagerly.

Alison gave her lip a twist as she thought. "Next Tuesday would suit. How if we say at around seven and I go straight to the hospital from the Uni?"

"Done. It's a date then."

"A date Max? You *are* a fast worker."

Max laughed. "Ye should see me in ma car, then." So it was left at that.

*******

The door was open as usual, Max rushed into Gil's house. "Gil I have met her!"

Gil did not look up from his Playstation.

"Ah said, ah've met her! Yon Alison Jeffries ah saw at the party!" Max was almost jumping up and down with excitement.

Gil did not share his friend's enthusiasm. "Met who?"

"Are ye no listening? Ah said, ah've met yon lassie at the party and am goin oot wi her next Tuesday. Ah can hardly wait!" Max rubbed his hands in glee, his eyes sparkling at the prospect.

"Oh her." Gil had not taken his eyes off the screen during his friend's outburst of excitement, or his bursting into his home.

Max took a hasty step forward and switched off the set.

Gil swung on him angrily. "Whit did ye dae that for? Ah was winnin for aince."

85

"Sorry pal but ah need yer help," Max quickly apologised, having no wish to annoy his friend especially at this moment.

"Whit again?"

"Aye, ye see I'm goin oot wi her on Tuesday - tae the hospital tae be precise."

"Didnae waste ony time did ye, Max? It widnae be tae the clinic by per chance," Gil laughed, setting his game aside.

Max drew him a look of annoyance. "Dinnae be daft. This is serious. As ah was sayin, am seein Alison at the hospital tae visit this guy that got slashed on his way hame frae that night o' the party. It seems he was her cousin or something," Max explained.

"Was it that boy ye were jealous aboot? Ye widnae have had anything tae dae wi it, wid ye Max?" Gil looked straight at his pal, as if he already knew the answer.

"Whit wid ah dae a thing like that for? Ah didnae even know the poor sod."

"Well, ye had a bit tae drink. And ye ken whit ye can be like efter ye have had a few."

"No enough tae blind somebody," Max lied. Now he felt uneasy. Should his best friend think this of him, would there be others when they discovered he had been at the same party?

Daily, he had kept himself up to date, scanning newspapers for any development, or mention of the assault on Alan Hunter. There had been very little, with scarcely a mention of the attack, which was not surprising, considering it had been the New Year and the police would have been busy dealing with more serious cases. Evidently, the police had not linked the attack on Alan Hunter to someone at the party, the assault having taken place some distance away. And further inquiries had failed to reveal the victim having had any words of disagreement when he was at the party. Max felt a surge of

86

relief. Had they suspected anyone that had been at the Laird's house he would probably have been sought out and interviewed by now.

"So what were ye goin tae ask me?" Gil asked picking up his game.

"Just this. Ah was thinkin o' taking her oot for a bite efterwards, if she was up for it."

"Ah bite o' what Max?" Gil tittered.

"Ah bite tae eat ye eejit. But ah cannae dae that without some dosh in ma pocket."

"So ye need yer dear auld pal, Gil the eejit, tae help ye oot. Is that it?"

Max shrugged, and felt the blood rush to his cheeks. F.. you Gil, he thought to himself, some day I'll get my own back.

"Aye, that's aboot it. Ah was thinking maybe ye could see yer way to lending me enough tae buy something decent tae wear…besides something for ma pocket for the meal."

"McDonalds no good enough for her is it no?" Gil chuckled enjoying his friend's discomfiture, now that he knew what he was after.

"I'll pay ye back pal," Max promised. "And wi interest for aw ye've done for me."

Gil felt an inner satisfaction at the pleading way Max had said it. "How are ye goin tae dae that? Sell that car o' yours? If so, ah think I'm entitled tae first refusal."

Max was aghast. "Ma car? Never, it's ma first … No," he corrected himself. "Now ma second love. And ye ken how hard it was for me tae save for it. Besides, what am ah tae tell the gang if ah had tae let it go?"

What an opportunity to do just that, Gil thought. Here, he had his friend by the short and curlies. What a thought it would be to humiliate Max in front of his fellow boy racers when he, Gil, turned up at their rendezvous in Max's car. Or better still, with Max as a passenger. Now was the ideal time to do this to his love sick friend. Max must have it really bad, as he had never seen him so anxious or excited over a girl before. And with Max's good looks there had been plenty.

. "How much dae ye need?" Gil toyed with the controls of the game in his hands.

"Well, ah was thinkin o' getting some new claes as well... besides havin something for ma pocket for the meal...only if ye can manage it, of course, pal," Max added tentatively.

Gil pretended to calculate his friend's debt by gazing at the ceiling. "Ye owe me for ten slashed tyres." He stopped. "It's aboot time ye pit an end tae that wee boy Lamont's tricks. Ah thought it wid have stopped aince ye had pit yer car away in that lock-up ye are renting."

"So did ah, Gil, but the wee bugger must have found oot where it is. And it's no exactly burglar proof either. Ye could knock a side doon wi a paper bag fu o' raffle tickets, if ye threw it hard enough. Next time ah catch him I'll tan his arse." Right now the damage to his car was of secondary importance to his pal loaning him the money.

"Then there is the money for the new alternator. No tae mention what ah gave ye for Road Tax and MOT," Gil continued absently, his fingers pecking away at the controls of his game.

"Ah ken, ah ken, but ah will pay ye back." Max was growing more impatient by the minute.

Gil shook his head sadly. "Am no pushin ye for the money, pal. It's just ye are getting yersel deeper in debt. Am no worried aboot ye no payin me back, for ah ken ye will no 'doo' me. The fact is, ye are no bringing in that much in the way o' money."

"I ken. Freddie gies me as much work as he can. But ah hive tae pay ma share o' the mortgage and still find money tae feed masel and put petrol in the tank. As it is, Cammie pays maist o' the mortgage and the food, no tae mention the gas and electricity."

"Aye, aw right then. Where were ye thinkin o' goin for these new claes and things?"

Inwardly Max was relieved. He was going to get his loan. "Ah was thinkin o' goin tae Ocean Terminal."

"OK. When?"

"The morn?" Max asked hopefully.

"Better make it the efternin, if ye want company," Gil suggested, turning back to his game.

"Aye, fine, Gil."

Gil looked up from his game. "Better make it ma car, then ah will no have tae gie ye petrol money."

"Thanks again pal, I'll no forget tae pay ye back."

"And how", Max uttered under his breath.

*******

Harry Lamont closed the car door and with a much lighter step, strode to and opened his front door. Matters had much improved at home since Peter's attempted suicide. Had it almost taken the life of their remaining son to have made things better, he wondered?

It had not been easy for the family; Peter's 'accident' was not something that could remain hidden from neighbours, especially neighbours across the street like auld Jimmy Moffat and his wife.

Both Moffats had heard the ambulance siren as quick as they themselves had, Harry reflected, and were in the street before the vehicle had drawn to a halt. Considering the state he was in, it had taken him all of his willpower not to shout at them to get away from the ambulance when poor wee Peter had been carried out on a stretcher, for had the nosey couple stood any closer they would have been in the damn thing. And if so

89

they would have needed an ambulance of their own.

Being at home Alex had borne the brunt of it. Of course all sorts of rumours had flown around the town with some inquisitive Belter or other stopping the old man in the street, who, under the pretext of being anxious about Peter's health had simply wanted to find out what really had happened to the boy.

The genuine Belter had the courtesy not to ask and to them he was thankful. Being at work he had been spared these confrontations, but not so his wife who had to bear numerous phone calls from concerned neighbours who had 'just found out what had happened to the poor wee soul,' or to similarly inquire when meeting her in the main street whilst out shopping.

Harry sighed. He remembered Peter coming home from his first day back at school.....

They sat around the dinner table only the clank of dishes broke the silence, each afraid to ask the boy what his day had been like. That was until Alex had taken it upon himself to ask.

"How did ye get on the day son? Have ye missed much o' yer lessons, being off for awhile?"

Harry heard his wife's sharp intake of breath. Peter shrugged. "No much. Ma pals were aw keen tae see the cuts on ma wrists." As he said it, his face broke into a wide grin. "Am famous ye ken. Everybody wanted tae see them. Ah should have charged them aw a viewing fee," he said with pride. "I'll ken better next time."

Jean's fork dropped on to her plate with a clatter, tears came to her eyes and she let out a howl of anguish, her chair crashing to the floor as she ran crying from the room.

"Peter!" Harry yelled at him. "Whit the hell made ye say something like that for, ye stupid wee eejit. See whit ye've done tae yer mother, and her getting better an aw!"

90

"Easy, Harry," Alex said quietly. "The laddie didnae mean tae hurt his mammy."

Peter's face drained of colour. "Ah didnae tell ma pals whit really happened, but ah did tell the head teacher when he asked me, when he had me in his office the day I came back."

"And whit was that son?" Alex asked. Although he had asked the question as calmly as he could, his insides were shaking, in apprehension of the answer. Would the whole of Tranent know the full story? Already he could see busybodies nodding their heads as if they were already privy to the truth.

Peter looked from father to grandfather. "Ah telt them ah cut ma wrists because ah couldnae live without Colin."

The boy heard two simultaneous sighs. "Did ah say the wrang thing?" Peter looked from one grown up to the other.

"Naw, son," Harry grinned, there was relief in his voice as he added, "noo away and tell yer mammy that ye are sorry for whit ye said and tell her whit ye have telt us."

As Peter left to do as he was told, Alex shook his head in admiration. "Ye have a right wee son tae be proud of Harry."

"Ah ken Alex - That the laddie wid take the blame - It takes an auld heid tae think up that yin. So Jean has nae need tae worry on that score. Noo, we'll maybe get back tae normal."

*******

"Is that you Harry?" the cheerful female voice asked from the kitchen.

"Aye, who else were you expecting?" Harry called back in the same cheerful tone.

Jean met him coming into the kitchen. "Are you no a wee bit early?" she asked, drying her hands on a small hand towel.

91

"So that was why ye were asking who it was," Harry teased.

His wife grinned. It was nice to see how much Jean's moods had improved since…he stopped his thinking at that.

"So what have you been up to during your day off?" he asked, lifting up the lid of a steaming pot on the cooker.

"Not much. I cleaned out Peter's room. Honestly, the rubbish that laddie can hide away."

Harry chuckled, happy that she had not said Colin's room. "So, what's this you are cooking up?" Harry stared into the boiling pot.

"Wait and see. It's a new recipe I'm trying oot, I saw it on TV the other night."

"Better no let the auld yin hear ye saying that. He says there is that many cookery programmes on TV he doesn't know whether he's watching TV or a microwave oven." Jean joined in his laughter.

"Where's yer faither and Peter? Usually they are here before me, as they can smell yer cooking frae as far away as Macmerry."

"Speak o' the devil!" Jean exclaimed, "I think that's them noo."

"Hello Mammy," Peter greeted his mother from the kitchen door. "Smells good, whit is it?"

"Wait and see," Alex suggested, pushing past his grandson into the kitchen.

Jean pretended to scowl at her father. "And you can wait too, for I ken you are fair itchin to ken what it is as well." She gave him a gentle rap on the wrist with her spoon.

"Away and sit doon, the lot o' you. It will be ready in a minute or two," she said as she shepherded the men into the dining room.

"That was guid Jean. Whit's it caed again?" Alex asked, licking his lips.

"Chicken something or other. I'll have to read the packet again." Jean winked at her husband. "Why, did you no like it Faither?"

"Ye must be slipping grandfaither, usually ye say that the chicken tasted fowl when ye are asked," Peter chuckled, for they had heard the old man's quip on occasions too numerous to mention.

The diners sat back, each happy in one another's company, Jean making herself believe that Colin was out training on his beloved bike and the others endeavouring to look as if there had never been an accident at all.

Harry was aware of his wife's face gradually darkening as she stared at the centre of the table and he knew she was thinking of her absent son. "I bumped into Jimmy Campbell the day."

"You should hiv watched where ye were goin Faither," Peter laughed. He too was aware of his mother's mood having changed.

Harry gave his son a stare at having interrupted him, though, not one of malice. After all, any attempt at humour was to be welcomed, which is why he had started this particular story. "As I was saying," he halted, to look at his son, daring him to interrupt, before continuing. "I met Jimmy Campbell the day. He was telling me he has had a hell o' a time wi that wife o' his. It's something to dae wi his budgie."

"He should see the doctor aboot that," Peter quipped with a giggle.

"That's enough oot o' you my lad," Jean's head jerked up, returning from her day dreaming. "Now listen to your father's story," she warned him.

Harry threw his hands in the air in exasperation. "Ahm ah goin tae get telling this story or no?"

"Aye, on ye go son, before I begin tae wonder whit's for supper." Alex frowned.

"Jimmy was telling me that he and his wife have this budgie." Harry halted, looking at each of his family in turn awaiting further interruptions and when none were forthcoming, continued, "and how they couldnae get it tae talk. Then, as it happened, yin night a neighbour asks Jimmy tae look after her dog while she and Jimmy's wife go oot tae the Bingo. Anyhow, Jimmy falls asleep and the dog decides tae go for a wee walk by itsel. When the women got back, the wee dog was missing. Jimmy's wife goes clean aff her heid and accuses him o' havin been doon at the pub for a quick yin and no lookin after the dog. So, Jimmy asks the budgie tae talk up and gie him an alibi, but he says the wee bugger takes the Fifth Amendment and just sits there refusing tae say anything. Later, Jimmy puts some twelve year auld malt whisky in tae its dish tae teach it a lesson."

"Whit happened then Faither, did it start tae sing?" Peter chuckled, and saw his mother's face light up as she followed the story, she too, eager to hear the end.

"Naw, son. But Jimmy says he was sure it said something as it fell off its perch. He says it sounded something like what he says when he watches his horses coming in last on the Telly." Jimmy let out a loud laugh, and looked around the table at the faces staring at him in bewilderment.

"Is that it? Is that whit I've been sittin here waitin tae hear?" Alex shook his head in disappointment.

"Well if that's it?" Jean rose with a scrape of her chair. "You can help me clear the table and wash up." She rose with a shake of her head, lifting a sauce bottle and milk jug, and disappeared into the kitchen.

Peter too got up. "Take some advice frae yer son, Faither, still keep yer day job."

"Thanks son," Harry replied, giving the boy a playful slap on his backside as he passed his chair.

Alex gave his son-in-law an appreciative grin. "Every

wee bit helps. At least ye got oor Jean tae listen. That's something."

"She is getting better, Faither. When I asked her what she had been doing aw day she said she'd been cleaning oot Peter's room...no Colin's. Ah thought that was a great start."

"Aye, son, so it is, each day life will get that wee bit easier tae bear, though the pain will no go completely away. Aye, time is a great healer so they say. And they're right. I still miss oor laddie and the wife, but as ah said, it gets that wee bit easier."

Harry watched the old man lift some dirty dishes and toddle with them to the kitchen, sadly wondering just how much Colin's death had also affected him.

*******

Max drove to where the red sports car was parked in the hospital car park, reversing into the empty space beside it. Locking the car, he walked briskly to the brightly lit reception, catching his reflection in the glass doors as he stepped inside. The new dark blue cords he wore suited him, as did the leather jacket. It had cost him a bomb...well Gil rather.

Max found the ward and walked a little nervously down the corridor. He was going to see her again. Once more the young man reflected on his good fortune and gave little thought at having to come face to face with his victim. At last he reached the little single patient room and saw Alison standing at the side of the bed.

He had almost gone into the room before he was aware of the other two visitors. Of all people, these were two whom he did not care to meet.

Doddie Shaw, looked up at Max standing in the doorway, unable to disguise his surprise as well as disgust at finding the man he most hated in the world standing there, and why he should be here at all.

Alison turned round interrupting her conversation with the man in the bed. "So you found us?" She gave Max a warm smile, having expected him to call off the hospital visit, but not on seeing her later.

Max nodded, now aware of Sadie sitting in the chair in the corner, her eyes blazing hatred up at him.

"This is Doddie and Sadie," Alison introduced the two visitors.

"We ken Duffy," Doddie said through pursed lips.

Alison looked from one to the other, having seen the look of contempt on Doddie's face and Sadie's horrified expression clearly saying to her, that she could not possibly be involved with anyone the likes of Max Duffy. Alison decided not to ask any questions. Later she would ask Max what it was all about. "Say hello to my cousin, Max." The girl forced a smile.

Max gave the patient a brief nod. Now he saw at firsthand what his handy work had done, although most of it was hidden by several layers of bandages over his right eye.

"Sorry for what has happened tae ye pal." And he meant every word, once again having realised the effect of his over impetuous nature.

"Thanks." The voice was soft, weak. Fear showed in his one good eye. Not of Max, for he was unaware that he faced his attacker, but for himself and his future.

Max nodded again. "Hope ye get better quick, like." He felt awkward in front of everybody. "I'll leave yees aw tae it then. I'll just wait ootside."

As Max made to turn, he heard Sadie say. "No, it's aw right, we were just leavin. Ye can have a word wi Max, Alan."

It was the way the girl had said his name that angered Max, for she had almost spat it out as if it had been something vile on her tongue.

96

Alison gave Max a look implying she did not understand this hostility, when Doddie came unexpectedly to the rescue. "We'll say cheerio for noo, Alan. Sadie and I will ca again next week, if ye like."

"That would be nice. And thank you both for taking the time to see me." The patient's voice had grown perceivably fainter and tiredness had drawn black lines under his one and only uncovered eye.

"Ah think we should go tae, Alison, yer cousin looks as if he could go a nap," Max suggested, not for the patient's benefit as all he wanted now was to get away from here.

"I *am* a wee bit tired, as Max says. I would like to close my eyes...." He halted and a tear came to his eye. "Close my eye," he tried to make a joke of it, "before they come around with the tea and biscuits." Alan pulled the covers up to his chin.

Alison leaned forward and kissed Alan gently on the cheek. And this time Max did not feel a pang of jealousy and had he not done so at the party, he told himself, things would have been different, especially for the young man lying there. Then again, he might not be seeing this girl tonight.

Max would have walked past the hospital cafeteria had Alison not stopped him. He drew her a look of disappointment. "Here?" he asked. "I thought we could have a real meal in the toon." He had not considered running to a candle lit dinner, but hoped to have taken her a wee bit more up-market than a cup of coffee in a hospital cafeteria.

"Why not?" Alison pulled out a chair near her, signalling him to sit down at the table. "I'm not in the mood for eating, tonight, Max." She gave him a look, hoping he would understand.

Max saw her hands shake. Seeing the condition, in which her cousin was in, had evidently shocked her. "Ok. How's aboot a coffee and somethin?"

Alison nodded. "A coffee would be just fine... milk, two sugars....and a biscuit if you don't mind."

She watched Max head for the counter, not quite knowing what she saw in this boy. There was no doubt that he was good looking...as to anything else? It could never lead to anything, as their lifestyles were poles apart. Yet there could be something there?

Max returned with the coffees, set them down on the table, and produced a wrapped chocolate biscuit from his pocket.

Alison sipped her coffee but made no attempt to unwrap the chocolate biscuit.

"Did I get the wrang kind?" Max pointed to the biscuit on the table.

"What? Oh no, I like them well enough, thanks. I was just thinking of poor Alan up there, and how his life has changed," she said sadly.

Max lifted his cup. He did not know what to say. What to do. It had been a mistake to have come here at all. But he did want to see Alison again.

"How come you know Doddie and Sadie, Max?"

Now more than ever he wished he had not come. How could he tell her the truth?

"I knocked doon Doddie Shaw's pal when he was oot cycling yin day. Him and Sadie still think it was my fault, though the polis say it wasnae."

"That accounts for the way Sadie spoke to you in the room." She put her hand on his. "You poor thing."

Max felt a surge of excitement at her touch. He could milk her sympathy for all it was worth. Somehow, he couldn't bring himself to do it. How unfair it would be, to take advantage of this girl, he, having caused all the trouble in the first place.

"That's how Doddie knows Alan, they are both in the

same cycle club. He was in it before he went to study in England," Alison told him. "It must be agony for Alan lying there wondering if he will ever be able to race again. Or even ride his bike."

Max didn't want to hear anymore about her cousin, or Doddie, or of cycling, come to think of it.

"So ye don't want tae go for a meal, then," he asked, hoping she had changed her mind.

Alison shook her head. "Not tonight, some other time maybe."

Max did not like the sound of 'maybe.' "Is that a date then? Or do ye no want tae see me again?" He held his breath, fearing the worst.

"Of course." She gave him a sympathetic smile. "But not tonight."

"When? Just say the day, and I'll be there."

Alison lifted her cup, amused by the look of expectance on the young man's face. He really had it bad, she thought. The trouble was, how to let him down gently when the time came, although right now she did enjoy his company, if not more so, his attention.

*******

"Where were ye Faither? Ye are never this late for yer dinner. I was getting really worried about you," Jean scolded the old man, but not too unkindly, as he sat down at the table beside Peter and Harry.

Alex salted his mince and tatties. "Ah took wee Damien tae the park."

"Faither, will ye stop calling the bairn that name, he'll start answering to it outside. Then what will Jenny and Glen say to that, do you think?"

"Och, it's only ma wee joke. The bairn is aw right. It was that ah never noticed the time. There's this auld guy,

99

Davie, ah get talkin tae. He aye cheers me up." Alex gave a chuckle. "He was tellin me aboot the time he was in hospital getting a new hip. The day afore his operation, they wheeled in this middle aged man. 'Whits wrang wi you pal', Davie asks him. 'I'm too embarrassed to tell you', the bloke says. 'Aw we're aw the same here' says Davie 'we don't have secrets frae wan another.' So the bloke says,' well I have just started to faint at the sight of blood.' 'Och that's nothing' says, Davie. 'At least it's no life threatening.' ' It is for you' says the bloke, 'I'm your surgeon!"

Harry was the first to laugh, the rest following as they envisaged the scene.

"Ah don't think that's true." Peter rose. "For, if he needed a new hip, they wid have taken him tae the hippodrome," he said throwing back his head in mock disdain.

Alex caught the boy's sleeve preventing him from leaving. "But that's no aw, he was telling me. Efter Davie's operation, they telt him tae take up dancing tae help strengthen his leg. So Davie says, 'I tried that Riverdance but nearly drooned. Next, ah tried Barn dancing, but fell aff the roof. And ma last attempt was at Line Dancing, and ah nearly got run doon by a train." Alex let out a howl of laughter, as the others looked at him as if he had lost his marbles. "Well ah thought it was funny. Maybe it was the way he telt it," the old man suggested, letting go of his grandson's sleeve.

Now free, Peter gave his grandfather a gentle pat on his head. "Keep takin the tartan pills auld yin and it will keep us frae visitin ye in ye know where."

"Honestly laddie, that's your Grandpa, your talking to," his mother said aghast.

"Well, there's hope for him yet Mammy, if he still minds it was me who reminded him aboot the pills."

"Ah'll gie ye pills! Ye have cut me tae ma incontinent pants. "Alex gave the boy a playful slap on the leg."

"Did ye see that Mammy?" Feigning pain Peter rubbed his leg. "Faither, whit is the phone number for 'Child Line'?" he asked Harry, sitting by the fire reading his paper.

"Better still laddie, go and see them directly," Harry advised his son.

"Where's that Faither?" Peter hobbled to the settee.

"Main office is in Portsmouth," Harry replied, turning a page of his newspaper.

"That's guid," Alex agreed. "By the time ye get there, ye will be ower auld tae complain."

Jean smiled at the banter of her family from the sanctuary of her kitchen. Now if only she had heard Colin's voice chipping in, she would be the happiest mother on earth. As it was, she still had Peter, and for this she should be thankful, especially after the way she had treated him. Please God, keep him safe, especially from folk like Max Duffy, she prayed.

*******

# Chapter 5

It was the first time Max was to meet Alison at her home. To say that he was nervous was an understatement. Max shivered, fully expecting the reception from Alison's daddy to match the freezing temperatures of this February, Saturday evening. He turned the car around in the gravel driveway in preparation of making a hasty departure, should Alison's father give him the thumbs down.

Taking a deep breath he pressed the doorbell and stood back.

It seemed forever before he saw the silhouette of a figure appear through the glass panel, halt and unlock the door. Then she was there, standing smiling at him.

"You're on time." Alison leaned forward as he entered the hall, allowing him to kiss her cheek. "Daddy is in here." She took Max's hand and led him into a large dining room.

It was as the boy had expected, having seen so many scenes such as this on TV or in old movies. 'Daddy' stood with his back to the fire, where flames rose from imitation logs.

"So you are Max, are you?" Nathan Jeffries, made no move to shake Max's hand, but just stood there appraising this 'person' who was dating his one and only daughter

"Aye, that's right, Mr Jeffries." Max made a point of not attempting to speak politely.
If he were to meet this man again, should a relationship flourish between himself and Alison, it would only serve to establish how false he was if he were to feign a posh voice now.

Max was aware of the man's eyes examining him from head to toe, and he was glad that he had bought these new clothes, as jeans and hooded jacket would not have gone down too well, he reckoned.

"And what do you work at, Max?" The man had made

no sign of offering his guest a seat.

"Maistly I am self employed, Mr Jeffries. Ah will take any job that is offered tae me, although, Freddie Stewart usually has some plumbing jobs on the go."

Nathan Jeffries showed he was impressed. "I know Freddie, he also does some sub-contracting for me now and then."

Max nodded. "Ah ken, he has telt me this afore. Maybe ah did some work for ye that ye didnae ken aboot." Max gave a nervous smile.

"Are you thinking of taking me out, Max Duffy, or do you mean to stand here all night gabbing?" Alison rose impatiently from the chair where she had been sitting.

Max felt a surge of relief. Alison's father was no fool. One could not afford to be, to have achieved what this man had. He was afraid that should the conversation - or should this be interrogation - have turned to hobbies etc, he would have been found out, in one way or another, as his not being good enough for his one and only daughter. Then again, who, in this man's eyes, would ever be good enough for his precious Alison and who could blame him? Now that there was no Mrs Jeffries, Alison would be the only thing in the whole world left to him.

Max looked at his host, as if asking permission to take his daughter out.

Alison's father gave Max a smile as if to say, now you know what I have to put up with. "Away and enjoy yourselves." He gave a wave of his hand as if urging them to leave. And as the couple reached the door, they heard the man call out that Alison should not be too late in getting back.

"What did you think of Daddy?" Alison asked, as Max turned the car into one of Haddington's one way streets.

What could he say? Evidently the man had been sizing him up and wondering what prospects he had. What was a

103

bloke like him meaning to do with his daughter?  Not that he, Max had the slightest chance of getting anywhere, or at least not for now.  He still could not believe his good fortune, that she was actually in his car with him and on their previous dates had actually allowed him to kiss her.  The first time that she had, he believed that he had the world at his feet, if not by the short and curlies - that was if the world had in fact short and curlies.  Maybe the world's equivalent was the Amazon Rain Forest or a jungle somewhere.

"I asked what you thought of my father?"  Max had been unaware of not having answered.

"Eh?  Oh, aye, nice bloke."  What else could he say?  "You and yer daddy must miss yer mammy.  Was it cancer, by the way?"  It was not a subject he wanted to dwell on, diseases being the realm of the old.

"Cancer?  More Capricorn really.  New Zealand to be exact."  Alison made a show of looking out of the side window.  "Someone from Kiwiland, who had come over here on a working holiday and started to work for Daddy.  One day Daddy sent him up to the house on an errand.  That's how it all started, so I believe."

Max turned on to the bypass, heading for Edinburgh.

"Where dae ye fancy goin the night?"

"There's a good film on at Ocean Terminal, if that's not too far away?"Alison turned to look at him, awaiting his answer.

Max mentally calculated how much he had to spend, which had him recall a previous conversation with his brother Cammie on this same subject of money…or the lack of it.

He had just arrived home when Cammie collared him in the living room.  "Look pal, I ken yer doin yer best but I cannae keep payin for everything in the hoose."

Max knew what his brother was saying was true.  However, as things had not gone well for him recently, this was almost the last straw. "Whit dae ye mean? Don't ah pay ma share?"

Cammie shook his head. "Afraid no Max. Jist think what that car o' yours is costing you wi Road Tax, insurance MOT, no tae mention petrol and repairs, and they tell me ye keep getting yer tyres slashed. Who the hell's doin that? I thought ye had a garage for that."

"A garage for having ma tyres slashed!" Max joked to give himself time to counter attack.

"Nane o' yer kiddin Max, things are getting gey serious. Whit, wi the heating and electricity, no tae mention food." Cammie gave his brother a look of despair. "Oor parents left us the hoose aw right, but we still have the mortgage tae pay. It might mean us havin tae sell up."

The unexpected news had Max sitting down, his mind reeling at the thought of having to move away from his friends, and now, more to the point, Alison. "Where dae ye think we will end up? It cannae be Edinburgh, ye hiv tae pay a fortune tae live in a cupboard, and no a very big cupboard at that."

Cammie saw the humour in it. "God help us if it ever came tae that. I don't think I could put up wi yer farting. They would find me deid in the morning."

Max's laughter filled the room. "Could be the perfect crime - nae fingerprints or anything - nae sign o' foul play..." Max trailed off.

And that's how it had ended.

"Not very sociable tonight are we Max?"

The question jerked Max back to the present. "Sorry, Alison, ma mind was elsewhere. No as much work this week. I'm a bit short, as any lassie will tell ye."

Alison gave him a puzzled look.

"Ach, never mind, it was only ma wee joke. What picture is it we are goin tae see anyway?"

"Did ye like the picture?" Max yawned as they stepped into the cold night air. He was glad that Alison had declined his offer of a bite to eat, for some of the places in the centre charged like the Light Brigade.

"I know *you* didn't, I could not hear the gunfire for you snoring."

Max drew to a halt mortified that he had fallen asleep. Ah wasnae snoring was ah?"

Alison took his hand and they walked to the car. "Only now and again, but I will forgive you this time."

"Just the same I would still like tae go for a bite tae eat. How aboot you, Alison?"

They had almost reached the parked car, when Alison asked, "Where do you usually go, Max...with your pals I mean?"

With his pals? That was the last thing he wanted. To him his pals were all right, but to this posh girl they would appear to be nothing less than heidbangers. "Ah like a hamburger at Mcdonalds, but its well oot the way."

Alison got into the passenger seat. "There is one at the Fort," she said as Max slid behind the wheel.

"Well, ah was meaning tae take ye straight hame on the bypass. Efter aw, yer faither said no tae be late." She could not have made a worse choice, as this was the usual haunt of his pals, and should they meet, he did not want Alison to know how he spent most of his other evenings. To a girl of Alison's upbringing, sitting in a car in the Asda car park until the early hours of the morning, chatting to your pals, and making the odd dash here and there, could only meet with her disapproval.

Certainly, he had not done this as often since meeting the girl. This and the fact that he did not have enough money to spend on a girl and petrol as well. Max gave an almost imperceptible sigh. He just had to make more money, as he wanted the best of both worlds by keeping his girl as well as

106

his pals.

He did not see his pals cars parked outside McDonalds until it was too late. Max ran a jaundiced eye over them as he locked his car door. Gil's car was there, Danny's Vauxhall Corsa as well as wee Joe's Ford. Under his breath, Max let out an oath and followed Alison inside.

It was as he feared; his friends greeted him with loud shouts of welcome from where they sat at the table.

"Friends of yours?" Alison asked, as she turned to look up at the selections above the counter.

Max saw the amusement in her eyes at his embarrassment. "Aye, in a way. What would ye like?" He pointed to the various choices available.

"I think I will have a cheeseburger."

"With chips?" Max asked, as the table where his pals sat had quietened down.

"No. But I would like a medium size coffee please. I'm paying. You got the pictures."

"Nae chance," Max said seriously. The last thing he wanted was his pals to see Alison paying for his meal and have them take the piss.

"Ower here, Max!" Wee Joe, stood up, gesturing that he and Alison should sit beside him at his table where he sat alone.

Max guided Alison to a seat opposite his friend and sat down beside her.

"No goin tae introduce us Max?" Danny asked, a wicked smile on his lips.

Max eyed the slim fair haired boy who did not look his eighteen years which continually angered him at having to produce some sort of identification in the many places that he visited. "Aye, aw right," he said seriously and daring wee Joe to say, or do anything that would upset him or Alison. "This is Alison Jeffries, she lives in a posh hoose in Haddington," he said with a smile that swept over his pals, his message loud and clear that they should mind their manners.

"Ahm Danny." The boy gave Alison a wink as she returned his introduction.

Max took it from there. "That's Gil, my best pal ower there, tearing intae his burger. Ye would have met him at yon New Year party that ah first saw ye at."

Gil set down his burger and wiped his hands on a napkin. He rose and held out his hand across the table. "Nice tae meet you, Alison. Ye will no mind me being at the party seein that there were that many comin and goin that night. Sorry tae hear aboot yer cousin getting it wi the knife."

Alison shook the proffered hand. "Pleased to meet you, Gil. And thanks for asking about my cousin."

Max turned as a girl approached the table. "And this is Myra, she's wee Joe's bird." he explained. God, he thought to himself, what will Alison be thinking? She's showing a bit more cleavage than usual and if her skirt was any shorter she would have to put lipstick on a different place.

"Alison." Alison introduced herself to the girl……..

Myra gave a nod and sat down next to her boyfriend.

"So you two met at a party," Danny said, stuffing a napkin and a few unwanted chips into his empty coffee cup.

"Not really. I met Max by chance when he was in Haddingon," Alison explained.

"Some chance," Wee Joe tittered. "Last time he was wi us, he couldnae stop talkin aboot this bird he had seen at the party and couldnae keep his een aff."

Max blushed as the company found wee Joe's disclosure highly amusing. Underneath the table he felt Alison squeeze his hand as if understanding his embarrassment, though her face showed how she appreciated the compliment.

Taking her hand away, Alison bit into her cheeseburger, as Danny asked, "When are ye comin oot tae the carriageway,

Max? Freespace nearly got yer record on Thursday night."

Max gave a shrug of indifference and took a drink of his coffee.

"Yer no geein it up cause ye've got a bird are ye?" Wee Joe said, curling a lip in disdain.

"No Joe." Gil pushed his empty cola carton away. "Max is still the champ, and he has the record and car tae prove it, for noo."

Max's eyes met that of his best pal. What had he meant by that remark? Did he mean he had the record for now? Or did he mean the car for now? It was as if Gil was deliberately mocking - challenging him.

"Just you finish yer cannabis sandwich Gil, and keep quiet." The others laughed, although Alison did not quite understand the quip. Max stared directly at his pal and gave him a wink. He should not have offended his pal, not when he was his only real source of steady money.

"What's this about a record?" Alison had directed the question at no one in particular.

It was Danny who answered first. "Dual carriageway between the Pans and Longniddry; doon and back as fast as ye can. It's the turn at the end o' the carriageway at the Longniddry end that makes the difference. Ye have tae be able tae shift thae gears jist right, or it's no worth yer while tryin," he explained.

Max felt ashamed, ashamed that as grown men they had nothing better to do at night other than drive as fast as they were able to, down one side of a mile long dual carriageway and back. Although the runs usually took place around midnight or so, sometimes there was the odd car on the road, which meant having to overtake, and likely as not, scare the shit out of the unsuspecting driver.

"It must be quite exciting," Alison sounded genuinely pleased at the image of boy racers, of which her man was the

109

champion. "I must get you to take me along at your next attempt, Max."

Max rose to his feet. "Aye maybe, sometime. Ah think it's aboot time ah got ye hame."

"I'll just go to the little girls' room, as they say." Alison smiled, clearly enjoying Max's discomfiture.

"Guid idea Alison. I will come wi ye." Myra rose and together both women started for the toilet.

"She's awesome!" Danny's eyes shone. "Ah widnae mind a piece o' that. She's got a right cholesterol body aw right."

"Ah think the word ye mean is celestial," Max corrected him with disdain.

"He has me tae thank for finding oot where she lives." Gil sat back in his seat toying with a plastic spoon.

"She disnae look as if she's short of a pound or two." Joe commented. "Gil here tells me her auld man has a construction business. Seems ye'll be aw right there if ye play yer cards right."

"That's no if ye havenae already played them," Danny tittered. "What's she like? Is she for it? Aw thae rich birds cannae get enough."

"Whit would you ken aboot rich birds, ye bammer?" Wee Joe sneered.

Suddenly Max was sickened at the way the conversation was heading. Except, had he himself not said the same thing, or acted in the same way when one of his pals had shown up with a new bird? Now he realised how humiliating it must have been, should any of them have cared for the person they were with at the time, as much as he did for Alison. So why should he feel angry now? Was it in fact because he cared more for Alison, and subconsciously hoped it would lead to something further than sex? No, it could never be, Mr Jeffries would make sure of that. So, perhaps all he would get out of it

110

was a few dates, and if he was lucky a night or two of sex. Whatever, he would settle for making love to that lovely body, even if it was only once.

They were well on their way to Haddington before Alison spoke of Max's friends.

"Is that what you do, Max, of an evening, race around in your car?"

It was what he feared she would ask. Now she had seen him for what he was - a right waster. He slowed down believing that this was the end and she would dump him when they reached home. Well, he would get his final kiss and, if he was lucky, a grope or two, even if she slapped his face.

Max gripped the steering wheel tighter, angry at the prospect of not seeing her again. The past few weeks had been the happiest that he had ever known, now it had come to an end, all because of meeting his moronic pals.

Max's anger mounted. What was all that shite about from Gil, getting his oar in about him having the lack of the readies. Some pal to put the boot in when he was down. Well, he would show them - show the lot of them.

"It must be really exciting, just to be in a car and speed as fast as you like. My car is pretty nifty but Daddy says that if I ever get a speeding ticket I lose my wheels. And I can't afford to, as it would be a bind commuting into the town from Haddington, especially in this weather." Alison sounded surprisingly excited by Max's boyracing friends she had met earlier.

"Yer daddy wouldnae approve Alison o' ye keeping that kind o' company. I'm a bit o' a bammer masel, though ah have tae admit it does gie me a buzz."

Max turned on to the road leading into the country town, astonished to think that Alison had not been horrified by what she had heard from his pals. There was no lecture either on breaking the law as he had expected.

111

It was as he drove up the main street that he saw the two teenage boys, one of whom he thought he knew, being chased by a gang of about four or five of similar age. As he drew parallel with the panic stricken pair, he saw, that in fact one was the Lamont, kid. Max squealed the car to an abrupt halt, and leaning over a surprised Alison, rolled down the window on her side to shout to the boy.

The car had stopped in front of the court house, when, Peter Lamont, heard Max call out. At first he was not sure who was calling his name. All he knew was that this car was a means of escape. He changed direction heading for the car, slipping on some ice on the pavement, when he heard his name called again, this time from some little distance behind him.

Peter turned, his pal Simon was on the ground the gang kicking him as he lay there. Sobbing, terrified, Peter, halted, he could not leave his pal and do nothing. Yet, what could he do, there were too many?

"Get in!" Max shouted to him, as he himself got out. In an instant Max had the boot open, grabbing a car lever and running to where the screaming boy lay in a huddle, his hands up to protect his face.

Too set in enjoying themselves, the gang did not see Max running at them until it was too late and he had struck the nearest youth with a blow to the head with the lever. He had started in on a second before the other two realised he was there. Neither waited to see what damage Max had inflicted on their pals before taking to their heels.

Max stood there, his breath coming in gasps as his two victims hurriedly backed away. Recovering his breath, Max ran at the nearest youth who was holding his hand up to his jaw, fear in his eyes as Max struck him in the neck. Without a whimper, the stricken youth crumpled to the ground, while his pal made off as fast as his injuries would take him.

With a last look at the fleeing youth, Max bent down

and helped Peter's friend to his feet. "Aw right pal?" he asked, helping the boy to his feet.

The shaken boy nodded, mumbling his thanks, his dazed eyes on the remaining assailant lying unconscious on the pavement.

"He got what was comin tae him,"Max said indifferently. "So let's get oot o' here before the polis arrive. Ok."

Peter came and helped Max to lower the injured youth into of the back seat of the car, the latter with one eye on the lookout for more trouble, either from the police or a reinforced gang.

"We'll take them to my house." Alison's face was chalk white. She had never been involved in anything like this before. Although she was sickened by what she had seen this gang of youths do to one of the boys, it was Max who had frightened her the most. Yes, he had gone to their aid, especially to the one on the ground but it was the way he had set about the youths, as if this was nothing new to him, and how he had hit that already injured boy a second time. Moreover she was sure she had heard a bone crack.

Alison's house was only seconds away. Max drew up sharply in the driveway and almost before he had switched off the engine the girl was out of the car and inserting her key in the front door and calling him to bring in the boys.

Max put an arm around Simon and helped him from the car into the house where Alison stood anxiously, ushering him into the kitchen, with a pale looking Peter Lamont a little behind.

"Sit down there," Alison instructed Simon, pointing to a high backed wooden chair.

"This might hurt a bit, but I will have to clean the cuts," she said as she wiped at the cuts on his face with a cloth she had held under the hot water tap.

Max leaned against the side of the fridge, his eyes following the would-be nurse at work. The boy would feel it in the morning he thought as already there were signs of bruising on his cheeks.

The boy gave a jerk and a gasp.

"Sorry." Alison bit her lip, unaware that she had leaned against him.

"It's my ribs or something, where they kicked me." Simon put a hand on his side.

"Take your jacket off and pull up your top, let me see," Alison ordered.

Max stepped forward and helped the boy to raise his arm high enough for Alison to take a look at his side.

"Does it hurt here?" she asked sympathetically, as she touched his ribcage.

"Aye, Och!"

"Could have been worse," Max stated not too kindly.

"How come?" Simon winced, as Alison continued her work.

"Well you could have a bad back as well, then ye would ken how the Hibees feel for they've got two." Max gave a little laugh. "Only jokin pal."

Simon curled his lip. "Doesnae bother me. I'm a Jam Tart supporter."

Alison swung to Peter who had sat down on a chair by the door, his head in his hands staring at the floor. "Let me have a look at you now, Peter - is it?" she asked

The boy looked up. "Aye. But I think am aw right."

"Let me be the judge of that." Alison put a hand under the boy's chin lifting his head gently up to the light. "I will have to put a plaster on that cut you have above your eye. How's the rest of you?"

"Fine thanks. It was Simon that got the worst o' it. He tripped as we were running away."

Alison cut a small strip of plaster from the green first aide box she had taken from one of the cabinets

"What's going on?"

In the confusion no one had heard Nathan Jeffries enter his own kitchen.

"Oh, Daddy, these two wee boys were attacked by a gang of youths, just outside the courthouse." She pointed with the cloth at Simon. "Simon came off the worse. It would have been much worse had Max, not gone to their rescue."

If Nathan Jeffries was impressed by Max's action, he gave no sign.

"It would be best if you took them to the hospital." He stepped forward, all the better to take a look at Simon. "You'll have a braw keeker in the morning son." Nathan gave him the briefest of smiles as if daring the boy to argue.

"There's no A and E in Roodlands, Daddy. And should we have to take them to the Royal…well they may have to wait for hours to be attended to. After all, it is Saturday night." Alison wrung out the cloth she had been holding and took a closer look at Peter's right eye.

"Then I'll call an ambulance. They will give them a look over and if there is anything serious they will take them to the Royal.

Holding his cheek, Simon gently levered himself off his chair. "Ah will be aw right"

"Wait. Let me put a band-aid on that cut. It's started to bleed." Alison took a large strip of plaster out of the box.

"Thanks." Simon ran his hand gently over the strip of plaster that Alison had put on him.

Peter rose and together the boys made to leave.

"Don't you want to phone or text your parents?" Alison asked anxiously.

At the mention of the phone, Simon clutched at his pocket. "Oh sh…" He quickly stopped himself, and stared at

115

the company. "I've lost ma mobile," he said despairingly. "What am ah tae dae?"

"Can't you breathe without it?" Jeffries let out a loud laugh. "That's all you youngsters seem to do these days. If your brain went as fast as your fingers on these things we would have a country of geniuses."

"Daddy," Alison scolded her parent. "Not now please."

And the company felt that this was one of this man's pet hates - people with mobiles.

"I've still got mine." Peter confirmed his remark by producing his own mobile.

"Then use it young man and let your folks know you're all right, and let them come and fetch you home," Nathan suggested.

"Nae need, Mr Jeffries, ah will see the laddies hame, they live just aroon the corner frae me," Max offered, moving to assist the stiffly moving Simon.

Nathan Jeffries nodded and stood aside to let the three young men past. "Very well, then we can all get to bed."

At the door Max blushed when Alison gave him a peck on the cheek. "Is it too much tae hope, tae see ye again?" He had asked the question as quietly as he could, aware that all eyes were upon him and his girl.

"Why not?" Alison was taken aback by what she saw as nothing more than an absurdity.

"It's just efter the night. You meetin my pals, and kennin what they are like. Then this." Max gave a little gesture at the boys.

"I'll see you on Tuesday, Max Duffy at the same place. Ok?"

She stepped forward and opened the door to let them out. Max had one foot on the top step, when he heard Nathan call out that he wanted a word before he left.

Max threw Alison a look and took a step back inside.

116

Now the old man was going to tell him to piss off and never to see his daughter, nor bring trouble to his doorstep ever again.

Nathan came into the hallway, his face showed no trace of what he was about to say. Max prepared himself for the worst, embarrassed that the two boys might hear him being chastised by this rich man. Instead, Max heard the man say, "Look up my site manager where we are building those flats just outside of Macmerry. If you want work, that is?" And at Max's nod and a grin. "He'll know that you are coming. Be there by seven." Adding severely as he turned. "Seven in the morning that is."

A happy Alison, gave Max another kiss as he left.

Max had not chosen to take the bypass back to Tranent, but instead drove on what had originally been the A1 and had almost reached the village of Gladsmuir before he asked. "So whit were yer baith daen in Haddington then?"

Simon lay couchant in the back seat with his eyes closed. He hurt all over and just could not be bothered to answer. So it was left to Peter sitting beside the driver to answer the question. "We met these two lassies at the Fort last week," he started to explain. "They telt us aboot a party they were haudin in Haddington. They seemed tae want me and Simon tae be there, so we went along.

Things were goin aw right. Simon was up dancing wi yin o' them and ah had this other yin hingin on tae me. Well, as it turned oot, the boyfriend o' the bird Simon was pullin was there. Of course we didnae ken she had yin. Seems she only invited us there tae make him jealous. When we saw what was happening, we decided that the best thing tae dae was leave. Hopefully, withoot bein noticed. However, when we got ootside, they were there waitin for us."

"You mean that mob ah saw chasin ye?" Max asked, speeding up as he left the village behind.

"Aye. We made a run for it and managed tae hide

amongst the trees doon by the river. Then, when we thought we were safe, we decided tae try for the bus, but they were waitin for us at the bus stop. So we ran as fast as we could just tae get away frae them. Then Simon fell...."

"That's when ah saw yis then." Max nodded his understanding.

Aye ,if ye had no come alang, hell knows whit wid have happened tae us, especially Simon there." Peter jerked his head back to include Simon in his assumption.

"Dae yer folks ken where ye've been? Or mair tae the point where ye were goin?"

"Ah texted ma mammy," the small voice said from the back seat. And to Max it was as if the boy had had only enough energy to say what he had said.

"And you, Peter?"

"Ah asked Simon tae ask his mammy tae let mine know where ah was."

Max's laughter jerked Simon upright, so loud and mirthful had it been.

"Feart frae yer mammy, is that it pal?" Max said amused, while applauding the boy's ingenuity.

"Yer dead right." Peter made a face. His head might hurt, but it was nothing in comparison to what his mother would do to it when she heard he had been at a party in Haddington. First thing she would do was smell his breath to detect if he had been drinking. Peter shuddered, thankful what little alcohol he had consumed would not now be traceable.

Max drove up in front of Simon's house, got out and helped the injured boy to the door. The house was dark; as it was now well past midnight.

"Have ye got a key?" Max helped the boy to stand steady as he groped in his pocket for the elusive key.

At last he found it and held it up to Max for confirmation. "I think this is it." His voice was low and he

118

choked as he spoke.

"Best get yer folks tae get a doctor tae have a look at ye." Max sounded concerned as the boy fought to keep his balance. Perhaps he should have let Alison's daddy phone for an ambulance after all.

Max took the key from the boy and inserted it into the lock, gave it a turn and the door opened in to the darkness of the silent house

"Thanks pal," Simon muttered. "I'll be aw right noo that ahm hame."

Max stepped down on to the top step. "Are ye sure? Ye don't sound too good. Maybe ye should get a doctor tae see ye the night."

Simon dismissed the suggestion with a flick of his hand. "I'll be aw right." He gave Max a weak reassuring smile and closed the door.

"He's no so good is he?" Peter asked, as Max slid into the driving seat.

Max started up the engine. "Naw he's no but he'll no see a doctor. If ah were his folks I'd have wan in the night. But I suppose he'll be feart tae tell his folks. Just like you." He gave his passenger a brief look as he pulled into the main street.

Max drove quietly into Peter's cul de sac. "So yer hame. Hope everything turns oot aw right."

Peter got out. He turned and leaned on the open door looking down into the car. "Thanks for whit ye did for Simon and me. If ye had no been there we would have had oor heids kicked in and big time." Much as he wanted to, he could not bring himself to say Max's name. In the short time he had been in this man's company, he did not appear to be someone who would have intentionally knocked down his brother. Perhaps Colin had been at fault after all. But right now he did not want to think that this could have been so.

119

Max stared up at Peter. His saving the boy had been purely selfish as he wanted to let the wee bugger know he was on to him as regards the slashing of his tyres.

"If ye think onything of whit ah did the night, then stop slashing ma tyres. I ken ye think ah was at fault for knocking doon yer brither and this is yer way o' getting yer ain back, but enough is enough. For if ye don't I will gie ye mair than ye got the night. Ye are costing me a fortune, ye wee bugger."

Peter stared down in disbelief, as Max's eyes blazed up at him. Any liking, however brief he had had for the man had instantly dissipated. "Ah havnae slashed yer tyres, no since ye caught me yon night. Honest!" He took a hasty step back as Max showed him his clenched fist.

Max stared back. Somehow he believed the kid. So if he was not to blame then who else was?

He started up the engine. "Ok then, ah, believe ye. But if ye find oot who it is, that is at the gemme let me know."

With a nod and a sense of relief, Peter closed the door and his rescuer sped off, leaving the boy to wonder who else had it in for Max the fanny. Although he was still indebted to him for what he had done tonight.

Peter quietly walked up the garden path, fumbling for his key. As he reached his front door, a light was suddenly switched on in the hallway. "Bugger it," Peter swore. "Nae chance noo at goin tae bed without their kennin."

The door opened to reveal his father standing there, his shirt tail hanging over his trousers. "Where have you been to at this time of night? Or should I say morning?"

"Sorry, Faither we missed the last bus."

"We?"

"Simon and me." Peter stepped into the hallway, one eye on the stairs, hoping for an early escape, only to find this blocked by his mother coming down them at a rush, her dressing gown flapping over her night wear.

"And where do you think you have been to at this time of night?" was the first question of her son.

How was it Peter wondered, his mother endeavoured to speak politely when she was angry. And when she did, he knew he was in trouble, whereas at other times when she was not working in the department store she mixed her Scottish words with her polite ones. Tonight, Peter had no doubt about his being in trouble.

"As I said my boy, where do you think you have been until this time of night?"

"Is that a trick question Mammy?" Instantly Peter knew this was not the answer he should have given his angry mother.

"I'll give you trick question you wee devil." Jean was inches away from her son. The son, ready for the expected 'dunt on the heid' backed up against the door.

Fortunately for Peter, his father came to his rescue. "Can we no discuss this in the room, instead oot here in the hall where it's freezing?" Harry turned and irate mother and scared shitless son followed.

"Noo Peter, ye're mammy asked where ye've been tae until this time o' night. Ye ken she worries aboot ye when yer ower late comin hame." Harry had sat himself down on an arm of the settee as he spoke.

"What's this?" Jean pointed to the plaster on her son's forehead and took a few rapid steps forward, aware of her son's bruises for the first time. She placed a hand on each side of his head and tilted it back none too gently, in order to study the wounds better. "Ye've been in a fight!" Jean declared letting go of the boy's face.

There was no use his denying it. Peter gave a shrug of his shoulders, having already surrendered under his mother's interrogation. "We were at a party in Haddington."

"Who is we?" Jean sat herself down in one of the

121

armchairs by the electric fire, her eyes daring her son not to tell her the truth.

"Ah said before, Simon and me. Did, Simon's mammy no phone ye?"

"And what was wrong with your fingers? You can use them well enough when you are texting your pals."

"Then what happened?" Harry interrupted his voice calm, as if by doing so Peter would be unafraid of telling what had happened, however unsavoury it might be.

"Simon and me were chased by a gang when we left the party for the bus. If it had no been for, Max Duffy, we would have been mincemeat, there was that many o' them," Peter said sullenly, his eyes fixed on the design of the carpet at his feet.

"Max Duffy!" Jean's exclamation was so loud, that Harry gave her a sign that she might have aroused her father from his sleep.

"So that's whose car I heard." Harry gave a click of his teeth.

Peter nodded. "He was takin his bird hame when he saw us bein chased." Peter gave a short laugh. "Ye should have seen what he did tae those guys." Peter's eyes gleamed. "He wis awesome - disnae seem a bad guy efter aw." He waited the reaction to his words.

For a moment there was complete silence in the room, until with a sigh, Jean rose. "Come on, and I'll have a look at those bruises for you." Her son knew better than to argue.

*******

122

## Chapter 6

Max was slightly apprehensive when he arrived on site on Monday morning to be greeted by the site manager in his portacabin. He was a strong muscular-built man of around forty or so. "So, ye are Max Duffy, eh?" he motioned the boy to sit on the other side of his desk. "I see ye have come well prepared." He pointed to Max's leather jacket and heavy jeans.

"Ye will get a florescent jacket, overalls and the compulsory helmet." Max saw that he referred to a metal locker standing in the corner. "Ahm goin tae start ye on the ditches. Then, if ye are needed, on tae helping the plumbers wi their pipes." He halted to ask, "Mr Jeffries says ye were an apprentice plumber until ye got paid aff?"

"That's right, Masons in the toon." Max hoped that the Manager would not check up on this, for although he had been employed by Masons he had in fact been dismissed for having taken too many Mondays off, the result of too many hangovers.

"If ye have no brought some sandwiches wi you, ye can get somethin in the wee shop doon at Macmerry, or there's Tranent, if ye have time. Ma name's Gordon by the way, and ye can ca me Archie. That's whit the rest ca me." He stood up. "At least tae ma face," he grinned.

Although much of the digging was done by mechanical shovel there were trenches that these giants could not manoeuvre into and it was one of these that Max was instructed to complete. The foreman left him to it with the measurements that he wanted the remainder of the trench to be dug to.

Max started digging with a will and although the morning frost had not yet evaporated from a late rising, wintry sun, the young man was already drenched in sweat. Halting, he took off his yellow jacket and discarded his leather jacket underneath.

"Too much for ye already?" The voice came from a

123

man in his mid twenties grinning down at him from the edge of the trench. "Ye havenae done much seein as the hole was a metre deep afore ye started."

Max squinted up at him, not quite certain if the man was joking or not. He put up a hand to shade his eyes from the slanting rays of a sun still low in the sky, deciding, as he did so that this man was not joking, at least not in a friendly way.

"Whit are ye using tae dig? A teaspin?" Laughing, he kicked some earth into the trench and turned away.

Angry at the criticism of his efforts, Max started to climb out of the trench. "Slimy bastard, I'll show you what it's like tae get hit ower the heid wi a teaspin." He was out of the trench, his eyes on the receding figure of his critic, ready to do battle, when the thought of what it would mean to Alison should he lose his job on the first day, came to him. And should he clatter this clown with his shovel, maybe his freedom as well. With a final oath, Max jumped back into the trench.

Max had brought a flask of tea. He unwrapped the rolls he had made up himself, and sitting in another large portacabin looked around him at the five other inhabitants, all of whom appeared to be engrossed in the daily newspapers.

One man who looked in his mid fifties lifted his head to reach for his cup on the rough wooden table. "You the new laddie?" he asked, taking a sip of tea.

"Aye, I'm Max."

The man nodded. "I'm Brian, the carpenter."

"Whit dae ye mean yer the carpenter? There's another five besides you." Another reader jerked up his head as if ready to dispute this statement, giving Max a wink.

"I'm the only one any good here," Brian said with conviction. "As for the rest, if they made wardrobes oot o' they're ain heids, they would have enough wood left ower tae make a chest o' drawers."

Max laughed at the good natured banter.

"Where did ye work afore?" another asked, setting down his newspaper.

"Masons." Not again, Max thought.

"Oh ah ken them. Ma bother-in-law works there."

Max took a bite of his roll in anticipation of further inquiries relating to his former employment. Instead, much to his relief, the inquirer returned to his newspaper and the sports page.

Now left to his own devices, Max mentally noted that he too must bring in a paper if only to pass the time and not feel as awkward as he did right now. He finished his roll. It had not tasted very good. Why was it they never did when you made them up yourself? Yet, it was a way of saving money.

Contemplating leaving to take a stroll outside rather than sit in silence in the cabin, Max started to rise as the door opened and in walked the former critic of his trench digging.

"So ye made it oot yer wee hole, did ye?" His adversary greeted him with a laugh. "Although that widnae be hard as the hole wisnae that deep. It's a guid job ye wernae in the Great Escape or they wid still be digging their way oot." The young man guffawed.

"Sit yer're arse doon, Andy and leave the laddie alain," an older man ordered, staring at the tormentor. "Dae ye have tae f***in dae that wi every laddie that starts here. Nae wonder nane can stick it."

Andy gave a shrug, his eyes still on Max and mentally contemplating what further mischief he could create with this newcomer as he opened his vacuum flask.

The door opened and a tall slightly built man came in. He looked around him, his eyes falling on Max. "You the new boy?" he asked cheerily.

Max smiled back, instantly liking the man who he already saw as an ally.

"Whit made ye want tae work wi a mob o' bammers

like these?" he asked sitting down at the table and unwrapping his sandwiches.

"Maybe he's on an ASBO and his Social Worker sent him." The taunting Andy, let out a loud guffaw sending bits of the sandwich that he had been eating across the table.

One man reared back, as the chewed bits of bread landed in his lap. "Ye mockit effin bastard!" the man exploded rising to shake himself clean. Unperturbed Andy sat a smile on his unshaven face. "I'll gie ye effin smile." The man sat down, swiping at some crumbs that had fallen on to his newspaper, glowering at the nuisance across the table. "How the boss pits up wi ye beats me!" the man growled.

"It's because I'm guid at whit a dae," Andy said, sarcastically.

Guid at effin causin trouble," another piped up.

Max sat listening to the banter pleased that this adversary of his was not a popular person.

Andy pointed a finger at Max. "Ye ask *me* whit I'm daein here? Whit aboot him that can hardly scoop a wee bit dirt oot the grun whithoot havin tae rest?" Andy leaned forward until he was staring Max in the face. "Maybe ye think you should get a JCB ?"

Max took his time to answer. "Naw pal, ye can keep yer medals, just pay me a bonus then, OK!"

Andy sent his chair crashing to the floor as he stood up amidst the laughter at Max's answer. Here we go Max thought, as the angry man stood glaring at him across the table. Then with shrug and a mumbled, "Whit's the point, he'll no last the week," he made for the door.

Watching him leave, Max instantly knew he had made an enemy.

*******

"What picture dae ye want tae see the night?" Max asked Alison as he moved the car into top gear.

"I thought we might go for a drive in the country, just to get away from it all for a little while. I'm a bit tired with all the Uni work I have got to do." Alison sighed and sat back in her seat.

"Aye if ye like. Come tae think o' it, we've been goin oot for a wee while noo, and ah have never asked ye what ye study at Uni anyway."

"Mostly the boys," Alison chuckled, searching Max's face for his reaction.

"Nice yin, Alison, I thought I did the jokes?" He gave her a quick sideways glance. "And don't say ye thought ah was a joke," he cautioned her.

They passed the Brig Inn, turning left at the traffic lights, then on to Elphinstone Road.

Alison gave a little gasp, looking back through the side window. "Did you see all those pigeons on the roof of the Brig, there must have been at least three dozen?"

"Must be a doo on, eh?" Max spluttered a laugh.

"I see what you mean by you being the joker." She shook her head sadly.

Max accelerated past the thirty sign. He had never been more happy- A bird that anyone would die for, a good job and money in his pocket - what more could a guy ask for?

"Ah asked ye what ye were studying?" Max asked the girl again.

"Scottish History. I'm researching, the Highland Clearances."

Max slowed as he neared Elphinstone. "Ye mean the January sales in Inverness or something?" he asked tongue in cheek. "That's when Flora Macdonald made a fortune in America was it no, selling margarine and hamburgers?"

It took Alison a little to catch on. "Oh Flora margarine,

127

Mcdonald's hamburgers.  How clever."

"Ah'm no just a pretty face ye ken."

"No, I would say, Max Duffy you are neither pretty nor ugly."

"Just pretty ugly," Max finished the quip for her.

"Now you've spoiled my joke." Alison petted her lip.

They drove, talking about everything and nothing, passing through the village of Pathhead and Max turned right, on to a country road that would take them up over the Granites.

"What a marvellous view." Alison stared past Max at the scene unfolding beneath them - green pasture land, villages and towns in the distance, the view clear all the way to the Forth, glinting in a weak evening sun.

"Let's pull in here."  Alison indicated a little unpaved road.

"No much tae see in there."  Max said a little puzzled by the girl's choice.

"Depends on what you want to see." Alison shot him a teasing smile.

Hidden from the main road by the lie of the land Max drew up, and before he had time to undo his seat belt, Alison had her arm around his neck, pulling his face on to her lips.

Things could not get any better in his world he thought. His breathing was heavy, and he thought he would suffocate from the lack of air.  At last Alison released her hold and sat back, with a deep sigh of satisfaction.

Max turned in his seat to look down at her.  "Ah thought that was ma place tae dae that?  See you Uni types…" his observation halted by the girl having her hand on his zip.

"Well hello big boy," she gave him a mock smile, dropping her head to look down at the bulge in his trousers. Max choked, and gave out a sigh as Alison set to work.  He had been manhandled before, or should that be woman handled? He didn't want her to stop but his own sap had put paid to that.

He took out a handkerchief and cleaned himself. Now it was his turn, but before he could do or say anything Alison had dropped to her knees. Here we go again he thought his heart racing. Here we go again.

*******

It was Saturday night and Alison had gone through to Glasgow for the weekend to visit her grandparents, leaving Max at a loose end. Driving into the Co-op car park he did not take much notice of the boy racers, their cars parked against the far wall. He would buy a six pack and a few crisps and watch a new DVD he'd bought and text Alison before turning in.

Max had reached the open doors of the store on his way out, when he again thought of Alison and wondered if her asking him not to disturb her grandparents by phoning had been an excuse as she might be ashamed of him. After all she went to the Uni, and he had only managed High School with low exam marks.

Max chuckled when remembering how he and his pal, wee Joe, had called at the Careers Office in pursuit of a job, to be interviewed by a wee Welsh lassie in her first day in her new job in Scotland.

"Now Joe," she had started, "have you any type of work experience at all?"

Joe nodded, "barryin' staines."

"Is that a firm in Edinburgh?" she asked in her Welsh lilt.

"Whit dae ye mean is it a firm in Edinburgh?" Joe looked at her as if she'd lost her Welsh Rarebit. "Barryin stanes is no a firm, it was the work ah did."

It was then another Careers Officer came to the hapless girl's assistance. "He means he was wheel barrowing stones."

The lassie turned a bright red. "Oh I see." But she

didn't. Max laughed as he walked into the car park. An old woman making for the store gave him a queer look, her expression telling him he should not have been out on his own. However, it was the next question this wee foreigner had asked that had him splitting his sides. "So you carried stones in a wheelbarrow. Very good. How about skills?"

"Oh Aye," wee Joe piped up, "Preston Primary then the High Scuil."

Max was at his car and still chuckling to himself when the sound of a car horn jerked him back to the present. Another boy racer had arrived, drawing up his car beside the others, with a final loud roar.

"Here's Mike," someone shouted, happy at seeing this new arrival.

Max inserted the key in his car door, only mildly interested in what was taking place. He had the door open when he saw the new arrival open his boot and extract a hockey stick, amidst hoots of delight from the coterie.

Max shook his head. Somebody looking for trouble, he mumbled.

"We'll get oor ain back the night boys," one of the bystanders shouted, to Max the voice sounded strangely familiar. He drew his foot back out of the car, and looked across the intervening dark space of the car park. He was right. He had not been mistaken. It was the voice of Simon, the boy whom he had saved from a kicking in Haddington, a few weeks past. Then a voice he clearly did recognise, encouraging Mike to declare what he had in mind, the wielder obliging by demonstrating with a few swings of his weapon.

Closing his car door, Max crossed to where the boys were gathered. "Peter, Simon." He acknowledged both boys with a nod. "Where are ye'se off tae then, at this time o' night?"

Peter took in a deep breath and looked at his friend

130

Simon for support.

"It widnae be Haddington by ony chance would it?" Max drew closer to Peter so that he could read the expression on the boy's face.

"Suppose so." Peter gave Max a defiant stare that said that it was none of his business.

"Ye ken whit will happen? Ye might belt up a few o' they Haddington guys the night, then they will be up here next week wi mair o' them and the hale thing will get oot o' hand. Then the polis will step in. Dae ye want yer folks to have that tae contend wi, eh?"

"It will no come tae that will it boys?" the bat owner declared, holding up his weapon as a symbol of assurance.

"And if they too have things like that, or even worse?" Max pointed to the bat. "What then?" He looked slowly around the seven or eight youths who had now grown closer to hear what he had to say. Most knew him as a hard man and someone to be avoided when angry. "You ken what happened last time ye were there, Simon?"

"Aye, but there were only two o' us that time and we wernae looking for a fight," Simon answered defiantly.

" Aye, and ye were in hospital for a couple o' days so I heard. It could be worse this time."

"No it'll no," Simon mumbled, staring at his feet and feeling a little guilty that Max had reminded him.

Max swung to Peter leaning against a car. "And you Peter, what will your folks say if ye get hurt? Or just get caught by the polis."

For a moment Peter was tempted to say something that would hurt this guy. Angry that what he said was right. But how could he back out now in front of his pals, to be branded by them as a coward?

Max suddenly swung to his left, tearing the hockey stick out of the startled boy's grasp. "Noo away hame the lot o'

131

ye and watch TV or something."

For a moment the boy who had lost his weapon took a step towards Max, his fists bunched, his eyes blazing at this humiliation.

Max looked him squarely in the eye. "Seems as though ye might as well get a f***in doin here and save yersel petrol money tae Haddington, son." He raised the hockey stick as if ready to make use of it.

This was the opportunity, Peter needed. "Maybe we should ca it a night this time, Mike. Maybe Max is right."

"Feart are ye, Lamont," one boy challenged, levering himself off the bonnet of his car.

"Only sensible, boneheid," Max replied, inwardly pleased that he may have prevented Peter Lamont from doing something he could regret physically or mentally for some time to come.

"Drive me hame Drew." Peter turned to address a young man standing near to his car. "I've a guid DVD ye will want tae see."

A few looked first at Mike, waiting to see what their hero would do now that he had been disarmed, Then when they saw that Peter and his driver were about to leave, closely followed by Simon climbing into the back of Peter's pal's car, they too reluctantly decided to call it a night.

On his way back to his car, Max felt a certain satisfaction at having done something worthwhile. Yet, why did he also feel uneasy when confronting young Lamont? And deep down he knew it was guilt. Guilt at what he had done to that boy's brother.

*******

It was now Max's second month in his job. After his first week at digging trenches too close for the mechanical shovels to dig because of the newly laid pipes, he had been

132

transferred to help with the cement mixing. It was all heavy manual work and he wondered if this had been intentional in order to see if he would last. Maybe the boss himself had been behind it, in order to discover if he was a worthy suitor for his daughter.

He didn't mind the work although the money was not so much more than what he had earned when working for Freddie Stewart and the Unemployment money he conveniently forgot to mention to the authorities. However, he had rectified this by writing to inform them that he was now in gainful employment and would they cease his Unemployment Benefit, which they probably had done as he had not signed on since his starting work with Jeffries.

It was close to his dinner break. The cement mixer churned away and he threw a last shovel full into it.

"That will haud it for noo," Euan his partner for the day suggested, standing back to lean on his shovel while the machine gave a final turn before stopping.

Max stepped forward and tilted the bucket to let the contents spill into the barrow.

"Whit the hell's that?" Euan swore, lifting out what looked like a paper parcel. Still swearing, the man lifted the object out of the wet cement and held it in his hand.

Max drew closer. "Christ, it's ma sandwiches!" he exploded recognising the paper he had wrapped them in that morning.

"How did they get in there?" Euan handed Max the bundle of wet cement with bread and pieces of meat seeping through it.

"Ah ken how and who!" Max exploded. "It's the kind o' daft thing that heidbanger Andy Gemmel wid dae."

Ewen threw down his shovel. "We'll coup this last lot in tae the hole and break aff for dinner."

After it was done, Max and his partner headed for the

portacabin, Max in a frame of mind to have it out with this nuisance.

Max opened the cabin door in full anticipation of hearing the guffaws of laughter from his tormentor. He was not to be disappointed. Bunching his fists, Max glared at Andy across the table, only vaguely aware of Euan holding him discreetly by the arm.

"Did ye enjoy yer sandwiches? Ah bet it was a real solid meal, eh?" Andy sipped his tea enjoying his joke and looking around at those sitting at the table as if eager tell them what he had done.

"No f***in funny, Andy," Euan told the laughing joker.

"Yer a right heidcase, so ye are." Max sat down.

"Ye tryin tae say am an arsehole?" Andy's face twitched with anger.

"Naw, Andy, I wouldnae ca ye an arsehole. An arseholes a useful thing."

The laughter emanating around the table was too much for the practical joker as Euan placed a ham roll in front of Max. "Here son, there's too much for me, help yersel."

*******

Max had not wanted Alison to get involved with his pals. She had asked him how he spent his time of an evening when she was too busy with her studies to see him. It was then he had told her that he met his pals and went for a spin in their cars. To his surprise, or disappointment rather, she had asked him to take her to meet them.

So here he was in the car park at Longnriddry Bents waiting for the last of his boy racer pals to arrive. Wee Joe and his girl Myra had already arrived and they left their car and came to stand by the side of Max's Honda.

"Nice tae see ye again, Alison," Joe greeted the girl.

"Thanks. It's Joe isn't it?" Alison peered up at the boy through the open window. "And I know you are Myra," she said smiling at the girl.

"Aye, that's me aw right." Mrya's eyes roamed over Alison's attire of jeans and woollen top. "Didnae think ye wid be up for this, though?"

"Up for what?" Alison knitted her brows in wonder.

"Did ye no tell her?" Joe asked leaning forward with his hands on the roof of Max's car.

"No the night, Joe, ah just came tae watch and let you morons flip yer cars." He had said this without a smile. The last thing he wanted was to involve this girl - this precious girl- in their madcap racing stints along the coast road towards North Berwick.

Before Joe answered, Danny Glover arrived, spitting up red ash and stone chippings as he skidded his Corsa to a standstill beside Max's car. Lowering his window he grinned across at Max. "Where tae the night, big man?"

"I'll gie it a miss the night, Danny, ah just ca'ed tae say hello," Max replied, resting an elbow on the door frame.

"Where's the rest?" he asked Danny, referring to others of the gang.

"Freespace is no comin. Got a touch o' the flu' so he says," Danny explained.

"Aye, Gil's no feelin well either, must be something goin aboot," Max decided.

"Max's has something tae, *bird* Flu ah think it is," Joe, tittered across the roof of the Honda. He's also a bit chicken, if ye will pardon the pun."

Max's face reddened at the insult.

Alison gave him a look. "It's all right by me, Max, I trust you. Besides, I could do with a little excitement." Why had she said this, she thought? Was it because most of her life was boring? If she was not with Max, she was studying. Max

135

had brought a little excitement into her life. At first she had thought him nothing other than a rough yokel - someone to show her the other side of life. Now, if the truth be known, she had fallen for his good looks and rough manners. That their relationship would lead nowhere was certain, but for now she enjoyed being with him.

Danny turned on the ignition, revving up his engine.

"How aboot a spin doon tae Dirleton then back up the middle road?" His suggestion was nothing less than a challenge to their leader.

"Come on, nae fun sitting here," Joe called out, turning to climb into his car, Myra by his side.

"Go on Max, don't worry about me, I trust you." Alison gave her boyfriend's arm a squeeze. "I'm not made of cotton wool you know."

"Ok. But I'm no goin tae show aff just tae please thae bammers." Max started up the car and slowly drove out of the car park and turned left, heading for Aberlady.

Alison sat back in her seat, looking out of the side window at the twinkling lights of the Fife coast. It was quite warm for the month of April, though a chill breeze blew across the Forth.

Max raised his speed by only a fraction, determined not to put this young girl's life at risk. At last he had something worthwhile to look forward to. Now he had a steady job, and if he played his cards right, a bright future with the firm. Already he had been given the chance of working beside a plumber, and Archie Gordon had hinted that they might consider allowing him time off to attend college and resume his apprenticeship. At nineteen he was a bit on the old side, but better late than never.

He was round the bends now at Aberlady, accelerating on the short straight stretch of road determined to keep under six thousand revs and out of vtec before heading past the bird sanctuary and the climb up towards Gullane.

It was here as they were almost at the bend of the road that Danny attempted to pass, honking his horn, laughing and waving at Max to get out of his way.

"Bammer," Max said in disgust at his pal's action, while slowing down. Danny shot past, rapidly accelerating to cut in front of Max as a car came round the bend in the opposite direction.

"Phew! That was close," Alison exclaimed, letting out a shriek of laughter. "Does he always drive like that?" she asked referring to Danny.

"Maist times," Max said sullenly. It was the first time that Glover had ever passed him, now he would never hear the end of it.

At the road junction just before Direlton, Max followed Danny as he turned right on to the 'middle road' as it was called by the locals and down to the village of Drem. On the descent he was again passed, this time by Wee Joe, Myra signalling their success with a thumb up.

By the expression on Max's face, Alison knew he was not happy. "You're not enjoying this are you?" The girl half turned in her seat to stare at him.

"I'm no in the mood. Ah telt them that, did ah no? Ah could be comin doon wi something an aw."

Max was angry now. Angry at the ribbing he would have to endure from his pals at being overtaken by them for the first time since they had started these runs together.

At last they drew up in a lay-by just past the roundabout at Meadowmill.

Danny was out of his car standing beside a grinning Joe and his girl as Max drew in beside them. "Guid job the other two wernae here as well, or ye wid have come last," Danny exploded, unable to control his excitement at beating their chosen leader.

"Ye would think ye had won a Grand Prix or something," Max growled up at him through his open window.

"Maybe, maybe no. Ye'll be tellin me next, that yer warnae tryin, eh?"

Max shrugged. "Maybe next time, when ah feel like it."

"Aye, maybe we could have a wee bet on it? What dae ye say, pal?" Danny could not contain himself at having beaten Max for the first time. Now he was certain that his girl had made him soft. He was no longer King of the Road and he could not wait to tell Gil and Freespace how he had given their top driver 'a doin,' and all because of a bird.

*******

Gil did not really need another shirt but, when he was feeling a bit under the weather, buying something always cheered him up. His shopping over in the mall, Gil decided on a cup of coffee so made his way to a tiny bistro he knew. It was as he made for an empty table in the corner that he spied Alan Hunter sitting alone at the next table.

"Hello! I ken you frae somewhere," Gil said, putting down his coffee cup at his own table and pretending that he really did not know where he had seen this young man before.

Alan squinted up at the speaker through his dark glasses. "You will have to excuse me, I cannot remember where."

Gil snapped his fingers as if having suddenly remembered. "Ah ken noo where it was. It was a party at New Year!" He sat down, swinging his chair round to face Alan.

It never failed, Alan thought. The mention of that particular party still had him dwelling on what life was like before this. How different things would have been, had he taken the lift home offered to him by Alison's father. His only reason for not having done so was because he did not want to make a fool of himself by throwing up in Mr Jeffries car. A triviality now, but major at the time. If only ... if only, he had repeated over and over to himself how many times since that night that had changed his life?

"I don't remember you having been there."

Gil tore the little sachet of sugar and emptied it into his cup. "Naw, ye woundnae, ye were too busy dancing wi a wee blonde thing aw night."

Alan remembered instantly who it had been. "Alison Jeffries, a far out cousin of mine."

"No so far oot the way ye were haudin her," Gil joked.

"We hadn't met for some time. I was at Uni in England, and had just been back about a month and was fortunate enough to find a job in Edinburgh. It was sheer coincidence that we met at the same party. I didn't even know where she lived. Although I understand, Uncle Nathan has a business in Haddingon."

Gil nodded. "Aye, that's how Max got in tow wi Alison. He had me find oot where she lived an aw." Gil let out a laugh which had a few customers look in his direction. "He couldnae keep his eyes off her aw night. Fare jealous he was o' you, dancing wi her. Ah never saw him sae angry afore and boy," Gil twisted his lip, tilting his head a little to one side, to add emphasis to what he was saying, "was he no angry." Gil lifted his coffee to his lips, his cup partially hiding his eyes as he watched for Alan's reaction.

"I never knew that. This Max..."

"Max Duffy," Gil informed him.

"This Max Duffy came to see me in hospital with Alison." Alan stared into space as he spoke. "Now I remember, it was him who knocked down Colin Lamont. Alison spoke about it the next time she came to visit me in hospital."

139

Gil got to his feet pushing back his chair. "Well, nice talking tae ye pal. Look efter yersel. Ye've no had an easy time, wi yer eye an aw. I bet ye would like tae get the bastard that did it tae ye? And for nae reason at aw, so it would seem."

Gil left the bistro with a sly smile on his face, and wondering if he had done enough to plant the seeds of suspicion into Alan Hunter's mind as to who might have been responsible for his affliction. For in his own mind he had no doubt as to whom it was that had done the deed.

Alan watched Gil Robertson leave the bistro and wind his way through the throng of shoppers in the concourse. He had a bad taste in his mouth and it was not from the coffee. Robertson's description of Max Duffy's behaviour at the party now had him believing that it could well have been he who had attacked him. After all, he had not been robbed and jealousy was as good a motive as any.

Alan's hand shook as he raised his coffee cup to his lips, recalling his admittance to hospital that fateful night. The A and E had been pandemonium with nurses and doctors hurrying and scurrying about, determined looks on tired faces having done this all too many times before, each knowing exactly what they were doing, and in the background the dark blue uniform of a policeman.

He had been seen by what he believed to be a triage nurse, who literally had to pull his hand away from where he held his eye, too afraid to let go less his eye - or what was left of it, as he was sure there could not be much left - popped out. He had squealed, not so much from the pain but out of sheer terror. No matter how patient and reassuring his nurse had been he could not help himself from screaming. Alan took another sip of his coffee blushing at what people must have thought of his cowardice.

He remembered the smells of the hospital - his lying in a ward amongst various sounds of moaning, weeping and

yelling, in an atmosphere that had further frightened him.
He had closed his eyes to shut out the sights, but could do little against the sounds.

Fear had kept him awake well after most of the noise had abated, his brain fighting to deny what had happened to him and that his life would never be the same again.

Alan took a look around the bistro, his eye seeking out those with spectacles or dark glasses, as if by doing so he would not feel so alone, or isolated from those healthy people hurrying about outside with not a care in the world.

At last had come the time when he must face up to his first day back at work.

It had been awkward at first with his fellow workers not knowing what to say or how to express their sorrow at what had happened to him. Eventually the tension eased a little and by the end of the week it had almost returned to normal. Alan allowed himself a little smile. He had even made a joke about how he now qualified as a football fan, as most of them were one eyed anyway. It was a joke he wished he had never had had to make.

Alan nursed Gil Robertson's assumption that it had been Max Duffy to blame for the attack. Oh how he wished he had known this at the time of his hospitalization, it would have given him a figure, a real person to focus his hatred upon, instead of an imaginary one, who, when he caught up with, would return the compliment. He knew, of course, this he could never do. Although it gave him a smidgen of comfort to think that he could.

Alan finished his coffee and rose. His fears were behind him now - not all, but most. It had been a long haul, one that he fervently wished never to repeat. But as regards Max Duffy? Well, first he must make sure that it was indeed him, then he would see.

*******

141

Jenny burst into her mother's house. "You will not believe what I have just heard!"

Still reeling from the news, Jenny banged herself down at the kitchen table, her face a bright red.

Jean turned from the sink where she had been washing the dinner dishes. Eyebrows raised, curious, as well as concerned by her daughter's distress, she asked quietly, in order to calm the girl. "What is it oor Jenny? It cannae be that bad to have you in such a state. Don't tell me the supermarket has put up its prices again?" She allowed herself a wee laugh.

"It's no funny, Mammy"

"Whit's no funny, Jenny?" Alex came into the kitchen.

Jenny swung to her grandpa. "

"Grandpa, you'll no believe what I've just heard." Jane's voice shook with anger.

"Ye'll have tae tell me first." The old man made a face, making light of it, for surely his granddaughter's news could not be that bad.

"I just heard from Sarah Mckenzie," Jenny swung to her mother. "Ye mind, Mammy, Sarah came with us yon weekend?"

Jean nodded. "Awfy nice lassie."

Jenny drew in a deep breath annoyed by this irrelevance. "Anyway, Sarah told me she had heard that, Betty Smith was goin out with, Cammie Duffy... he's Max Duffy's brother, for God's sake!" Still unable to digest what Sarah had told her, she stared at her mother across the table, fully expecting an eruption of anger from her at any moment.

Instead, to her and her Grandpa's surprise, Jean said calmly, as if fate had decided that this should be so. "As I said before tae Betty, that it was her life and she's still young. So, if, Cammie Duffy is the one for her..."

"How can ye say that Mammy? Jenny was beside

herself with anger. "She was Colin's lassie for..." Jenny, spread her hands, "over two years. What would Colin think if he knew she was goin with the brother of the boy that killed him?"

Alex thought it time to intervene. He did not want his daughter upset, not when everyone - ironically including Jenny - had helped bring her back to normality and to finally accept her son's death. "Ah think we should leave it there for the minute, Jenny." The way Alex said it was a warning to the girl not to take it further. "Maybe this Sarah that telt ye has only heard it frae somebody else. Ah would wait and if ye see Sarah again, ask her where she got her story frae."

Jenny was still fired up by what she took to be an insult to her dead brother. She rose sharply, accidently knocking over her chair. "Well, if that's how you see it, it's fine by me." Choking back her anger, Jenny bent and righted the chair. "I'll see you both the morn, then." she said as calmly as she could and left the house, mystified by her mother's reaction, or more to the point, lack of it.

*******

"So the word's oot. The Lamonts ken ye're goin oot wi me?" Cammie handed Betty a cup of coffee.

It was the first time she had been in his house, his and Max's. She felt strange at being here, in the lion's den so to speak. Much to her surprise, the house although missing the woman's touch was neat and tidy. And it spoke well for two young men living on their own.

"Aye, I kent they would be upset, but Jean...Mrs Lamont seemed to understand."

Cammie understood Betty's uneasiness at being here. He was surprised when she had knocked on the door. Now he understood why. "We could go oot for a drink if ye like." he

143

suggested, sitting down opposite her, his voice full of concern. It could not be easy dating the brother of the boy who had knocked down and killed your fiancé. This, he had understood from his previous conversations with the girl, had been the case.

He and Betty had met by chance in a pub he frequented in the town. She had been on a night out with some of her workmates when he saw her. He smiled across at her. It had been a smile conveying his condolences at what had happened to Colin and the effect it must have had on her. She had smiled back before turning away to resume her conversation with her pals.

It was later; again, by chance that he bumped into her, literally, as he came out of the Gents as she was heading for the Ladies. He thought both of them must have blushed and she was the first to burst out laughing.

He had stood there, clearing his throat before asking, "How are ye Betty?"

She shrugged. "Fine thanks. And yourself?"

It was his turn to shrug. "Fine tae, thanks."

"Aye, that would be fine, Cammie, I could do with a drink."

Cammie looked at her now in the house, as if not quite understanding what she had just said. Then he remembered having asked her if she would like to go for a drink.

"Oh, aye, I'll just put ma jacket on." He got up as the front door opened, and his brother strode into the room.

Max pulled up at the sight of Mary sitting in his chair, *his* chair by the fire

"Whits this then?" Max swung angrily to Cammie, his face a deathly white, awaiting an answer.

"Ye ken Betty, don't ye Max?"

"Bloody silly question, Cammie. How would ah no ken the bird o' somebody ah accidently knocked doon." Max swung on his heel and headed for his own bedroom, banging the door shut behind him.

Max threw himself down in his computer chair. How could his brother bring someone like Betty Smith here, of all people? Just when things were looking better, Cammie had to go and do this, especially now that he had a steady job and a bird like Alison. Max played with the computer mouse. Now Cammie had to muck things up for him. How could he come home and find that bird sitting in his house? Had his brother no sense; no thoughts as regards to his feelings?

As he looked at the blank computer screen, Max was aware that this was not the crux of his anger. Earlier, Gil had let it be known he had met Alan Hunter ... accidently of course. His pal had had a sly look on his face, one that Max well knew as to be nothing other than trouble. So what had Alan Hunter and his best pal discussed, he wondered? Max banged the mouse down with a thud. He would not let the wee nyaff spoil it all for him. He had ambitions. He would stick in at work and prove to Nathan Jeffries how good a worker he was. Already, Archie, the site manager had said that after watching him work with the plumbers that the boss had considered letting him off to continue his apprenticeship. He would be a bit older than the rest, but if he stuck in ... Max stared up at the ceiling. He could do it. Put away what had happened in the past, to Colin Lamont and Alan Hunter. Aye, he could do it. But why did his own brother have to spoil it for him now?

*****

145

# CHAPTER 7

"Fish suppers!" Peter exclaimed, as Glen followed his wife and child into the Lamont kitchen. Glen put the suppers down on the table while Jean went about bringing plates out of the cupboards.

"Dae we need plates Mammy? They taste better in the paper!" Peter cried in dismay.

"You will eat them the right way and no show off your bad manners," Jean chastised him.

"Och, Glen is wan o' the family, he'll no mind," Peter assured his mother.

"Dae as yer mother tells ye Peter or ye'll no get any at aw," Harry warned his son.

Peter sat down at the table in disgust as his mother emptied a portion of chips onto his plate.

"Must have cost ye a fortune Glen, let me gie ye something for them." Harry dug into his pocket for an appropriate sum.

"Nae bother Mr Lamont, it's my pleasure." He saw the look the man gave him and smiled. "Sorry, ah mean Harry," he apologised.

Glen had always felt awkward at calling his father-in-law by his given name, but the man had insisted and he had done so, when he remembered. As to his mother-in-law, the same offer had applied, although, for some reason, he could not bring himself to call her Jean.

"What have you been up to these days, Grandpa?" Jenny inquired of the old man, ladling some chips on to his plate

"No much hen." Alex raised a hand to stop Jenny. "That's too much. Gie some o thae chips tae somebody else."

"Since when have you no been able to eat as much, you

146

auld blether?" Jean challenged her father from across the table with a tut, tut.

"I asked you Grandpa, what have you been up to? You haven't been around to take wee Drew to the park. He really misses you."

"Aye, he will have tae learn tae shoot straighter." the old man said dead pan.

"He's been banned from the park, Jenny," Jean informed her, shooting a hostile stare at her father.

"Who banned you, Mr Henderson?" Glen asked reaching for the salt.

"I did," Jean said firmly.

"How come Mother? Grandpa loves the park. He has an auld pal there, so the bairn says." She looked down at her son at the table next to her. "Is that no right son?"

Drew munched on a chip, nodding his confirmation and happy at not having to speak and lose out on some more chips on his daddy's plate.

Jenny sprinkled salt on her chips. "So how come you have banned Grandpa from the park, Mother?"

"Because he is a health hazard, that's why."

"A health hazard?" Jenny was mystified.

"Aye, Jenny, to himself. Is that no right Faither?"

"If ye say so, daughter." The old man picked at his fish and threw Glen a wink.

"So let's hear it, auld yin," Harry asked, quietly amused.

"Well, ah take the bairn tae the park, and sometimes ah meet auld Davie there and we have a crack thegither whilst the wee yin plays on the swings, but recently there is this bigger bairn that has started tae bully the rest. Tuesday there, he had maist o' them greetin as he widnae let ony the bairns near the swings. So, ah just got up and went ower tae him. Who dae ye think ye are, say I, Lord o' The Swings or something?"

Around the table the family let out various levels of laughter, except Jean who was not at all amused as she already knew the outcome of the story.

"Then," Alex went on, "would ye believe it, he gies me this awfy moothfu! The size o it! So, I gave him yin on the bum and there was mair than stoor came oot o his trousers, ah can tell ye."

"Oh you didn't Grandpa!" Jenny was horrified. "You can get the jail for that."

"That's what I told the auld goat," Jean agreed, whilst the rest of the company disguised their laughter by lifting their cups to their lips.

"Good for ye auld yin," Harry applauded the old man. "If there was mair like you there wouldna be sae many cheeky bairns aboot."

"But listen to this Jenny," Jean addressed her daughter, with a sharp downward thrust of her finger. "Go on, Faither, tell us aw what happened next."

Alex took his time in drinking his tea and fishing a bone from between his teeth. "Well, when ah gave him yin on the bum, he went runnin tae this fat red heided wumman just comin in the gate; seems she was his mother."

"On no!" Jenny put a hand up to her mouth. "Senga Lees."

Alex shook his head in disgust. "Naw, she disnae come frae Africa, no wi hair yon colour."

"I don't mean she was Sengalese, that's her name!"

Peter's knife crashed down in his plate as he howled with laughter, the laughter infecting the other male members of the company, including Alex who now saw the funny side of it all.

"It's no that funny," Jenny warned them. "I don't want big Senga at my door wanting to know who belted her bairn." She turned to her mother. "You would mind Senga, we were at school together? She was Senga Wright then, before she got married."

Jean screwed up her face in an attempt to recall who Jenny was talking about. Suddenly it came to her. "That's no the same lassie that used to run the hundred metres in the school sports wi you?"

"Aye the same one, she's like a house end now."

"Yer right there, Jenny," her Grandpa agreed with a nod of his head. "If she were tae run the hundred metres noo, it would be in, lanes two three and four, aw at the same time!"

"Aw at the same time!" Peter repeated, exploding with laughter and Harry had to keep his son from falling off his seat.

When Glen, Jenny and wee Drew had left, Jean sat down by the fireside. There was a colour in her cheeks that Harry had not seen since Colin had died. Perhaps things were getting back to normal. He thought again of the evening, and his father-in-laws escapade at the park. It was a true saying that time was a great healer and that laughter was the best medicine.

*******

Alison looked around the lounge, walked to the fireplace and lifted the silver trophy that sat on the shelf above.

"Yours?" she asked Max, examining it.

"Naw, Cammie's for running when he was at school."

"You don't have one?"

"Aye for running away when ah was at school," Max joked.

"So this is your home, Max Duffy?" Alison said cheerfully, looking admiringly around her

"No up tae yer standard, but, aye, it's hame."

"There's a world of difference between a house and a home, Max. Yours is a home."

Alison's face turned to a deep frown as she sat down.

"Whit's wrang wi your hoose, it's ginormous?"

"Maybe so, but it's empty since mum went away."

Max was in the act of sitting down beside her, aiming to console her when Alison rose.

Her mood suddenly changed. "And where is your room?" she asked feigning coyness.

Max's heart beat faster. Surely, this could not be happening. His thoughts returned to the incident in the parked car that past evening in the Granites. Here could be even better.

While Max's thoughts had been elsewhere, Alison explored the house, first opening Cammie's bedroom door, then, his own. The girl stepped inside, swung one way then another, taking in the computer, stereo, posters on the wall and other little items that seemed to hold her attention.

Max breathed heavier. He must not rush things, although he could scarcely control his desire. "Fancy a drink?" He had his back to her, ready to dive down to the kitchen in order to give his ardour time to cool.

He felt her hand on his, turning him around to face her. "I can't stay overnight."

"Just as well." He swallowed. "Cammie will be back the night."

Alison let go of his hand and took a couple of steps back. Slowly and provocatively she undid her skirt, then her top." Do you like it so far?" There was a seductive twinkle in her eyes, daring him to suggest otherwise.

Max darkened the room and swiftly took off his shirt. He advanced towards her and gently placed her on his bed.

The clock on the bedside table said ten fifteen. Max turned on to his side looking at the lovely naked body sleeping beside him. He drew a hand across his eyes to make sure that this had not been all a dream. If so, he very much wanted to fall asleep again. Alison gave a little moan and turned on her side towards him. He drew closer and kissed her on the lips, then down her body, hearing her moan and tense a little as he reached her legs.

His thoughts still on last night, Max cheerfully set about his work. Even the thought of having to put up with Gemmel's stupid irritating banter did little to damping his well being. If it had not been raining, he would cheerfully have sat outside to eat his sandwiches, something he was wont to do when the weather was fine. On some days, when he had a little money to spare, he had gone into Tranent to buy his sandwiches in order to have a change from his own sandwich making and also to get away from the moron's jibes.

Max's fingers itched to text Alison, but she was at Uni and would not want to be disturbed. Again he thought of what had taken place last night, now knowing that it was more than just lust for this lovely creature: he was in love. He thought of her body again and the sheer joy of it.

The few already sitting around the table offered him a brief greeting as he came in before returning to their newspapers. Max sat down next to Joe and unwrapped his sandwiches, delighted by the absence of his arch enemy. A delight not long to last, as Gemmel, shaking rain from his yellow, waterproof jacket entered the cabin. The man looked around him his eyes coming to rest on Max. He smiled, a lip turning up at the corner of his mouth as he formulated his taunt. Max strove to ignore him. Somehow, he knew that today would be different. When work had not gone Gemmel's way - he was on bonus work as well - this was when he was apt to take it out on someone, and that someone was mostly him.

"Well, Max how did it go last night, get it in did ye?"

Max's head shot up, various thoughts flashing through

his mind such as how did he know about last night? Had Alison told anyone which in turn had made it back to Gemmel?

He was aware of Alison being on Facebook, though he had no doubt in his mind that this would not be a subject she would discuss, even with the most intimate of her friends.

Gemmel saw that he had the younger man rattled and continued with his assumption. "Whit was she like, Max, soft and juicy eh? It widnae be her first time though, that yins been aroon the block a few times and you are her new block!"

Gemmel's laughter was much louder this time, as if by doing so it would somehow help to eradicate his miserable morning, and his loss of bonus.

Fighting to control his temper, his face drained of colour, Max bunched his fists. This is what the moron wanted, for him to hit him. Maybe, so that he would get his books. Or was it that Gemmel thought he could take him and by doing so further humiliate him?

"That's enough Gemmel." Brian looked up, as the others had done, all shocked by Gemmel's crass remarks.

"Enough? I havenae f***in started yet." He swung his glare back to Max. "Still have a hard on thinking aboot her, have ye?" Andy Gemmel's mouth seemed to twitch in a mocking smile, daring Max to do something about his remarks. When Max did not react, Gemmel started again. "Or maybe ah hiv got it wrong. Maybe ye cannae get it up at aw. Maybe yer pipe's bent and yer just hanging aboot wi the boss's daughter just tae keep yer job. Though ah don't think ye'll keep her happy for long if yer no givin her yin, eh?" Gemmel's roar of laughter filled the room.

All eyes were on Max, awaiting his reaction. He rose, fighting to keep his hands steady as he slowly wrapped up his remaining sandwiches, lifting his cup to empty the contents back into his flask. The entire time, a hush had fallen around the room. Then just as slowly, he walked to the door, the silence broken only by the taunting laughter from Andy Gemmel.

Max's breathing came in gasps as he fought to control his anger and hatred of the man, whom he had left back in the portacabin. He sat down just inside the doorway of one of the unfinished flats and unscrewed the top of his flask, pouring the remaining tea shakily into his cup, unaware of some of the hot liquid burning his hand. He had lost his appetite. All he could think of, besides Gemmel knowing about last night, was the way he had intentionally degraded Alison. Perhaps, if he were to tell her what Gemmel had said about her, it might move Nathan Jeffries to take some action in defence of his daughter's good name. Or would it? It would mean Alison having to disclose what had passed between them last night. Somehow he did not think Mr Jeffries ... his Boss, would approve of his daughter giving herself to someone with his background.

A shadow fell across the doorway, it was Brian.

"Dinnae let that f***in eejit upset ye son." The older man passed Max and sat down on a step.

"How come Mr Jeffries allows someone like that tae work for him? Surely Gemmel's no such a guid worker that he cannae gie him the shove?" Max looked angrily at the man, awaiting an explanation.

Brian shrugged. "Ah think it's something tae dae wi Gemmel's auld man. Maybe something that happened in the past and the boss feels obligated tae him, so this is why he tolerates Andy. Of course am only guessing ye will understand. However, this ah dae ken and that is, that young Gemmel went oot wi your Alison. Only yince, ye understand." he assured the boy. "Then she dumped him and who could blame her," the man chuckled. "This is why ah think he has taken a dislike tae you. You have whit he has always wanted, a lassie o' his ain, and in this case, the boss's lassie. The yin he sees that should be his. This, and aw that goes wi her," Brian declared. The man took a look at his watch. "We better get started back."

They began to cross to the flats opposite, making their way round puddles of muddy water. The rain had steadily grown heavier and Brian stared up at the sky. "No much doing ootside the day, Max," he declared. Max muttered his agreement, still angry at Gemmel, and what he had said about Alison.

Max heard his name called and turned in that direction. It was Archie, the site manager, beckoning him from the door of the site office. "See ye, Brian." Max turned, making his way across the muddy ground.

"Hell o' a day, Max." Archie greeted him with a look of dismay at the sky. "Take the van doon tae the timber yard at Haddington. Ye'll ken where it is as ye've been there before." He handed the boy a sheet of paper. "Get whit's on that list. Nae hurry … no much daein the day and ye cannae help the plumbers as they're away on another job elsewhere this efternin."

Max got into the van, relieved to be doing something away from the site. He slowed down as he approached Macmerry, cutting his speed at the flashing lights when nearing the school. Kids were lining up to go back in after their dinner break. He gave them a look of jealousy as he passed. That had been him a few years back, when he had been a different Max Duffy. He accelerated a little as he left the school behind and shook his head at the thought. No, he had always been this same Max Duffy. Trouble had always followed him. Even since the age of seven - that was his earliest recollection of beating up a bigger boy at school for stealing some sweeties from a wee girl. The same wee girl he saw shopping and wheeling a pram in the main street of Tranent. Christ, he thought, what a way to start being a mammy, at nineteen. Of course, that was if it was her bairn.

He was twelve and just going to the High School when his mother had decided to leave. His father did not seem to care. At least he thought he had not. Then his father had begun to come home later each night from work. Poor Cammie had taken the brunt of his father's anger. Or was it frustration? It had got so bad, he remembered, they had sat in their room with the light out, hoping father would think them asleep and leave them alone. It had seldom worked.

Max checked his speed at the roundabout, raised his speed on the other side and slowed down again as he drove through Gladsmuir. His father died less than a year after his mother's leaving and an aunt had came to look after them in their home, which had been left to them by their parents, complete with mortgage. By this time Cammie was working and making good money for his age. His brother had managed to pay the mortgage payments from the money his parents had left them. This was the only contribution his mother had ever made to their welfare.

Max was almost at the junction to Haddington. A few years later, he himself was earning money as an apprentice plumber and by doing so thought himself a 'big man'. He had spent most of the money left to him by his parents on a car, the first of many until he had come to afford the one he had at present, his pride and joy. It was the first real fall out Max had had with his brother. On reflection, Cammie had been right. He should not have spent most of his legacy on a car when Cammie was struggling to make ends meet.

For the first time since Gemmel's outburst, Max cheered up. Now he could pay his own way and when things improved a little more he would make it up to Cammie in appreciation for what he had done for him. Max sighed. Nothing had really changed, trouble still followed him. Was this the reason he had taken to drink? It was also the reason for him losing his job while still an apprentice. He liked to drink;

155

it made him forget, at least for a while. Then again, he shuddered remembering that night of the party and what he had done to Sadie Muir. How would he feel if someone like Andy Gemmel was to do this to Alison? Max shivered again, ashamed of himself and also what he had done to Alan Hunter. This was his trouble; he lost control of his temper too easily. He just did not stand back and take stock of the situation before barging headlong in, especially after downing a bucketful.

By the time Max had loaded up and headed back to the site, the rain was torrential. So much for Global warming he cursed, as the windscreen wipers - what was left of the rubber on them - scraped the glass. Max had sat for a time outside the timber yard, Archie having hinted that there was no need for him to rush back. Perhaps, the man had heard about the incident at dinner time and believed this was the best method of keeping Gemmel and him apart. It was as he was about to turn on to the site that he saw the solitary figure of Andy Gemmel up on the scaffold. Instinctively, Max quickly reversed back on to the road, the fermentation of a plan forming in his mind.

Two hundred yards or so down the main road in the direction of Macmerry, he turned the van into a field, just past a gate. For a moment he sat there reminding himself of what his impetuosity had cost him in the past, but only for a moment. His mind made up, Max thumped the steering wheel with both hands. Let's do it, he said aloud.

By crossing the field from where he had left the van, Max entered the rear of the site, shielded from the main office and portacabins by the partially completed flats. The heavy rain was in his favour, as it kept most of the workers indoors working in the flats opposite. Max crept to the foot of the scaffolding where Andy Gemmel was working above and began to climb. Should anyone come out of the flats opposite, or happen to look out of the unframed windows, they could not fail to see him. If they should, how was he to explain the reason for his being there? There was none, he told himself.

On the next landing, Max heard the carpenter whistle a tune. He cautiously poked his head up a little and rain ran down the back of his neck. He wiped his face dry, as best he could, from rain stinging his eyes and made out Gemmel working by himself at the edge of the platform. The carpenter was unloading window frames from a hoist. Max levered himself up on to the next floor, his hands red and aching from the slippery wet scaffold tubing.

"Watch what ye're doin!" Max heard the warning from someone below who was evidently helping to winch the frames up to the carpenter. Max cursed and waited. He could not wait here all day for he was sure to be seen, especially if it was at the end of the day's work when the men would come out on to the site to where their cars were parked.

"Haud on Andy, ahm away for a piss and be mair careful wi thae frames in this wind." Max heard from below.

The stalker watched the figure cross the muddy space to the Porta Loo. If he was to do it, now was his chance, Max decided. A blue tarpaulin flapped in the wind, momentarily hiding him from his intended victim. He tip toed closer as the carpenter unharnessed the window frames from the hoist, which now free from its load swung back sharply. It was all that Max needed. Picking up a spar of wood, he launched himself at the unsuspecting figure who still held the bulk of the frames close to his chest. Max hit him on the back of the head with all the strength his pent up anger could muster and as the man fell over the side to the ground below, Max was already on his way back down the scaffolding.

Max waited a few minutes in the van until the ambulance and the police car had gone. A little later he pulled up on the site and got out of the van, an expression of wonder already on his face. "Whit's happened? I saw the polis come

157

oot o' here."

Archie pushed back a strand of wet hair and replaced his helmet. "There's been an accident. Yer pal, Andy Gemmel fell frae the scaffolding up there." He pointed up to where the hoist swung in the wind. "He shouldnae have been working in this wind and rain but he said he needed the bonus money. A lot o' good that will dae him noo," he said turning away.

"Ah telt him tae be careful." The man who had helped with the hoist said simply, with a shake of his head. "Ah telt him that when a left for a piss."

Max knew he had to be careful of what he said and not let slip that he had seen the man leave.

"What happens noo?" Max asked of those standing around. "What did the polis say aboot it?"

"There will be an investigation intae it. They took names and things when they were here."

"Aye." another said. "They wanted tae ken where we aw were at the time."

"Lucky for you ye were oot in the van." Brian moved in amongst them.

Max choked a little and changed the subject as quickly as he could. "Is he hurt bad?"

Seems he has two broken legs, maybe a collar bone as weel," the first man informed him.

"Hit his heid aff the cement mixer," added another.

"Well that's the end o' the cement mixer then," Max chuckled.

"Aye, you'll no be sorry tae see him oot o' the way for a while. Puir bugger's likely tae be in hospital for some time.

"Ye'll no be taken him floors, ah widnae think," one of the labourers commented, aware of how much taunting Max had taken from the injured man.

Max gave him a wicked smile. "No unless they're pee- the-beds!"

158

Next morning Nathan Jeffries arrived in expectation of the police calling at the site. By lunch time, their investigation complete, they left, satisfied that the industrial accident had been caused by Andy Gemmel himself and there would be no need for further inquiries, the invalid having testified that his fall had been due to being hit from behind by the hoist.

Nathan Jeffries met Max as they crossed the site. "I'm told you work well, Duffy. Keep it up." He moved on before Max had a chance to thank him.

*******

Doddie had decided to call at the Lamont home in order to discuss the forthcoming memorial cycle race. He had trained hard as he wanted to do well in the race. It was to be held as had other recent races, on the Gifford circuit. This course did not really suit him as the long climb out of Bolton was where his added weight had its drawbacks and favoured the lighter riders, who inevitably *were* climbers.

Doddie drew in a deep lungful of fresh air, and the smell of wood smoke brought back memories of Colin. Again he raised his pace, sprinting for thirty seconds before resting for a minute, to repeat the same format over and over again. How he hated this interval training, especially on his own. It was pure torture but it had to be done. Once more he forced his aching, reluctant body to do it again. Why was he doing this? Why would anyone in their right mind want to put themselves through this torture, all in the name of sport?

After three hours of steady riding, alternated with interval training, Doddie called it a day, including a few four letter words. Before leaving the house, he had packed a small haversack with fresh clothes as he would be calling on the Lamonts to discuss Colin's race. With this in mind he had decided to take his car and park it in a quiet spot just outside of

Haddington and commence his training from there. The night was warm with scarcely a breeze, something that any rider could appreciate. Doddie stood leaning on the bonnet of his car, drinking in the peacefulness of the scene - the different shades of trees, the colour of wild yellow gorse dotted in among the different shades of grass. He took a sip of his water bottle; put in down and pulled off his race jersey. From his bag he produced a towel, deodorant and a wet cloth.

Doddie knew what it was like for other people when cyclists arrived at a café or tea room smelling to high heaven of sweat and other odours. He smiled, remembering a particular café in Dunbar that had clients rise and bolt down their meal at the arrival of a half dozen or so sweaty cyclists, the riders pong reaching as far away as the beach. He had been told from older riders, that in their day, when the number of cyclists was greater, that it had been worse for the owners when wave after wave of cyclists had descended upon their premises, so much so, that the unfortunate place had looked and felt like a sauna from perspiring bodies. Old people had been known to faint from lack of oxygen and many a male cyclist had appeared to expire in the hope that some young female would rush to their aid. Doddie put his bike into his car and with these thoughts still in his mind, drove off in the direction of Tranent and the Lamont household.

Young Peter Lamont was mowing the front lawn when Doddie arrived. Looking up the boy came quickly to a halt. Switching off the machine he waited for Doddie to come out of the car.

"Pleased tae see me young Peter? Or is it ye just want an excuse tae stop work?" Doddie grinned

"Am aye happy tae see ye big man," Peter replied, his face lit up by the prospect of such cheerful company.

"Have ye stopped already?" A voice from within the house asked through an open front window. The owner of the voice quickly appeared at the window. "Doddie, son! How nice tae see ye."

Relief flowed through Doddie's body. He gave Mrs Lamont a wave as she stood at the window. The woman appeared to be her old self again. Now there was more colour in her cheeks and her hair had more sheen to it.

Soon Doddie was sitting at the table, a welcome plate of soup before him.

"Been training hard for Colin's race?" Peter asked Doddie eagerly.

Doddie smiled to himself at the word 'Colin' "Sure, but it's no goin tae be easy, Gifford course is no tae ma liken, but ah will dae ma best," Doddie assured him.

"It would be nice to see you win it son. Colin would have liked that." Jean placed some buttered bread down in front of him.

"I'll try ma best Mrs Lamont, but don't haud yer breath." It had been on the tip of his tongue to have said that he might have done, had he been as good as Colin, but instead he chose a piece of bread and chewed on it eagerly.

"Hello, Doddie." Alex came into the kitchen where they were all seated. "And what have you been up tae?"

"Nothing much. And yersel?"

"Ye see it aw son." The old man sat down at the table and helped himself to a cup of tea from the pot.

"Ma faither was telling me aboot the other day when he went oot canvassing. Ye mind me tellin you he was retired," Doddie began. "Well, he was trying tae sell some things for the Braeburn Burgh Police Pipe Band. So he says there was this street where he would only get as far as opening his case tae show them what he had for sale, when they would shut the door on him. He says tae me 'Doddie ah had more open and shut cases that day than a lawyer has in a life time.'" He halted to laugh and the rest joined in. "So, he gets tae this door and knocks, and this pair of eyes peers at him through the letterbox. 'Whit dae ye want?' the owner o' the eyes ask. I'm selling a few we things for the Braeburn Burgh Police Pipe Band he says. The door opens and this wee wumman no five feet wi her haunds up says, ye'll have tae talk up, am a bit deaf.' So, faither starts again, 'am selling a few wee things for the Braeburn Burgh Police Pipe Band. Its nae guid says the wumman a cannae hear a word ye are sayin.' So again faither says, 'I'm selling a few wee things for the Braeburn Burgh Police Pipe Band…..'It's nae use says the wumman ah still cannae make oot what ye are sayin.' By this time, faither was fed up repeating the same thing ower and ower again, and it was comin on rain, so he decides it wasn't worth it. So he says, 'ah was just tryin tae sell you these wee things for charity,' but the wee wumman just shook her heid and said, 'sorry son ah cannae make oot a word yer sayin. Never mind says faither and closes his case and walks doon the garden path, and just as he reaches the gate, the auld wumman shouts oot tae him 'Mind and shut ma gate.' So faither shouts back 'Aw tae hell wi you and yer gate', and the auld wife shouts back ' Aye, and tae hell wi you and yer Braeburn Burgh Police Pipe Band."

Jean's cup crashed down on the table with a thud, her laughter ringing around the kitchen. Harry, who had come in at the end of Doddie's tale could do nothing but laugh himself, not so much at Doddie's tale but at seeing his wife looking so happy and enjoying herself for the first time in a while.

Doddie got up still smiling at the picture he had painted.

"Well, I'll see ye aw at the race."

"What time have we tae be there Doddie?" Harry asked. "And dae ye want me tae gie something in the way o' prizes?"

Doddie shook his head and pushed his chair a little way under the table. "Naw Harry, yer giving the cup will be enough. The winner gets tae keep it until next year, but maybe ye can pay for the engraving. However, we'll decide that when we come tae it. I've got enough prize money as well."

He looked at Mrs Lamont, thinking that what he was about to ask the woman might be too much of an ordeal for her.

"Will you present the cup and prizes, Mrs Lamont?" he asked, apprehensive of her answer.

"Of course, Doddie, I would be happy to son." She gave him a smile as if understanding what he had been thinking.

"Good." He turned to young Peter. "Will you give the prize for first Junior?"

Peter's look, suggested doubt. "How much dae ah get paid?"

"I'll gie ye paid you wee monkey!" Jean exclaimed, horrified by her son's question.

"Only kiddin, Mammy. I'll dae it Doddie, nae bother."

"This next one is a bit tricky." Doddie made an apologetic gesture with his hands. "Which one o' you two men should ah ask tae present the Veteran Prize?"

"Him!" Harry and Alex pointed to one another at the same time.

Doddie shook his head. "Aye, aw right then, maybe ye can toss for it."

His farewells said, Doddie climbed into his car. The relief at completing what he dreaded as being nothing other than an ordeal had gone smoothly. No tears, no real talk of Colin, even though each of their thoughts were for the missing boy.

Doddie drove off, pleased that his wee joke about the salesman had gone down pretty well. He only hoped none of the Lamont family would ever mention it to his father.

*******

Max believed that his luck had changed for the better. With Andy Gemmel safe in hospital for a time, there would be no more taunting at work. His love life with Alison was also improving after each encounter. Now the single thing that threatened his good fortune was his pal Gil.

Max had been suspicious of his pal's intentions for quite some time. Gil's not too subtle remarks, such as accidentally meeting Alan Hunter, and hinting to that man, how he, Max had fallen head over heels for Alison upon seeing her that first night at the New Year Party, and how jealous he was of Alan when up dancing with her, had him believing that Gil was intentionally trying to frighten him. Or, was he reading too much into it? Then again, he thought, as he drove to his pal's house, he had seen a little of the same reaction when Gil had met Betty Smith one night when dropping him off at his house and the girl had been on the verge of leaving. How Gil had expressed his condolences, belated as they were, for Max running down her boyfriend. Max seethed that when referring to Colin Lamont's accident, it never was just that - an accident, but always his running down of the cyclist.

It had come on a heavy rain when Max got out of his car and knocked on his pal's door. Receiving no answer, he turned the handle and stepped inside. A single step told him Gil was on a high. The place reeked of it. In the dining room, Gil sat slouched in an arm chair, his eyes staring up at the ceiling.

"Christ Gil, what are ye up tae?" Max stood over the drug addict.

Gil gave him a sheepish grin. "Am cool man, am cool!" He waved his hand, letting it drop as if it weighed a ton, his grin even wider.

"Cool? Yer that cool yer brain's frozen." Max sat down in a chair opposite.

He had come to have it out with his pal, but now he was not sure that if he did, Gil would ever remember what he had said.

"How's that bird o' yours pal?" Gil's mouth twitched a little as he spoke, peering at Max as if through some dense fog.

"O K. And that's how ah want it tae stay. That's what ah have come tae see ye aboot."

"Whit's that then pal." Gil fought to be serious.

"Only this. First, cut oot thae sly remarks about me knocking doon, young Lamont. Ok?"

"But ye did, Max, ah was there. Or dae ye no mind?"

"It was an accident," Max shouted. "And ah don't like the way ye keep on about it tae everybody as if it wasnae, as if ah had set oot tae kill the puir bugger."

Gil gave an almost imperceptible nod.

"And as for meeting, Alan Hunter, what did ye say tae him?" he asked, this time a little quieter, though still angry at his pal.

"Say tae him about what?" Gil drew on what remained of his cigarette.

"Aboot his face ye bammer, and how he got it." Max could feel the anger swell up inside him. He had to be careful. He had too much to lose by being too impatient, and he had intentionally refrained from swearing and losing his head.

"Oh his face? Oh he was a wee bit cut up aboot it." Gil's insane laughter, filled the room.

"Cut the jokes Gil." Max bunched his fists..

"Whit ah telt him was how much ye had fallen for his cousin that night of the party. And that's another thing ye should be grateful tae me for, 'cause if it wasnae for me you would no have kent anything aboot that party." It was the first time Max had ever given it a thought as to his being there at all. "Ah was there on business." Gil drew on the stub of his cigarette. "Aw them there were ma clients, so tae speak." He saw the look of surprise on Max's face turn to one of disbelief. "Naw naw," Gil assured him with a wave of a heavy hand. "Alison wasnae wan o' them." As the look of relief spread

165

across Max's face, he added. "Neither was that cousin o' hers by the f***in way."

Max twisted his lip. "So that's why ye were all dolled up. It was for aw thae posh clients."

Gil had closed his eyes as if keeping them open was an effort, one in which he did not appear to be winning. He belched, and suddenly came to life again, his dilated pupils mere pinpoints as he stared across the room to where his pal sat so very far away. "Am on a f***in high, Max ma pal. Ma only pal."

Max thought he was going to cry. "Yer on a high aw right ye eejit. So when ye come doon aff the ceiling, ah want tae have a word wi ye."

"Ah will need an effin parachute if ah dae." The cigarette fell from Gil's lips as he let out a guffaw of laughter. "Whit aboot, eh?"

Max picked up the fallen cigarette and stubbed it out in an ashtray. "Ah will tell ye what aboot? The Honda."

"Yer car? Whit aboot it?"

"Ye know how ah kept havin ma tyres slashed, even when the car was in the garage?"

"Aye. It was wee Lamont."

Max shook his head. You ken it wasnae him, Gil. It was a wee laddie by the name o' Eric Thomson."

Gil sat as if he had not taken in what Max had just said.

"Ye paid him tae slash ma tyres, Gil, kenning fine that ah wouldnae put in a claim tae the insurance as it would affect ma no claim bonus. This, and the fact ah had tae pay the first two hundred on each claim if ah did." Max waited to see what affect this disclosure would have on his friend. "What ye didnae ken was, that ah paid wee Thomson no tae slash ma tyres although he telt ye he had and ah pocketed yer loan for the new tyres for masel. Ye kent at that time ah didnae have a steady job and it would be hard for me tae pay ye back. So why did ye dae it? We were supposed tae be pals."

"Pals!" Gil slumped forward a little in his chair. "So did ah, Max. But ah just got fed up wi your makin a fool o' me in front o' others, especially oor pals. So ah decided tae learn ye a f***in lesson. When ye couldna pay me back ah would take yer car, then we would see who was the best boy racer, eh? It's yer car that makes ye guid, Max Duffy, no yer driving. In fact yer drivin is shite, by the way." Gil returned to his formal position in his chair and drew in a deep breath as if having shed a great load off his mind.

It was always the same when Gil had a doze, his swearing came to the fore. Max sat silent for a little while. It was something he had suspected for some time, that Gil was jealous of his car. Or was it he and his car? Yet, somehow, he had thought it had been more to do with his being a witness to the accident with Colin Lamont.

Gil suddenly sat forward again, lifting a can of lager he took a swig, and then threw it on the floor in disgust. Max bent and picked it up.

"See ye've spilled it aw ower the floor ye mockit bugger." He could not care less about Gil's carpet; it was to give him time to calm down, to coordinate his thoughts.

"So tell me Max, - honest noo pal- why did ye knock doon Colin Lamont? It wasnae as if he had done something bad tae ye. "

Max's anger rose again, this time almost to boiling point. "Ah telt ye it was an accident. He just came oot o' that road without lookin." Max hurled the words across the short space between them. "How many time must ah fu...," He stopped midway through the obscenity, "tae tell ye?"

Gil gave a grin that would not have looked out of place on someone who had a slate missing. "Come aff it Max, ye did it on purpose. Why, ah will never ken. But it has gied me a few sleepless nights thinking aboot it, and what would happen

167

tae us if the polis were tae find oot. Ye'd be up for murder and ah would be an acc..accup." Gil had difficulty saying the word and Max was in no way inclined to help him.

It was out, now Max knew for sure that he could not rely upon Gil keeping his mouth shut. He looked across at his friend who lay slouched in his chair, his head tilted back, eyes closed, skin clammy his breathing irregular.

Max rose and went to the fridge in the kitchen, took out a can of beer and returned to sit in his chair. Gil had not moved his breathing still rapid and irregular. Max pulled back the ring on his can and took a sip of beer. His eyes moved slowly from Gil's face to the table beside him. In amongst the litter of cigarette stubs and empty beer cans, there was a syringe, rubber band and a glass half filled with liquid. Also there were a few strips of tinfoil. Max sat for what seemed to him to be a long time before he rose; now knowing what he must do. He had only seen Gil inject himself once before. Could he do it? Get it right.

Max tightened the tourniquet on Gil's arm as he had seen him do. Putting the syringe into the unconscious boy's hand, he found a vein and injected the full doze he had added to the already half filled syringe, letting it fall to the floor with Gil's fingerprints on it. He had done it. Now there could be no going back. There was no time to lose.

Auld Mrs Archibald would find Gil in the morning. This he knew, as Gil had often told him how the old woman would call on a Saturday and Sunday morning with his breakfast: Her thank you to him for fetching her newspapers and groceries.

Not many people - if indeed any - knew that Gil, besides being a druggie himself also dealt in their selling. This is what concerned Max now. Should the police find any substantial amount in his house and arrive at the conclusion that Gil was a dealer, the obvious step was to contact him as

Gil's best friend. And should they suspect that he too-however wrongly- was as a dealer, things could become a little bit awkward. There was no accounting where their inquiries could lead; least of all his claiming Unemployment Benefit while working for Freddie Stewart, which in turn would not make that man very happy as he had always paid him in cash.

Max swore. Just when everything seemed to be going his way with Alison; his job...This had to happen.

Gil's bedroom was an untidy mess. T-shirts, boxer shorts and jeans littered the floor. Max waded through the assortment of clothes and drew back the door of the large wardrobe that stood against the wall. "Christ!"Max let out, as he stood back in amazement. There must have been at least a dozen suits hanging there, all of the best quality, and on the floor an equal number of pairs of expensive shoes. Obviously, Gil had been into drug dealing in a big way.

Max's mind went back to the night when they were on their way to the New Year party and his surprise at Gil wearing a Rolex watch. Now he knew how he had come to afford such an expensive item. He closed the door and stood back. He would have to search the house and should he find an amount of drugs, dispose of them as quickly as possible.

Fortunately the Rolex was easy to find. Max knew that had the police found this, they were certain to conclude he must have had an income from another source, and what more likely a source than drug dealing.

Max searched in all the likely, then all the unlikely places where Gil could have hidden the drugs. After close on an hour he gave up. He had not bothered about leaving his fingerprints in places he was likely to have been as a regular visitor to the house but had been more careful when searching places he was not likely to have been in.

Max sat at the kitchen table, his eyes roaming around the tiny room. In a last desperate act he tried under the sink once more, examining detergents and cleaning containers. He rose. Either Gil did not keep his supply at home, or he was in the process of waiting for another batch. What Gil himself had been taking lay on the table beside him. He could find no more around the house. His eyes drifted to the cupboard above the sink where dishes were untidily stacked, large plates alternated with saucers and smaller plates, cups stuffed together in a corner, though there were plenty hooks to hang them on.

Max shook his head. One more look, then he must be off. He did not know how forensics knew how long a body had been dead, but he did not want to linger too long and be accused of being here after Gil was dead. Max climbed on to a chair, the easier to examine this last place. There was a glass bowl, a plastic beaker and a few baking dishes all covered in a thin layer of dust. With a last sigh of disappointment, Max was about to climb down when he noticed a small indentation in the inside of the top of the cupboard. Taking a ten pence coin from his pocket he inserted it into the indentation and drew back the chipboard top. There was a slight draught from the dark space above. A lagged pipe ran somewhere into the darkness, and something white caught his attention. Max drew it to him, and with both hands, took it out of its hiding place.

The searcher stepped down off his chair, the shoe box in his hands. " So this is where ye stashed it, ye cunning wee man," he said in a whisper, while opening the box.

Max's breath came in gulps as he stood back in amazement. He had fully expected to find neat little packets of white substances, instead of which the box was crammed full of bank notes. "Ah wonder?" he climbed back up onto the chair and reached into the black hole, extracting another shoe box. By the time he reasoned that the hidey hole was empty, there were five more boxes on the kitchen table.

Max started to count the banknotes in one of the boxes and by the time he had finished there was eight thousand one hundred and fifty pounds, mostly in notes of fifty's and one hundreds, lying on the table. He passed a hand over his eyes. He would have liked to have counted the money in the rest of the boxes, but the sooner he got out of here the better.

. Max found a plastic bag and emptied the contents of the six shoe boxes into it. Next, he placed the empty boxes on the floor of the wardrobe and placed six pairs of shoes in them, carefully closing the lids on each. It would not matter if the names on the boxes did not match the brand of shoes, no one was that meticulous, he reckoned.

Max left the lights on in each room as Gil was apt to do. For a moment he sat opposite his dead friend, staring at the lifeless face, reminiscing over the good times they had had together, and feeling a pang of guilt at what he had done.

"Gil, oh Gil, ye daft bugger, why did ye have tae waste it eh?" Max got up, and approached the body as if expecting it to suddenly come to life and attack him. He put out a shaking hand and touched the cold and clammy skin of Gil's arm. He had never been afraid of Gil when he was alive, why now? He put his fingers around the dead boy's wrist and felt for a pulse. There was none. He stared at the face, glad that Gil's eyes were closed and he could not see the accusation in them. Had he not read somewhere that the dead held a last picture of what they saw in them?

Max closed the front door behind him, the Rolex watch in his pocket. It was still raining outside. He threw the plastic bag in to the back seat. It didn't matter if someone saw him or not. He frequently called on his friend, and tonight it would appear to be nothing different.

Max drove towards Gladsmuir, turning left on to the road that would take him down into Longniddry. Just before the junction, he turned right and passed a couple of cottages. Here, on the country road, he was likely to meet little traffic. The rain had grown heavier and it would be early dark. He drove along roads that twisted and turned until he had almost reached the junction of the Longniddry, Drem road, drawing up outside a derelict building.

Max looked around him before reaching into the back seat for the plastic bag. Opening it, he stared inside it for a moment, then carefully drew out a handful of notes and started to count. By the time he had finished he had counted fifty thousand pounds. Hastily he stuffed the notes back into the bag staring at the floor when he had finished. Rain beat against the windscreen and he turned the ignition key to start the wipers, as if afraid that someone would suddenly leap out of a hedge at him. The place was eerie in the half light. The sooner he made his mind up the better.

Max climbed out of the car, locked it, left the money inside, and walked down the weed strewn path to what remained of a farm building.

All that was left of the old building, except for the stone chimney piece, were a couple of walls no more than four feet high. And it was to the former that he made his way. Cammie and he had sometimes played here as kids, full of pride at having cycled all the long way from home. The place had deteriorated a lot since then, except for the chimney. Max kneeled down in what had once been the fireplace and stuck a hand up inside the flue. For a moment his hand groped around, his cheek pressed against the cold stone, and with a grunt of satisfaction finally extracted a little tin box.

"It's still there." He smiled down at the small tin box in his hand, which he and Cammie had placed there 'as their special secret'. He opened it and gave a smile as he took out the small photograph of his father and mother and Cammie, he himself, little more than a baby, now so long ago that he did not ever remember the photo having been taken.

Max put the box into his pocket and returned to the car. He had made up his mind, if the tin box had remained safely there all those years, what better place than this to hide Gil's money. Max took the watch out of his pocket and stared at it in his hand, reluctant to put it into the bag with the money. He had to take Gil's watch to prevent the police from finding it. Therefore, as he could neither sell nor wear the watch himself, the safest place to dispose of it at this time was with the rest of the cash. Perhaps at a later date when things had blown over, it would be safe enough for him to wear.

It had taken Max quite an effort to wedge the plastic bag in the chimney. He was not quite satisfied that it would not fall down. If it did, and someone did come along and find it in the fireplace, they would indeed believe there was a Santa Clause after all. Later he would come back with some wood and a strong sack and wedge it securely behind the flue. He might have to wait until things died down after they found Gil's body, for as sure as death itself the law would come knocking at his door.

Max's assumption proved correct. Early on Saturday morning came the knock on his door. It had not yet gone half past nine when Cammie, already dressed, opened it to a stone faced police sergeant and a constable standing on the doorstep.

"Are you Mr Max Duffy?" the senior officer inquired civilly.

Cammie shook his head. "That's my brother." He wrinkled his brows. "Is he in trouble?"

"Why should he be?" the younger officer asked.

"No reason, but trouble aye seems to follow him for some reason or another. I suppose ye'll want to come in." Cammie stood aside and the sergeant, followed by his constable stepped into the hallway.

"Max! Are you up yet? There's a couple o' polis here to see ye?" Cammie shouted from the foot of the stairs.

Max, in fact had been in the act of putting on his jeans, when the police had knocked on the door. He had expected them, although he had thought he would have had time for breakfast before they arrived. He should have risen earlier, but he had lain awake, going over and over in his head what questions the police were apt to ask, and the answers he would give. Although he knew that what he had done to his best friend had been in the name of self preservation he had not slept as well as he had expected. He pulled on a shirt, tucked it into the top of his jeans, and with a last stifled yawn went downstairs to meet them.

"Morning sir, I am Police Sergeant Watt, Lothian and Borders Police, and this is Constable Cummings." The senior police officer introduced himself and his colleague. "Might we have a word with you?"

Max gave a shrug. Silly bloody question he thought to himself as if he had a choice. "Aye come in." Max preceded the officers into the dining room, gesturing that they should take a seat.

"Would you care for something to drink, tea coffee?" Cammie asked from the dining room doorway.

"No thank you," the sergeant answered for them both, as he sat down at the dining room table. He took out a notebook and pen and looked up at Max still standing there.

"I believe you know someone by the name of Gilbert Robertson?"

It was the first time Max had heard his pal called by that name. It sounded strange, as if it was not about Gil that he had asked the question. "Aye, he's ma pal. Ah saw him last night for a wee while." He had been careful to use the present tense.

The sergeant wrote briefly in his book. "What time was this?"

"Why? Is it important?"

"The sergeant looked Max squarely in the face. "I'm afraid it is, Mr Duffy, you see Mr Robertson was found dead this morning."

174

Although he had already known the answer, it still came as a shock to hear it said out loud. So the shock on Max's face registered genuine surprise. "Ah bet it was an overdose -the daft bugger. Ah warned him aboot it last night afore a left, but he wouldnae listen," Max finished angrily.

"We won't know for certain that it was in fact an overdose, although it would appear to be at this juncture," the sergeant said calmly.

"Was it auld Mrs Archibald that found him?" Max asked.

The sergeant nodded.

" It must have been a shock for the auld soul." Cammie spoke for the first time.

"It was indeed. She is being treated for shock by her own GP."

Sergeant Watt returned to his notebook. "What time did you leave the house, Mr Duffy?

Max thought for a moment. "Aboot ten or eleven"

"Did you come straight home?" the young constable asked.

Max turned to look at him. Now he thought he had to be careful, and hoped no one had seen him take the road to Macmerry. "Aye. Straight hame. I fell asleep watchin TV."

"Do you know if Mr Robertson had any near relatives?" was the sergeant's next question

Mr Robertson. Again Max found it difficult to relate Mr Robertson to his friend. Max thought that he had never heard Gil ever having been addressed as Mister, in all the time he had known him. "Ah ken he has a brother living in England….Doncaster ah believe Gil said it was, if that's any help. Ah dinnae ken whit he does though. "

"If we have to get in touch with you during the day, where can you be contacted?" Sergeant Watt continued

"Ah work on the site just aff the Macmerry Road, for

175

Mr Jeffries frae Haddington"

"There was an accident there recently," the young constable commented.

"Aye, ah was picking up timber at Haddington when it happened."

"Lucky you." The young officer had a twinkle in his eye as he said it, as if implying that he knew more than he would care to say at present.

"How dae ye mean lucky?" Max was aware of having asked the question much too angrily.

"Only, that I mean, you missed having to see how much agony the poor bloke was in"

"Oh aye," Max nodded, now understanding the officer's comment.

"You've had more than your share of misfortune have you not Mr Duffy?" the young officer went on.

Max stared at the speaker. "In what way?"

"Were you not involved in an accident with a cyclist about a year ago?"

Again the question had put Max on the defensive. What was this young eejit up to? Did he think he was Taggart or something? "Aye, but it wasnae my fault, as ye weel ken," he said angrily.

Constable Cummings gesture offered an apology. "No. I understand that it was not." Following his senior, he stood up.

Sergeant Watt put away his notebook. "Thank you for your assistance, Mr Duffy. Should we need any further information we'll be in touch."

From the window, Max watched the officers walk down the garden path, and as they drove away, turned to his brother.

"Whit dae ye think that wee nyaff was on about, Cammie?"

"He only said he remembered your accident with Colin

176

Lamont, that's all."

"Aye, but it was the way he said it, the same way as he said about me working on the site."

"You're just upset Max, hearing that Gil's dead. It seems it was his own fault, so ye have nothing to reproach yoursel aboot." Cammie moved towards the kitchen. "Want a cuppa? Or are you ready for your breakfast?"

Max had never met Gil's brother before, and if the truth be known, he knew very little about his pal's family. Gil's brother looked nothing like him. Max shook his hand and the man introduced himself as Paul. He looked to be in his late twenties. Gil, Max knew was around twenty three or so, and had finished his apprenticeship, enjoying the wage of a full plumber for the last two or so years. But he had not saved the money or the clothes, he had on a plumber's earnings. Max wondered what the police had made of all those suits, shirts and shoes, and he was glad that he had found and pocketed the Rolex, thus avoiding any awkward questions.

"Gil spoke often about you Max, he said you were his best friend," Paul was saying.

Best friend who had killed him, Max thought. Out loud he said, "Ah suppose ah was. He was some guy. Ah telt him aboot taking yon stuff, but he just laughed, and said it made him feel good."

Paul nodded his understanding as they stood outside the crematorium. Max switched his stare to Alison standing talking to Danny. "Am sorry there wasnae more o' his pals here, it's the Edinburgh Trades and maist o his workmates will still be away on holiday," Max explained, by way of an apology for the very few who had come to pay their respects. "Ah texted the yins ah kent. Some said they couldnae make it as they were in Spain or some o' thae places."

"That was nice of you. I appreciate that."

177

"Is there anything ah can dae for you Paul?" Max spread his hands a little. "Ah mean wi you being doon in England and aw - the hoose and his things ah mean."

"The house belongs to the council. As to Gil's belongings, you are welcome to what you want. His clothes etc."

"Thanks Paul, but ah would have tae slim and shrink a bit tae get in tae them." Max gave a little laugh.

Paul smiled back. "I suppose so. If you know of any Gil's friends that they would fit, then they can have them. If not, I'm sure charities would be happy to have them."

"Aye, OK Paul." Charities, Max thought, those suits are too good for any charity to have. However, it was not any of his business to say so, if this is what Gil's brother wanted.

"Whit dae ye want me tae dae aboot Gil's car? Or are ye takin it for yersel?"

"No. I have my own car."

"Ah can aye try and sell it for ye, Paul, and if ye gie me yer address ah will send you the money, if ye like."

"Do that if you can, Max." Paul dug into his inside jacket pocket. "My address is on the card."

Max took the small white card Paul had handed him.

"So yer a big wig in a law firm?" Max said, reading what was on the card.

"Not exactly a big wig. But yes, I am with a law firm." Max's description appeared to amuse Paul

"So ah will ken who tae contact when ma next case comes up eh?" Max said with a laugh.

*******

178

# CHAPTER 8

Doddie, in company with Sadie, picked up Alan Hunter, to take him to the bike race at Gifford. It was a lovely July day, which was unusual as it was still the Edinburgh Trades holiday and the weather was usually less kind than it was today.

"How ye been keeping then, Alan?" Sadie asked, from the back seat, as they entered Pencaitland.

"Not so bad, Sadie thanks. It has taken a lot of getting used to." The young man gazed out of the car window through dark tinted glasses.

"Ah bet it has." Doddie sounded genuinely sorry for his passenger. "Are the polis any closer to finding oot who did it?"

Alan shook his head. He would have liked to have mentioned the conversation he had had with Gil Robertson, but it was not a subject to discuss with a rider before an event that he had trained so hard for. Instead he said, "How do you think you will do today?"

Doddie turned the car right at the war memorial, taking the road to East Saltoun.

"The Gifford course is no that hard, though the climb oot o' Bolton and Gifford can take their toll if the pressure's on and yer feeling a bit knackered by that time."

"How many laps is it?" was Alan's next question. Already he was feeling envious of Doddie and all those who would be participating in the sport he loved.

"Six. That makes it aboot sixty miles. The finish is just ootside Gifford. If I'm there at the finish, I've a good chance in the sprint." He gave Alan a smile.

"That's if *yer* still there," Sadie piped up from her back seat.

"Oh ye of little faith." Doddie gave a mock sigh of despair.

Alan stared out of the window. "There's not much wind and it's warm and dry. Unlike my last race in England when it was so wet the lead car was a motor launch," he laughed and the others joined in, especially Doddie who knew what must be going through the young man's mind.

The changing rooms or 'the strip' as it was known in cycle racing terms was the Town Hall. Although Doddie had planned on arriving early in order to ensure all was going well organisation wise, he found it difficult to find a parking space. Eventually he had to settle for one close to the park. However he was relieved to find the club members appointed for the occasion had everything well under control.

The Lamonts were due to arrive a little later to watch the race and Doddie hoped he would do well as he would like nothing better than to win, in memory of his old friend. Yet he knew deep down that there were too many good riders here to beat.

"Ah will see that everything is goin aw right," Sadie informed her beau. "So away and dae yer warm up and no worry."

Doddie left Sadie and Alan talking with some of the riders in the strip and did as he was advised to do, by starting his warm up The day had grown warmer, so he had agreed with Alan that the latter would hand him up a water bottle should he need it. They had decided that the best place would be at the top of the hill that climbed out of Gifford on the road to Haddington, where Sadie would park the car.

It was now almost race time, and as Doddie lined up with the other sixty or so riders he caught sight of young Peter Lamont, giving him a wave for good luck. The lead car took off and the race started, the' bunch' slow to start. A lone figure made a dash off the front of the bunch as soon as the neutralized zone was over and a few old wags let out a laugh, shouting to the rash rider that they would see him later.

It was now the third lap of six, and Doddie had managed to hold on to the leading bunch of a dozen or so riders. As they climbed the hill out of Bolton, he heard a shout of encouragement, and glimpsed Alison Jeffries standing with Max Duffy.

Alison had wanted to see the race and encourage Doddie Shaw to do well as she knew how much winning the race in his pal's memory would mean to him. She also wanted to meet her cousin Alan again, as he had texted her to say that he would be here.

"Doddie's doing well!" she cried excitedly to Max, giving the boy a nudge.

Max did not particularly want to be here. He could think of nothing more boring than watching a bunch of riders trying their guts out, the pain clearly etched on every face with the endeavour of keeping up with the man in front. He had considered letting Alison come to the race on her own, and although he did not relish confronting either Doddie Shaw, or Alison's cousin, he wanted to be present at any conversation that might pass between them. Max took an indifferent look down the hill at a small group of riders toiling up the slope, followed at various intervals by the odd rider struggling just to keep going.

The convoy of support cars had just passed when he recognised Danny Glover's Vauxhaul Corsa. Max had texted him and wee Joe, to let them know that he would be here. Not that he had any real desire to meet Danny or Joe, for in fact he had nothing in common with them except when out at night, racing in their cars: It was, that he simply wanted them to be here to give him a feeling of support.

Danny drew up beside them with a final noisy thrust of the accelerator, wound down his window and grinned up at them. "No much fun this, Max, except when ye get a wee bit close tae thae eejits on bikes and some nyaff in a car toots his

181

horn at ye, or wan o' thae guys on motor bikes draws up beside ye tae ask ye politely tae gie the riders room, or bugger aff. This doesnae float ma boat, mair like it sinks ma submarine."

Max grinned back. "Ah thought ye would be here earlier, Danny, ah wis sure ye wernae coming."

Danny's face turned into a scowl. "Got stopped by the polis, for no havin a Tax Disc. I telt him it was in the post. And he says, so is, Oor Wullie and the Broons but am booking you anyway, the bastard!"

Danny's look travelled from Alison to Max, both of whom were vainly trying to keep from laughing. "No funny, you two. Noo am up for a few quid plus a fine."

Max shook his head having failed to stifle a laugh as Alison turned away, the shaking of her body betraying her amusement.

At last Danny saw the humour in the policeman's witticism. "Oh well it is, whit it is."

"Have ye seen wee Joe and Myra anywhere?" Max's eyes still twinkled with amusement as he asked the question.

Danny screwed up his nose. "Last time ah saw them they were feedin their faces in a café doon in Gifford. Whit did ye want us to be here for anyhow? As ah said, no much fun this." He, as had Myra and Wee Joe, refrained from mentioning the absence of their late pal Gil.

"Do you not care to watch real sportsmen?" Alison drew closer to the parked car. "It's not pansy footballers you're seeing here you know." She had asked the question in a teasing way. "When cyclists fall, they don't look around for the referee you know and lie there writhing around pretending to be in agony."

"If they dae ah will just run them ower," Danny bellowed, as he and many motorists did not see cyclists - especially racing cyclists - as anything other than a nuisance on the roads, holding up traffic.

Max ignored Danny's humour. "Me and Alison will wait here and watch the race."

"And when it comes near to the last lap we will go to the finish," Alison informed the young driver.

Danny wrinkled his brows. "Where's the finish?"

"On the East Saltoun side of Gifford. You can't miss it, there will be barriers up etc."Alison explained.

"How long afore they'll be finished?" was the impatient Danny's next question.

"They are on their fourth lap, so they have two to go. We will make our way to the finish when the riders pass for the fifth time. I want to see how Doddie's doing."

Danny revved his engine. "Ok, see you there." And stamping on the accelerator, the small car took off with a roar, smoke pouring out of the exhaust.

Doddie felt quite comfortable in the remaining group of six riders, fearing only one rider who could out sprint him. Therefore, all he had to do, he told himself was to hang in there when the climbers lifted the pace on the climbs. All he had to do? He grimaced at the thought as the pace suddenly lifted, and one rider shot off the front in preparation for the climb ahead at Bolton. Another rider followed and Doddie had to work hard to get back on their wheels and into the safety of their slipstream. He took a deep breath, now not feeling as comfortable or confident as he had done.

The climb out of the small village took its toll on him, and Alan Hunter, at the top of the hill shouted encouragement as he struggled to keep up. One more lap of this he realised would be murder.

Passing the finishing line, the final lap bell ringing in their ears, the surviving riders raised their speed once more as spectators cheered them on, the Lamont family amongst them. Was he going to let them down? Doddie clenched his teeth and gripped the handlebars tighter.

183

Doddie had survived the last climb out of Bolton, now all he had to do was sit on the wheel of the rider whom he knew was the best sprinter in the group of four who had survived the climbers' last attack. One more dip in the road past the thatched cottage on their right and he could make this happen. Make it happen for himself, for Sadie but especially the Lamonts. He could see the finish now, the platform with the photo finish camera, and a fuzzy haze of spectators cheering them on. The riders slowed for a moment, no one wanting to be at the front when the sprint started. Doddie took a chance and jumped clear. Out of the saddle he wound up, already having selected the correct gear. He was almost on the wrong side of the road. He must not get himself disqualified: The commissare's car would not be too far away. Doddie gasped for breath as he made his bid for the line, aware of the other three riders close behind. Suddenly, a car approached from the opposite direction. "Christ!" he swore, why had no one stopped the stupid bastard? The car came on, and he had to swerve back on to his own side of the road, the other riders passing him as he touched his brakes to check his speed. Then they were across the line. The sprinter whom he had feared the most, his hand raised in the air in triumph.

Doddie stood astride his cycle, head bowed over the handlebars, as those who knew him, or sympathised at his ill luck gathered around, amongst whom was a tearful Peter Lamont. "Ye would have won Doddie, if it hadnae been for that eejit in the car," the boy declared angrily.

Sadie came and gave him a hug of commiseration, as he still stood slouched over his handlebars in despair. "Ah had it. Am sure ah could have held them aff."

As he rode slowly back to the strip with other riders, amongst whom was the eventual winner, that rider put a hand on his shoulder. "Ye had it won if it wasnae for that clown in the car. How did the marshals let him through when they knew the sprint was on?"

Doddie shook his head. Under the rules, officials could not legally halt traffic, but they usually asked drivers to wait for a minute or so in the name of safety, especially at the finish when the sprint was on. Usually drivers complied. However this moron had not. Doddie leaned his bike against the wall at the foot of the steps leading to the Town Hall. He would put his bike into his car after he had changed.

Doddie turned at the sound of a familiar voice, across the street, Alison gave him a wave, and he started slowly towards her, already anticipating her sympathy. As he drew nearer, he saw Max Duffy take her hand as they crossed the street to meet him. It was as he did so that he was aware of the Vauxhall car drawing up beside the pair. It was the same car that had caused him to switch during the sprint. Doddie broke into a run.

Before the grinning driver knew what had happened Doddie had him out of the car, his fists hitting the unexpected youngster in the face. He would have pounded the young driver into the ground had some of his fellow cyclists not run to hold him back.

"Ye could have got me killed ye eejit!" he hurled at the shaken youth. "There was nae need for ye tae play boy racers there, was there?" All his anger was at the boy and what it had cost him in endless hours of training, besides losing the race itself.

"I ken ma rights," Danny Glover retorted angrily, holding his face. "An am goin tae charge ye wi assault."

"In that case, include ma name." One of Doddie's club mates piped up, raising his fists in preparation of following up his remarks.

"Stop it! Stop it! That's enough!" Alison's voice cut through the air, her expression one of shock and incredulity. "I'm sure Danny did not mean what he said. Did you, Danny?"

185

Before the unfortunate driver had time to answer, Max thought it was time that he came to the rescue as mediator.

"Alison's right, Danny. Ye didnae need tae dae whit ye did. And if the polis come tae ken that whit ye did wis irresponsible and that ye could have killed somebody, it might no look too good for ye. And nae Tax Disc either, remember?" Max gave an almost imperceptible glance at Doddie as he spoke, in the hope that he might for once, think not unkindly of him.

Danny wiped the blood from his cheek with a handkerchief. "Aye, but there wis nae need for this," the young driver said angrily, pointing to his face.

Doddie turned away. If Duffy thought he was going to thank him for his intervention he was mistaken, and the same went for that young moron of a driver.

"You were lucky there, Doddie," the rider who had supported Doddie during the altercation said to him in a sympathetic but serious manner, as they made their way back to the town hall. "You could have been suspended for what you did to that guy."

"He cost me the race the bammer." Doddie was not to be chastised for what he had done. He would have done more had he known he was a friend of Max Duffy.

The main room in the town hall was crowded with riders, supporters and race officials. The noise almost deafening as riders discussed their hard luck with anyone who had the patience to listen, while they munched sandwiches and drank tea or coffee. Others nodded in apparent sympathy - most of whom had heard the same old reasons before - as to why that particular rider had punctured, or had been in the wrong place when the winning move was made.

Sadie saw Doddie come in and hastened to bring him a cup of tea and a plate of sandwiches and small cakes. "Hard luck Doddie. The Lamonts are devastated that ye didnae win.

186

Never mind darlin, there's always next year." She gave him a peck on the cheek as he took the plate and cup of tea from her.

Next year was of little consolation to what had happened today. All his hard training gone due to an eejit playing the daft laddie in his car, was Doddie's reaction.

Their club president thumped a trestle table with a pump to gain everyone's attention, announcing the commencement of the prize giving. Doddie could scarcely control his feelings when Mrs Lamont presented the trophy their family had donated in the name of their son Colin to the winner. His feeling mixed at the mention of his late friend's name, and his own emotions at not having won the trophy for himself and the Lamont family. The biggest cheer of the day, however, was when he had gone up for his fourth prize, everyone there knowing that he should have won. Perhaps not he demurred. The rider who had won, had the car not got in his way may have beaten him after all. This he was never likely to know but as Sadie had said, there was always next year.

Their farewells said to the Lamonts, with Doddie thanking them for how well they had presented the prizes, Mrs Lamont giving him a consolatory kiss and Peter waving him a sad goodbye, his young face still crestfallen that his hero had not won, Doddie, Alan and Sadie climbed into their car.

It was a good distance down the road before anyone spoke.

"Did you speak to yer cousin, Alan?" Doddie was the first to break the silence.

"Aye. I saw her at the finish. She said she didn't want to come into the reception." Alan hesitated a little. "I expect it was because of what had happened outside."

Sadie's eyes opened wide. She leaned forward from her seat in the back. "Whit's this yer no tellin me aboot? What happened ootside?" She clenched her teeth in annoyance, as she was never sure what this man of hers could get up to.

Briefly, Doddie explained the altercation between himself and Danny Glover and how Max Duffy had acted as mediator. When he had finished, Sadie sat back in her seat.

"Ye should have belted yon wee nyaff Duffy as well when ye had the chance." Sadie's unexpected angry comment had both men laughing at her belated suggestion.

Alan wished he had not gone to the bike race. True, he had gone in the hope of seeing Doddie win. It was meeting his peers, those he had until recently ridden against in the sport he loved, that had affected him. He had stood inches away talking to them, but he might as well have been a million light years away from doing what they could do and he no longer could.

He had known others who were partially blind who still rode. And although he would love to do the same, he believed he was not quite ready - not confident enough to try. Besides, he did not want to jeopardise other riders, as well as himself. Perhaps a little later he would have the courage to get back on his bike and take a ride in some quiet country road before even contemplating getting back into the sport.

Doddie dropped Sadie off at their house and on his way to Alan's home his passenger brought up the subject he had wanted to before the race. "I met, Gil Robertson one day at Ocean Terminal." Alan hesitated, now not so sure what he was about to say, or what his friend's reaction might be. "It could not have been very long before he died."

"Committed suicide," Doddie grunted. "Daft bugger. Thae druggies are aw the same, cannae face life without an armfu."

Alan sat quietly annoyed by Doddie's unexpected outburst. Now he would have to start all over again, just when he had plucked up enough courage to discuss it all. Perhaps if he told Doddie about his suspicions, his friend might think him paranoid.

"Sorry, ye were sayin Alan, afore ah cut ye aff? Ye

188

were tellin me ye met Robertson at Ocean terminal."

Alan swallowed, his eyes on a cyclist riding on the pavement. "Yes. He told me how sorry he was about my eye."

"Nice o' him." Doddie pulled up at a set of traffic lights.

"He told me that Max Duffy had his eye on my cousin, Alison, at the party, the night that it happened. He told me that he had never seen his pal so angry or jealous." Alan waited until Doddie had accelerated away from the lights before he continued. "It was the way he said it Doddie, as if he knew more about what had happened to me than he cared to admit. I believe, Max Duffy had something to do with my mugging...no, attack that night."

Doddie gripped the steering wheel tighter, at the possibility. "Ah wouldnae put it past the bad bastard. Are ye thinkin o' goin tae the polis aboot it?"

Alan shook his head as if unsure. "If I did, what could I tell them? And, with Gil Robertson dead..."

Doddie nodded, understanding Alan's dilemma. "The polis would probably make some inquiries as to where Duffy was at the time you were attacked. Probably it would be hard tae prove that he had anything tae dae wi it."

"And if he were to be convicted, he'd probably get very little of a sentence, while what happened to me is for life." The bitterness showed on Alan's face as he spoke.

"Maybe if the polis did interview Duffy, it might shake him up a wee bit... make him think, then there's always the possibility o' him gein himself away." Doddie drew up outside Alan's house. "Of course there are other ways o' gettin yer ain back."

Alan drew back in his seat, all the more able to see if his friend was joking or not. Doddie was not.

189

Alison had never been more proud of Max than she was right now. How he had defused the situation between Danny Glover and Doddie. Of course it had been a stupid thing that Danny had done, but he had only done it in fun. However the consequences could have been serious.

Alison sighed a little as she studied Max's face. He was handsome, yet he did not appear to be aware of it. Max had told her something about the night he had knocked down Colin Lamont, and how people, such as Doddie and the Lamonts, believed it to be his fault, although inquiries had exonerated him.

Max was aware of her looking at him. "Whit? Have ah got something stickin tae ma nose or something?" he asked, as he moved out from behind a slow moving tractor, on their way home after the cycle race.

"No." Alison laughed at the notion.

"What are we daein the night then?" he asked the girl, at the same time thinking what a way for a farmer to spend a Saturday.

"I think we've seen all the good films there are, unless you want to get a DVD?" She stroked his arm.

"Funny, ah was thinking that mysel. Cammie's away on another course. The hoose is empty. We could get in a Chinese if ye fancy it?"

"What, would he do the cooking and the cleaning up?" Alison quipped.

Max threw her a swift look then back to the road again. "Whit's makin ye sae cheerful? Ah never heard ye makin that sort o' joke afore."

Alison sat back comfortably in her seat. "Maybe I've never been this happy before."


Max heard the rattle of dishes from the kitchen. Yawning, he swung his legs out of bed and pulled on his boxer shorts. Alison was at the sink, her back to him, unaware of his being there until she felt his bare arms around her, and him kissing her on the neck. She turned her head a little and beamed up at him. "Did you sleep well? And don't say that you didn't, for you kept me awake with your snoring."

"Sorry," he apologised. "Naebody has ever telt me aboot it afore. Ah suppose that's because Cammie is in the next room...when he's here ah mean." He laughed at the girl's startled expression.

"It's a good job he's not. He wouldn't get to sleep either."

Max blushed. "You mean us?"

It was Alison's turn to blush. "You are an animal, Max Duffy."

"Whit kind? A cuddly bear ah hope."

Alison ignored the question. "I found some bacon and eggs in the fridge. How do you like your eggs?"

"Quickly. Ahm starving."

She laughed at his answer. "For that crack you will have to wait."

Max released himself from her warm body, and stood back watching her at work. He hummed happily and took two mugs and two large plates from the kitchen cabinet. This could be them in a few years ...no months time, if he played his cards right. Alison was on the pill and he also protected himself, so there was no way in which she could become pregnant. A pity he thought, for had she been, Daddy would have to come around to his marrying his beloved daughter, to prevent a scandal. Then he, Max, would be set for life. A good position in the family business...eventually, that was. Yes, things could work out very well for him. However, Alison was not in the family way. Max cursed himself as it had not been a nice thing to think about. He had not really thought of raising a family. A son would be nice, to inherit the family business, his business.

191

No, the world was not ready for another Max Duffy.

He set the plates and mugs down on the table. Alison swung the frying pan round from the cooker and placed two rashers of bacon on his plate. "Do you want more? There's still some in the packet?"

Max shook his head. "Naw this is fine." He sat down watching her put a rasher on to her own plate. He reached for the salt shaker and shook a little on to the egg that she had slid off the frying pan on to his plate. "Whit will daddy say at ye being oot aw night?"

"I told him a little white lie. I said I was at a girl friend's house in town. He didn't ask who, so I didn't elaborate."

"Ye've done this sort of thing afore then?" Max chewed his bacon, as Alison sat down opposite, sliding a mug of tea across to him.

"Once or twice. Are you jealous?"

Max gave a shrug. "Everybody tae their ain taste as the wumman said when she kissed the coo."

Alison laughed, and started on her egg.

"Ah mean, Alison, ah don't want any friction between you and yer auld man. Somehow ah don't think he would be pleased if he kent ye were wi me aw night, and whit we were daein."

"I'm a big girl now, Max. I know what I'm doing."

"Ah hope so." Max put down his knife and fork. "Ah really hope so," he sighed.

*******

Friday night came around again. Max had not wanted to meet his pals. Alison had her heart set on meeting 'Freespace', a member of the gang she had not yet met, so he had given in. Perhaps, Max thought, it had been his fault by

192

telling Alison how crazy the boy was. How Freespace - Max had forgotten his real name - had told the story of how, when a lot younger (he was still only eighteen) he had run out of a shop having stolen two Mars Bars with the owner hot on his tail, only to be confronted by a policeman who just happened to be there at the time. According to Freespace, that officer was usually sitting in his car at that late hour devouring one of McDonald's finest. Freespace had seen a mobility scooter whose owner he had flown past in the shop, parked outside, and jumping on to it had put it into top gear and made off, with the puffing policeman running beside him whilst taking details in his notebook and shouting 'pullover', to Freespace, who had replied that it wasnae a pullover but a jumper his mammy had knitted. No one had believed his story of course, but it had given Alison, a laugh and an urge to meet this so called ASBO delinquent.

He and Alison were the last to arrive, except for Freespace. Just as Max had climbed out of his car to greet wee Joe, Myra and Danny, Freespace drew up his Mini Cooper with a squeal of brakes, music blaring from his JBL Subwoofer, the car scarcely coming to a halt before the driver was out of the car and greeting them all with a big smile and a wave.

Freespace, as he liked to be known, at eighteen, still acted like a nine year old, and a not very bright nine year old at that. He was totally bald causing the tattoo on the back of his head which read 'this side up' stand out even more. He was of average height, dressed in a pair of army camouflage, three-quarter length shorts, his denim jacket covered with badges of various makes of cars.

"Hi folks how's it goin then? He walked towards them with a jaunty gait.

"Where huv ye been, Freespace?" Myra asked, kissing him on the cheek.

"Spain for a fortnight." His eyes fell on Alison as if

having suddenly realised that she was there. "And who's this then?" Freespace's eyes roamed over the girl in undisguised admiration.

"Mine," Max said, his voice nondescript.

"My name's Alison and I know you're Freespace." The girl stepped forward and held out her hand, smiling up at him.

Taken a little aback by the girl's politeness, Freespace shook the proffered hand and gave a little whistle. "Where did ye find this yin, Max, she's awesome?"

"She's no a car, ye bammer." Max was a little upset by the way Freespace had phrased the question.

"No, buy yin get yin free, eh?" Freespace chuckled. Then as if having forgotten the subject, asked of no one in particular. "Whit have ye's been up tae since ah left for ma holiday?" He looked at each in turn. "Sorry, Max, ah forgot ye've lost Gil. Puir bugger."

Wee Joe broke the awkward silence before Max had time to answer, "How was Spain anyway, Freespace? Did ye get yer leg ower some o' thae Spanish birds?" His question was followed by a queer, wee laugh, as if slightly embarrassed at having asked the question in front of the girls.

Freespace's face lit up. There was yin night, me and ma pals were just aboot tae leave this bar that was haudin a karaoke when this auld bird,- she must have been in her thirties grabs me as ah passed her table. She must have dooned a bucket fu o' Sangria, for she was fair steamin. "Where are ye goin, handsome?" she says.

"She should have gone tae Specsavers!" Danny laughed.

Unperturbed Freespace continued. "So, ah says, ahm just leavin wi ma pals. By this time they had left as they had their eyes on these birds that were leavin too. 'Sit yersel doon' Of course she says this in English." Freespace changed to what he considered to be an English accent. 'And meet my husband.' " So this bloke pits his haun oot and says 'I'm Bert, please to meet you.' "Just then, this big bloke tries tae squeeze past the wumman's table, whose name was Melonie by the way."

"Get on wi the story, Freespace, or it will be oor turn tae go on holiday," wee Joe snarled, his impatience beginning to tell.

Freespace, drew him a look at this interruption to his 'chronicle'. "As ah was sayin, this big bloke tries tae get past oor table. ' Sorry Frauline' he says by way of an apology. ' It's all right Adolf,' says Melonie, we're all on the same side now." ' Melonie!' Bert shouts, quite annoyed he was tae. ' Keep your voice down we're surrounded by Germans.' ' Just like the war,' "Melonie gies oot this big laugh and everybody turns tae see who it is. Then Bert gies another look aroon him and says." 'I think we're all right, they're mostly Spanish here.' "So ah thought tae masel, its time ye got oot o' here Freespace, afore Melonie mentions the lArmada, and we aw get oor heids kicked in!"

Alison was the first to let out a roar of laughter quickly followed by the others.

"That's a guid story Freespace, when did ye make that yin up, on the plane hame?" Danny gave a shake of his head in disbelief of the story.

Freespace was not to be deterred from continuing. "Talk aboot planes. Before we got on the plane ma pal, Hughie says tae the steward, how often dae these big planes crash? Only the once says the steward. Ah nearly fell aff the steps o' the plane laughing. Then this steward says, if you feel quite frightened, I will give you a seat near the tail. Oh, says Hughie, is that the safest place tae be? Well, she says, I have never heard of any of our planes backing into a mountain!"

Again there was uproarious laughter from the company, with the exception of wee Joe, who was impatient to be doing something else. Throwing his hands in the air, he exclaimed in desperation, "Are we goin tae staun here and listen tae this load o' shite aw night? Or are we goin tae dae something, like go tae Mcdonalds?"

Freespace's expression turned to one of dismay at such a suggestion. "Ah came tae go for a burn up. Ah havenae had a decent run in ma car for three weeks."

"Well ye shouldnae go away on holiday, should ye big man?" Danny chastised him. "Anyway, Max is no up for it. Are ye Max?" Danny turned a mischievous eye on his leader.

"Max no up for it? Since when?" Freespace asked incredulously.

"Since his bird came along." Danny knew he was taunting the one who had always considered himself to be their leader.

"This right Max?" Freespace studied the accused, his expression one of disbelief.

"Yes it is Freespace," Alison butted in, her face red with embarrassment. "Max does not want to take the risk with me in the car. Do you Max?"

"That says a lot for me then," Myra said sarcastically. "Joe kens ah like the buzz, Don't ye Joe?"

"And so do I, Myra," Alison defended herself. "But Max does not see it that way. After all my daddy is his boss, and I am made of cotton wool."

It was too much for Max. "Right, if ye want a burn up, I'll gie ye a burn up." He walked quickly to the car, and as he reached it turned angrily to face the others. "Well, what are youse waiting for, an invitation in writing?"

It had been decided that the race would be down the length of the dual carriageway on the road to Longniddry and back.

Max shot off with such unexpected speed that Alison was thrown back in her seat. She gave him a sideways glance, and settled down in excited expectation, Max, his jaw in a determined set. As they reached the dual carriageway, Freespace, in his Mini attempted to overtake him and Max simply increased his speed.

Alison let out a howl of delight. "This is cool! Who is that right behind us?"

Max glanced in his rear mirror. Danny was tailgating him, waiting for the right moment to come around him when Freespace had dropped back.

They were almost at the end of the dual section. A car appeared from the opposite direction and Max checked his speed, before making the turn, and as he did so, Danny seized his opportunity to shoot past.

"You are not going to let him get away with that are you Max?" Alison said in despair, remembering how Danny had niggled Max when he had beaten him last time they had raced.

Max watched as Danny geared down, then suddenly gunned the car, sending it sideways and fighting to bring it up straight again as it turned into the opposite lane, then he was away, blue smoke billowing from the exhaust. Max took the corner wide and Freespace passed him on his inside, then he too, was shooting up the dual carriageway back towards Prestonpans. Now only wee Joe was behind the gang leader and Max cut his speed so that he too could pass.

Alison was livid. She brushed back a strand of blonde hair, and swivelled round in her seat to chastise him. "What was that all about? You intentionally let everyone pass you! How do you think that makes me feel? That I am too precious? That I do not have a mind of my own? Humiliating me in front of your friends. Take me home please! And I do not want you to stop and have that carnaptious Danny...something..." she had forgotten his name "laughing at you again."

It was the first time Alison had been angry at him. He did not know what to say. He turned left at the roundabout at

Meadowmill and headed for the bypass to Haddington.

What had he done wrong? All he wanted to do was keep this lovely young girl safe. On previous occasions, when on his own, although aware of the dangers and the subsequent repercussions if things were to go wrong, he only had to think of himself. Now, with so much at stake he did not want to take the chance. It was as simple as that, he could not imagine life without this girl.

Eventually, unable to bear the silence any longer, his voice subdued, Max said. "Alison, ye mean everything tae me. If anything was tae happen tae ye, ah wid be devastated. Whit does it matter who wins thae damned races, as long as ye're safe."

If what Max said was to pacify the girl, or to have her think how much she meant to him, Alison did not show it. Max was nothing other than a rough diamond to her, someone with whom she could let her hair down, have fun with. After it was all over, they would go their separate ways. There never could be any future in it for either of them. Despite her anger she could not help but feel moved by Max's declaration. However, her pride would not allow her to admit it. Perhaps the time had come for her to move on, now that Max had become so drearily responsible. His type she could have in their hundreds at Uni.

Max dropped Alison off at her house. He had tried to make further conversation, including asking her when they would meet again, and she had answered that she would text him, when, and if, she wanted to see him again.

Feeling as though the bottom of his world had dropped out and needing a drink, Max left his car at home and headed into Tranent. His brain would still not absorb what the girl was on about. Had he been irresponsible, he would have understood. So why, when he was now trying to be the opposite for once - be responsible for his job, his future with

198

Alison – had she condemned him? Women! He thought, and downed his first Vodka.

Betty was in the toilet in Cammie's house, when she heard the front door open and surmised that it was Cammie returning with the pizzas. After drying her hands she opened the bathroom door, calling out Cammie's name as she made her way to the kitchen. It was as she passed the open door of Max's room that she saw the fully clothed figure sprawled out on the bed. She halted, looking down at the unconscious figure of the boy lying there, his breathing deep, contemplating how easy it would be to put a pillow over his face and bear down on it with all of her weight. Perhaps then she would find some peace of mind, perhaps too, the Lamonts. She felt her heart beat faster, her breath coming in shallow gasps with the thought of what she could do to the man who had killed her boyfriend, Colin.

Max had not stirred - had not made the slightest move - as she tip toed quietly into the room. Betty lifted the white pillow from off the bed. For a moment she stood over the unconscious figure, a kaleidoscope of thoughts flashing through her brain. Should she do this, she would be a murderer, no better than the person lying there. And if she did go through with it, would she be able to live with herself? As the thoughts hurtled through her mind, she took another step forward, blotting out her doubts as she made to place the pillow over the sleeper. It was then she heard the front door open and Cammie's footstep drawing closer.

"Whits this?" Cammie stood staring.

At first Betty believed it to be her holding the pillow to which the man had referred, until she heard him go on.

"That's the first time since he met yon lassie that he's been in a state like this." Cammie pointed to the figure on the bed.

"I was going to put the pillow under his head to prevent

him from choking," Betty lied, lifting Max's head and placing the pillow underneath.

"Serves him right if he wakes up choked." Cammie, made a face. He stepped into the room, handing Betty the red and green striped pizza box. "Here, you see to this, and ah will take his jacket and shoes aff. Thanks, Betty it could no have been easy for ye tae dae whit ye did. Max must have had a fight wi his bird," he commented, removing one of his brother's shoes.

"Seems like it," Betty said, relief flooding her body and wondering, should Cammie not have come back at that precise moment, would she in fact have gone through with what had been in her mind. This, she would never know, now that the opportunity was lost. She left Cammie to it, hearing at her back Max mumble Alison's name.

*******

It was a well over-used cliché in today's parlance, but to say the least, Max was devastated. He had texted Alison every day of the following week, and she had not replied. It was all over - she had dumped him. His work too, had suffered and he had been reprimanded more times than he wished to remember. Max found himself angry and ready to punch anyone who came near him, just to feel relief at what he was going through. Sadly, he was returning to his old self, too ready with his fists. He must take a grip of himself. If it was only a temporary setback in their relationship, it would not do to have him lose his job.

Friday night came again, the first for a while that he would be without Alison. He would be alone. Max drove without a clear idea where he was going, and with only a vague notion of meeting his pals at the lay- by. Max swore. Bitch, forcing him back into a way of life, that he had readily accepted as being well and truly behind him. Bitch he

200

murmured again, angry that love could so easily turn to hate. Yet, why did racing his beloved car not appeal to him now? Was it the fact that he had lost the urge to race, and not out of any thought of having Alison injured? Max shook his head. No, he had not wanted the girl to be injured. He gripped the steering wheel tighter, knowing that he could not live without the girl; could not bear not to have her near; ogle, if you like, that beautiful body; touch; make love.

Max found himself at the lay- by prepared to be taunted and baited by his pals. Perhaps he deserved it, for in a way he had deserted them, looked down on them since meeting Alison, and having a steady job.

Somehow, Max was relieved to see his pals there, as he had visions of them all going their separate ways. As he arrived, Danny threw him a wave of welcome as he stood leaning on the bonnet of his car, his face turning to a frown at seeing Max alone.

"Where's the bird the night?" Danny's smile did not reach his eyes. He hoped their former leader had been dumped: served the bastard right. How many times had he, Danny, taken insult and sarcasm about his driving skill...or lack of it, besides deriding his beloved car? Now it was his turn to turn the screw.

Max shrugged, saying nothing. He would not give this moron the opportunity to laugh at him, especially after the way he had taken care of Alison at the expense of these boy racer pals of his. Suddenly it came to him, now with Alison out of his life, these were the only friends he had left.

"Are ye up for it noo that yer bird is no here?" Wee Joe stood with an arm around Myra as he asked the question. Myra gave a smirk.

Max drew a little closer to the coterie, and was not immediately aware of the car drawing up behind him, until his pals let out gasps of delight and disbelief. He swung round.

Alison's red sports car stood there, its powerful engine throbbing gently, the girl herself, smiling up at him from behind the steering wheel.

"What a beauty!" Freespace exclaimed. "And ah don't mean yer bird either Max." He let out a whistle of admiration, slowly circling the car, inspecting every inch of the gleaming machine.

"Yer car's awesome. That would set ye back a bit." Danny stood looking down at Alison who had rolled down the window.

"Daddy actually," Max mimicked before the girl could answer.

It had been the wrong tact to use, Max realised. Now there would be no reconciliation. He gave her a smile in an attempt to make amends.

"Yes it can go a bit."

"So could ah," Freespace laughed, "and ah don't mean the car."

At any other time Alison would have been insulted by the remark, now however, she had the opportunity to get her own back at Max for his snide remark regarding her father.

"Are we going to go for a ride or not." Alison asked, and saw Freespace's face burst into a grin. "And not the kind you are thinking," she told him, giving the boy a big smile for Max's benefit.

"How aboot, The Horseshoe?" Danny asked.

"The Horseshoe? What's that?" Alison made a face indicating that she did not understand.

Danny obliged. "First we go doon the coal road, tae Port Seton, tae we come tae the camps....the holiday caravan park," he explained, "then we gie it a bit welly frae there tae the junction up at Dirleton, turn right doon past Fenton Barns, Drem, Lonngniddry and back, stopping just afore the roundabout up there." He pointed to the Tranent junction.

"Good. Let's go for it." Alison switched on her car engine and revved the accelerator a couple of times, giving Max a sideways glance, in order to see his reaction.

As Danny and Freespace gave a shout of joy and ran for their own vehicles, Max stood looking down through the driver's window at Alison. "Don't dae it Alison, it's too risky. Anything can happen wi thae bammers driving the way they dae." There was real concern in his voice as he said it. "That's why ah didnae drive like an eejit wi you in the car, ye mean too much tae me." He was glad that none of his pals were in earshot, as he felt a right pansy at having said what he had said, and the pleading way he had said it. He had never done so before with any other girl he had gone out with, but Alison was special - a girl he hoped someday to marry - or be his partner for life.

Alison gave Max a benevolent smile. "I'll be all right. I just want to try this just once for myself. I shall be careful you know."

Max felt a surge of hope spread through his body. They were not going to split up. He gave the side of the car a thump and stood back, a broad smile on his face. "Be careful, yer daddy will kill me if anything happens tae you."

Alison gave him a cheery wave as she started after the others, still not quite sure when the real racing would begin, although she understood it to be somewhere on the coast road. She gave a brief glance in her rear mirror, and her heart sank a little that Max was not behind her, or joining in.

Freespace, took off as he passed the caravan site on his right, and the rest speeded up after him. Alison was enjoying the sense of freedom and what speed could do. Her Mercedes Sports was capable of out running any of the others, and she waited for a straight stretch of road to overtake Freespace, already anticipating the look of astonishment on his face at being passed, and by a woman driver at that.

The River Forth lay a grey and blue under the night sky, here and there, darker, almost black where it was hidden by drifting clouds blotting out a pale moon.

Freespace was almost at the bend at the Gosford Estate. Alison beamed satisfaction. She would take him here just before the bend, her smile turning to one of astonishment as Danny overtook her. Alison stamped on her brake horrified at the thought that someone could be coming around the oncoming bend in the opposite direction. She pulled aside, ready for the anticipated crash at the same time as Wee Joe honked his horn and Myra gave her a wave as they too passed her. For a moment Alison felt herself shake, then with a determined shake of her head slid the gear into top and accelerated after the others.

After the double bend at Aberlady, she gained ground and passed wee Joe on the comparatively straight road by the side of the bay, birds taking to the night sky at this intrusion to their sanctuary.

By the time Alison had almost reached the road junction, just short of Dirleton, she was on the tail of Freespace. She was really enjoying this. Now she understood why Max had wanted to do this every Friday night. There was more excitement to this than all the blockbuster films put together. If only Max had joined in, then she could really have shown him what she could do behind a wheel, and that she was not the Miss Prim and dainty he had taken her for.

Max had watched them disappear down the coal road. At first he wanted to follow, if for nothing other than to see how Alison fared. He decided however, to drive in the opposite direction and watch them approach Ballencrief Crossroads. He would wait until they passed, and make sure Alison was still there, or as he fully expected, some distance behind his pals before following her to the finish. He would be happy when it was all over. Secretly, he hoped she would not want to do it again.

It was close on five minutes after he had taken up his waiting position, that he saw the first car approach the crossroads. "Christ!" Max exclaimed, for it was Alison's red sports car. Had there been an accident, or a hold up somewhere that had given her the lead? Strangely he found himself smiling at what would transpire when his pals came limping in behind a woman driver!

Max watched in amazement at the speed in which the red sports car approached the roundabout at the junction of the Ballencrief Crossroads.

Suddenly, from the direction of Aberlady a small blue car appeared. Max clenched his fists, his eyes glued on Alison's car. By right she would have to give way, but at the speed at which she was travelling, there was no way that she could draw up in time.

To Max, it all happened in slow motion. Aware of the sports car bearing down on him at such a high speed, the driver of the blue car jammed on his brakes in an attempt to swerve away from the speeding sports car.

"On no! Christ no!" Max shouted, yet unable to take his eyes off the inevitable crash. All too late Alison braked, sending the light car into a spin, a spin that had her crash into the side of the other car, and it seemed to the watcher, tear through its side not halting until both cars had spun on to the grass verge, and come to an abrupt halt.

In an instant, Max was speeding to the scene, tears flowing freely down his cheeks, and telling himself, over and over again, that no one could have survived such a crash, yet hoping all along for a miracle.

He was out the car in a flash, running to where both cars sat entangled on the grass verge, vaguely aware of Freespace close behind him, and somewhere in the distance, sounds of other cars.

Alison sat staring up at him as he reached the car. It was if she wore a metal cover up to her chin. He could see nothing else except that lovely head, the fair hair matted in blood, her body jammed somewhere in the mangled interior of the car. Sobbing uncontrollably and shouting that he had told her not to do it, Max tore at the smashed side of the driver's door, praying to the good Lord to give him the strength to pull it open and release this beautiful girl that he loved.

Freespace was next to him, trying to help. "Phone for an ambulance!" Max yelled hysterically at him, as he still pulled frantically at the damaged door.

Alison's eyes beckoned up to him. Max let go of the door, and got as close as he could to the girl and gently put an arm around the back of her head.

"You were right, Max," she whispered. "I should have listened to you." She gave a little squeal as if suddenly racked with pain, then a smile and a sigh. "It was fun though while it lasted."

While it lasted! Max was angry at her - at his pals - at the world, and at God for allowing this to happen. But mostly he was angry at himself for not having reached into Alison's car and snatched the ignition keys from her, before she had started on this crazy race. He saw her eyes dim, and panicked.

"Haud on Alison! We will get ye oot, the ambulance will be here in nae time." He bent further into the car and held her, as if by doing so it would keep her with him. He kissed her cheek, his tears mingling with the blood that had begun to run down from some cut on her forehead.

Max bent a little to the front of the car the better to see the injured girl's face. Alison's eyes were closed. He spoke to her, his voice gentle, coaxing her, urging her to hold on. There was no response. He would not believe that she was gone. Fainted with the pain or lapsed into a coma perhaps, but not dead, he told himself. There were cries of what sounded like hysteria around him. At first he thought it was for Alison until his fuddled brain told him that it came from the other car. There were strange folk all around it, pulling at it as he had done with Alison's car.

Myra came running across the short distance from where wee Joe had left his car. "Is she all right?" the girl asked, staring at the mangled wreck of what was left of the red sports.

"Don't be F***in stupid wumman!" Max howled at her. "How could she be, in a car that state."

All of Max's anger was funnelled at the girl. Alison was dead. He had known this while telling himself that she was only unconscious.

It had seemed an eternity before the police, ambulance and fire brigade arrived. Now the once empty country road was filled with cars full of curious onlookers. A few running about, some serious, others seeing this as some sort of reality show.

Wee Joe shook Max by the shoulder. "Listen pal, the polis will be asking questions o' us as eye witnesses. We have tae say what we saw. There is nae use makin up lies. The polis will ken by the skid marks on the road that yer bird was goin at a helluva rate o' knots."

"Aye, we will hiv tae tell the truth," Danny conceded. He was shaking as if cold. "If anything, we owe it tae they other pair souls." He turned in the direction of the blue car where ambulance men were hard at work, and Max saw what he took to be a body covered by a blanket being carried on a stretcher from the blue car to the ambulance.

"Two wee bairns. Ah believe yin is deid. Ah dinnae ken aboot the ither yin. Their faither was drivin. They have managed tae cut him oot." Joe kicked at the grass where they stood a little distance away from the crashed cars, and no doubt wishing he was anywhere else on earth, besides not savouring the forthcoming interview with the police.

Max stared at what was left of the blue car. Although it had been embedded in Alison's car, he had been too busy trying to extricate the girl from the twisted metal that he had been completely oblivious to everything else. This was something else they would all have to live with. "Christ," he said. "Whit a bloody mess. And ah dae mean bloody."

First the ambulance left, followed, shortly after, by the fire brigade and by the time the police had taken all of their statements regarding the accident it was late evening. The road was still closed. Other police arrived to investigate the scene of a fatal accident, and by the time Max and his pals were allowed to leave, it was almost midnight.

Max's head ached as it had never done before. Gripping the wheel tighter, his knuckles almost white he headed for the hospital. Why he was going there he had no idea, except that he must know, if by some miracle, Alison had survived. He was on the bypass now, his brain whirling that if Alison was to survive that she must at least be disfigured or crippled. Disfigured ! That lovely face? He shuddered. Or crippled. He would of course look after her. What a lot of crap he thought. A car passed him and his nerves made him slow down, now aware of what a lethal weapon a car could be.

Max arrived at the hospital. He wanted to run... find out where they had taken his girl. Instead, he walked slowly to the reception desk, not wanting to hear the news he expected and dreaded to hear.

He came out of the lift at the floor those at the desk had told him to. Nathan Jeffries sat across the room holding his head in his hands. A man standing next to him had his back to Max, who upon hearing his approach, turned; it was Archie Gordon, the site foreman. He nudged his employer on the shoulder, drawing his attention to Max, his face impassive.

Nathan Jeffries looked up, his eyes blazing hatred at Max crossing towards him. Suddenly and without warning the stocky man was on his feat. "Ye bastard, I knew you were trouble from the time I first set eyes on you! You killed my Alison!"

It would be useless to explain to the man that he had not been in the car with Alison, and that he had not even taken part in the stupid race. It was enough for this man that he had known his daughter and that in knowing her, he, in some way was responsible for her death. Max saw the blow coming. He took it full in the face and stumbled back, falling against a chair, and landing on the floor. He put up a hand to stop the blood flowing from his nose. He could have defended himself by dodging the fist, but somehow he felt he owed this man some kind of penance for what he had done to Alison and a few more.

*******

Max stood outside the gates of Mortonhall Crematorium, well aware that his presence at the service would not be appreciated. He waited in the slight smirr of the September day. It was over a year since Colin Lamont's accident. A day much the same as this, he reflected.

The cyclist's death had never really cost him much sleep, nor had that of Gil or his disfigurement of Alan Hunter, or to a lesser extent, Andy Gemmel. No, what he had done, with the exception of Sadie Shaw, he had done out of sheer survival. It was different now. Since Alison's accident, his night's sleep had been punctuated with dreams - nightmares, if he was honest with himself -.dreams that had remained with him long after he was fully awake and throughout the day, everyone still vivid in every detail.

Max was still deep in his reverie when the cortege

slowed down to enter through the gates of the crematorium. He looked on as the hearse passed, the coffin decked with wreaths, and tears came unashamedly to his eyes. She was there, the beautiful girl he would never see again. He could not bring himself to think what was about to happen to her.

Max was still staring when the next black car passed, the forlorn look on the face of Nathan Jeffries, turning to one of anger at the sight of the boy who, in his eyes had been the cause of losing his daughter. Max watched the cortege disappear and turned away, having said his last goodbye.

*******

Having signed on at the benefit office as required to do - though he would not receive any benefit money for a time as he had given up his job at the building site and with it any prospects for the future - Max walked the little distance to the supermarket. It was not that Nathan Jeffries had dismissed him, rather, it was that he could not face him or any of the workforce, especially Brian or the foreman Archie Gordon.

In the supermarket he climbed the stairs to the café, ordered a coffee and a sandwich and sat down at one of the tables that looked down into the store. He opened the cellophane wrapper and took a bite of the ham and cress sandwich, absently running his eyes over the busy shoppers below. How, at this time, he wished he was any one of them. Max lifted his cup of coffee. Although with his lack of luck, he would find himself either a shoplifter, pervert or someone terminally ill.

A man in his mid thirties slid into the seat at Max's table. He was smartly dressed in a dark suit, tie and white shirt. Max eyed him for a moment, wondering why he had chosen to sit at his table when there were plenty of others that were empty.

210

"You Max Duffy?" the man asked his voice deep for one with so slender a build.

"Aye. Whit is it tae you pal?" Max asked, his anger obvious. He was in no mood for a conversation, polite or otherwise.

Unperturbed, the unwelcome stranger continued. "You know, or should I say, knew," he corrected himself "Gil Robertson."

Max nodded and waited for him to continue as he tore open the little white paper sachet and poured the sugar contents into his cup of coffee.

"Gil worked for us." Max continued to look at the man. "Not his day job of course." He gave a little smile as if he had made a joke. "No, the one he did for us at night."

"You mean drugs?" Max said with the right touch of sarcasm.

The man looked around him as if fearing that someone might have heard. "To be precise, yes."

"Ah want nothing tae dae wi that sort o' thing mister."

"You can call me Frank."

Max smile was cold. Then I'll be frank, Frank, ah don't like bairns being selt stuff that does nothing other than harm them."

Frank raised a hand in protest. "We don't deal with children, only adults who have a choice, and of course should know better."

Max took another bite of his sandwich, followed by a mouthful of coffee. Frank sat patiently waiting for him to speak.

"What are ye askin me tae dae, exactly?"

"Gil said you were a good bloke, handy too in other ways if it came to the crunch. He also said that in the event of him being indisposed, as number one that you could take over for him, temporarily. And now that he is permanently ...."

211

Frank left the sentence unfinished.

"Don't ye have a number two?"

"Number two is right," the man smirked. "We gave this guy who likes to be known as, 'The Cat, a go. He made a right number two of it. He came up short of a few quid all because somebody could not pay that particular week." Frank spread his hands out, as he said, "you could see where that sort of thing could lead if we didn't nip it in the bud."

"So ye want me as a gardener?"

Frank looked puzzled, for a moment until Max explained.

"A gardener... tae nip things in the bud."

The man smiled and sipped his coffee. "Right. So, if you will consent, we can get down to business."

It was not something in which Max wanted to be involved. He loathed drugs, and had tried in vain to coax Gil off them.

"We can make it worth your while. On average you can make six hundred a week. That is what Gil brought in. What do you say? I should think that you could use the money now that you are unemployed."

"How dae ye ken that?" Max put down his cup, angered by the disclosure.

"We must be sure that we know something about you," the man explained.

"Who is this we ye are on about?" Max was becoming a little agitated by the man's self assurance. He must think he is Al Pacino, more like Al cupacino, and would have loved dearly to have taken him down a peg or two by telling him so.

To Max's question, Frank tapped the side of his own nose. "That's not for you to know. The less you know the better."

The better not knowing if I get caught, Max thought. Out loud he said, "Six a week? No bad money. Whit exactly

212

have ah tae dae tae earn this?"

The man looked relieved, convinced that by asking the question, Max had given his consent. "You will receive a shipment each week, which you will distribute to your number two, who, in turn, will distribute a share to the next down the line and so on. This way each dealer only knows the one whom he is directly dealing with. Your number two, will collect all the proceeds and return them to you. He will have already paid those involved besides himself, and will hand the remainder to you. You in turn will take your six hundred."

Max curled up a lip. "Doesnae seem ah dae a lot."

"On the contrary, you will be responsible for the number of sachets given out, and the return of any unsold. Should the latter be the case you will, you understand, not receive the full six hundred. If however, there is an increase, you will receive the appropriate bonus. Naturally, you will be unable to meet this increase until the following week. Do you understand?"

Max nodded.

"Should there be a discrepancy in the number sold and the money you receive, it will be your responsibility to find the defaulter and sort it out."

"Sort it, or sort him out?" Max asked sarcastically.

"Either or both. That's what you will get paid for."

Frank sat back in his seat and sipped what was left of his coffee as if his explanation of the system had taken a lot out of him.

"How, and when, dae ah get this first consignment?"

"You will meet me under the hump back bridge Monday night 8 o'clock precisely. And I do mean precisely. I will give you the full instructions etc for the forthcoming week. When you pass over the consignment to number two, he will give you the previous week's takings, count it and bring it to me here under the bridge the following Monday."

Max had digested each step explained to him. "Where dae a hand ower this consignment tae this number two?"

"This I will tell you on Monday, if you come. In the event that you have changed your mind ...," Frank gave a shrug.

"The less ah ken the better," Max confirmed.

Max arrived exactly on time as instructed. A little beneath where he stood under the arch of the old stone bridge, the Esk ran slow and silent under a late September moon. The night was dry, although there was a hint of rain in the air.

He did not hear Frank approach for the sound of the traffic on the road above - evening shoppers on their way home laden with groceries from the nearby supermarket.

"Good to see you here and on time," Frank greeted him. He put the small suitcase he had been carrying in amongst bushes hiding it out of sight. "Can't be too careful." He gave Max a smile devoid of any friendliness. "Now down to business."

Max said nothing, waiting until the man spoke again.

"You will meet the Cat, your number two up on the road that goes by Fa'side Castle, at nine tonight. You will introduce yourself as number one. Give him the case and take this week's money. There is a bag in the case there to hold it." He nodded in the direction of the hidden case. "Now..."

Before Max was aware of what was happening Frank stepped forward, put a hand around his neck and drew Max to him, kissing him on the mouth, and before the astonished boy had time to struggle, he heard a voice say from a little above where they stood.

"What's this then? You'd better take your affections off home with you."

Unsure of what was happening, angrily, Max managed to free himself from Frank's embrace. A policeman stood there, a look of disgust on his face, although the eyes read that

214

he had seen all this before.

"Sorry officer." Frank stood back from Max.

"Off with you both before I take your names." The officer ushered them up the banking. "And don't let me catch you two at it again. Do you hear me?"

His face beetroot red, Max moved his lips in compliance to the demand, and began to move up the banking, Frank just behind him. Both men reached the road and the police officer started back to his car, where he stooped to speak to a fellow officer in the driver's seat.

"Whit dae we dae noo?" Max asked, wiping his lips clean. "If yon cop ken who ah am, ma name will be shite in Tranent." He shifted his gaze from the car to Frank. "F***in mess, ah hope ye didnae enjoy that pal, for if ye did ah will tell ye where tae stick yer job."

"Wasn't much fun for me either, but it was either that, or answer a lot of awkward questions." Frank looked across at the police car. "We better keep moving until they are gone. I will go this way," he indicated right, " and you the other. When you think all's clear, come back and collect the case."

"Noo that oor rendezvous has been discovered where will ah meet ye next Monday?"

Frank thought for a moment. "Better make it the café on the corner. At least if we are seen together, it will be in public."

"Aye, aw right. But don't think this means we're goin steady."

Max's comment left Frank to wonder if he had been joking, or just downright angry.

"That's one of them," the elder police officer said, as Max walked past the police car.

His fellow officer dipped his head to take a better look at the young man passing. "That's the pal o' yon one that took the overdose. I interviewed him at his house the day after it happened. He works up on a site on the Macmerry road where one of the carpenters had an accident yon day of the rain and high winds, a while back. And if my memory serves me right, it was the same boss whose daughter was killed down at Ballencrief." He snapped his fingers. "Duncan was at that accident at Ballencrieff, his report will tell us the name of one of the witnesses. I'm sure he said something about one of the youngsters there being employed by the lassie's father, which could mean he's the same guy as we saw here."

"Gets around," the elder said. "Perhaps he's worth keeping an eye on?"

"We'll report it when we get back. Are you sure that's what those two were up to when you caught them?"

The other gave a shrug. "Could be your man might be doing other things. He doesn't strike me as the type to be kissing men. But these days you never know."

"Could be he's into the drugs as well. His pal was on the hard stuff, though there was no sign of him being a pusher. Maybe this one was down here for his usual fix, and not the kind you witnessed."

"We better do a wee bit prying. I'll look up the reports, his name will be in one of them."

Max took his time on going back to recover the case. He had waited until the police car had drawn away before returning. It was as he reached his car in the car park next to the stone bridge that he saw the police car return. It was the same officer who got out of the car and walked to where he had come across Frank and him as they stood under the bridge.

Max carefully took off, heading right, away from the town and on to the bypass at the Fort. There was no way he was going to chance passing the police car, not with a case full of drugs. Max was sweating. The fact that the police had returned proved that they must be suspicious of something, and he had not hung about to find out. Perhaps he should call it quits and pack the whole thing in before he got too deeply involved. Besides, at this precise moment, thanks to Gil's money he had no cash flow problems. Although Freddie Stewart had no work for him at present, he had said he was hopeful of finding some work next week, so things could get better.

On the bypass, Max took the slip road to Wallyford, his intention being to take a back road to Fa'side Castle. His mind was still on his earlier encounter. He could not shake off the feeling of foreboding. He had scarcely used any of Gil's money. Max sighed a heavy brooding sigh. The money had been for his and Alison's future. He had it all planned. Despite the fact that Nathan Jeffries was first and foremost a business man, he would not have let his son-in-law remain a common labourer for long. Or for that matter (should he Max qualify as a fully trained plumber), allow him to serve under such eejits as Andy Gemmel, but this was all elementary now. All his prospects had died with Alison.

Max reached what he believed to be the rendezvous. From where he stood outside his car, across the Forth, shimmering under a pale moonlight, were the twinkling lights of the Fife coast. Here and there a bobbing night light of a ship riding at anchor waited to enter the Forth Port. He glanced nervously at his watch, still unsure or not whether he had been followed by the police. He leaned against the bonnet of the car trying to convince himself that there was nothing to worry about....at least not yet, but for how long? This was a nasty business he had decided to enter, and he was not quite sure why. Perhaps it was the prospect of making more money...being someone. He gave a mirthless laugh, who was he kidding?

The sound of a car approaching brought him back to the present. He waited, still leaning on the bonnet, striking a nonchalant pose for the newcomer. He must convince this man straight away, who was the boss here. The car drew up a little distance from where Max stood, and a figure, dark against the backdrop of the fields walked to meet him.

"You the yin ah hiv tae meet?" The voice was clearly local. "Naebody gave me ah name, just tae be here as usual." The tone was one of resentment.

"Aye. Ye must be the yin that likes tae be caed the Cat. Whit are ye some sort o' pussy or something?"

Max was not close enough to see the newcomer's reaction, but heard a deep intake of breath.

"Listen f***in smart arse, ah dinnae ken why thae need somebody like you tae come in. Ah did this efter number yin topped himself. OK?"

"So ah believe, and it was you that made a right effin arse o' it. That's why ahm here. OK?" He mimicked his opposite number.

Max threw Cat the case that had lain at his feet. "Just take this and dae the business as usual. Is there any trouble that ah, and the Boss should ken aboot?" He had said Boss in a way that suggested he was familiar with whoever was responsible for running the whole affair, though probably this Cat knew as little as he did about him.

"Naw. Everything is cool. Ah'll let ye ken if there's any trouble. Trouble that ah cannae handle masel, that is."

"If there is, ye better let me handle it, that's whit am paid tae dae. Aw right?"

Max stood there in the darkness for a little while. The lights still twinkled across the Forth, little had changed in the world since his meeting with Cat, except he had this uneasy feeling that this Cat could mean trouble, his look of resentment had said it all - he wanted his job - wanted the extra money, but above all he wanted the power that went with it. If only he knew, Max thought. If only he knew.

*******

To Max everything was falling apart. There was no boy racing anymore, not since Alison's accident. He shuddered every time he thought of it, which was now daily. And if this was not enough to torture him, his nightmares had grown worse, so much so that he had difficulty distinguishing whether he was awake or not, so vivid had they become.

Perhaps tonight would cheer him up. He had already imbibed at home before making his rather shaky way to his local pub. Freespace of all people was emigrating. Max sat in the little restaurant staring at Freespace across the table.

"Aye," Freespace was saying, holding up his glass of vodka, a cheery, almost stupid grin on his face. " Canada here Ah come!"

"Whit harm did the Canadians ever dae you, Freespace?" Danny asked, laughing at his own joke.

"Never mind him Freespace. We will expect ye tae come back for Myra and ma wedding." Wee Joe squeezed his bride- to- be sitting next to him.

"Is that right, Joe, you and Myra are tyin the knot?"

"Joe wanted us just tae live thegither, but ah said ah wanted tae dae the right thing," Myra told them.

"Ye mean live apart?" Danny roared with laughter.

Max grinned and took another deep drink of his whisky, aware of others who were sitting at tables casting annoying glances in their direction. The expression from the older ones clearly stating that kids their age did not know how to enjoy themselves, unless they were semi paralytic- of course it was their upbringing, or rather the lack of it, was the cause- -they reasoned.

"Braw watch ye've got there, Max." Danny held Max's wrist to take a better look. It's no an Rolex by ony chance!" he exclaimed, letting go of the wrist. "How could you ever afford a thing like that?"

Max gave a shrug. "Alison gave it tae me."

Wee Joe gave a whistle. "She must have been loaded."

"She was, in mair ways that one," Freespace's laughter was quickly curtailed by the hostility on Max's face. "Nae offence big man," he apologised, with a wave of his hand, his eyes firmly fixed on his pal, awaiting his reaction.

Max got up.

"No leavin already are ye, Max?" Freespace sounded and looked disappointed at the thought of Max leaving so early. "Was it something ah said? Come on, ah was only joking. Ah ken ye miss her. Ah shouldnae have said that aboot your bird"

"It's aw right Freespace, yer forgiven, seein as am no likely ever tae see yer ugly mug again. God help the Canadians." Max turned. " Jist goin tae the wee hoose," he explained.

"Suits ye, Max, that's where aw the big nobs hing oot." Wee Joe pretended to choke on his beer at the hilarity of his quip.

"Aye, nice yin Joe. You'll no be oot o' place there either… ye dick heid."

Max made for the door as the laughter from his own party filled the room while others in the room shook their heads in disgust and disappointment at this generation.

Max walked down the steps from the restaurant, giving a quick glance into the crowded lounge bar as he passed. Cammie and Betty Smith were still there. The girl had given him a brief smile and a wave as she talked on her mobile, when he first arrived for Freespace's party. He had told Cammie earlier that he would be here, and to feel free to join them if he so wished. Cammie had answered that he would see what Betty said about it. So Max was not surprised when he saw them sitting in the bar lounge instead.

Max had no intention of returning to the party. His boy racer days were over. He had seen at firsthand what damage and grief irresponsible driving could do to so many lives. Besides, none of the gang had met since that fateful night of Alison's crash.

There had been a recent accident across the road from the inn. A drunk driver had run into the parapet of what had once been a railway bridge. The railway had long since ceased to exist and now the pathway leading to the Town of Prestonpans was known locally as Railway Walk.

Max crossed to it, the damaged stonework cordoned off with yellow and green tape, and a little mound of earth prevented anyone from using the pavement. He felt sick, perhaps a breath of fresh air would help.

Max leaned beside the broken wall, staring down into the walkway beneath, then up at the sky. He should do the same as Freespace, and get himself out of here before it was too late. The young man gave a little shiver. It was only a matter of time before he was caught at the drug game. And Cat would most likely be the cause. The man was too ambitious-too greedy.

Tonight's drinking had not mellowed him. It never did as it used to. As he stood there all his troubles seemed to pile on top of him with no way out. Such as the police seeing him under the bridge that first night in Musselburgh. It only took one officer to mention it to another to connect his name with that of Gil.-Gil who had been a witness to his accident with Colin Lamont-.the same officer who had taken a statement from him at Gil's overdose- the younger officer, who had mentioned him working on the same site as Andy Gemmel. It could all come together unexpectedly with pieces fitting together like a jigsaw.

It was enough. He would inquire into emigrating to Australia, New Zealand or Canada. If a country could take a person like Freespace, surely he himself stood a chance.

Max felt sick- sick at the thought of staying and being

caught- sick at leaving the only place he had ever really known. Tranent was not a bad place as places went, he assured himself most Belters were friendly and would not do you a bad turn if they could do a good one. No, it was folk like himself who gave a place a bad name.

Max leaned over the broken parapet and emptied his stomach, the contents cascading into the shrubbery below. He turned to wipe his face as the black shape came out of the shadows. He put up a hand to ward off the intended blow from the club, the drink slowing his reflexes. His feet stumbled amongst broken masonry and he fell backwards breaking the yellow tape.

There was no sound as Max Duffy fell on to the asphalt below, only the sound of a crack as his head hit the unyielding black surface.


"Where dae ye think ye are goin at this time o' night daughter?" Alex asked, leaving the light off as he came into the dining room

Jean looked up, surprised to be caught in the act of leaving the house. "Just goin tae Jenny's. I'll no be long,"she assured him.

"Pull the ither yin Jean. I ken whit ye are up tae."

Jean buttoned up her coat in preparation of meeting the chill night air. "Am sure I dinnae ken what ye mean Faither."

Alex motioned the woman to sit down. He leaned forward and switched on the electric fire, the glow from the three bars lighting up the woman's pale and drawn face, in the dark room.

"It's aboot Max Duffy is it no ?"

"How did ye ken?" Jean was taken by surprise by her father's revelation and her face twitched slightly.

"Ah had an idea something was up the night Jenny telt us aboot Betty goin oot wi Cammie Duffy."

222

The woman drew her father a look of non comprehension.

Alex gave her a wee comforting smile. "When ye get really angry Jean ye get aw polite, or ye just lose it aw thegithert. Yon night there was nae anger or even disappointment on yer face. It was as if ye had expected Betty tae dae what she did. Then again…" Alex's expression was an attempt to justify his own action. "Ah heard ye on the phone tae Betty that night o' Max Duffy's accident."

Jean looked crestfallen. "I thought we had it well planned, Betty and me." Jean sat up a little in her chair, as if by telling what had happened it would give her some comfort from the pain. A pain she never thought she would ever again experience after losing Colin.

"It was when they wouldnae let me see Colin, lying there,"Jean choked. "Maybe it was just as well, for ah wanted tae remember my laddie as ah last saw him passing the window goin oot on his bike- daein whit he loved tae dae, and no harming anybody. It was then ah decided whether it was an accident or no, that it was still Max Duffy's fault."

"So ye devised a plan wi Betty," Alex prompted. "She was tae go oot with Max's brother so as tae find oot what that bad bugger was up tae."

"Aye, though the lassie wisnae tae ken at the time she was goin tae fall for Cammie."

"Dae you no think that was a bit underhand-Betty ah mean leading the poor laddie on- And getting him tae tell you aw aboot his brother so that ye could dae what ye had in mind for him?"

"Maybe, Faither, but Max Duffy deserved aw he got," Jean said angrily with a slight nod of her head as if convincing herself that what she had just said was true and that justice had been done.

Jean blew her nose on her handkerchief and began to

explain, as if by doing so it would somehow help to lift the burden of guilt she was feeling,

"Max told Cammie that there was a party on Saturday night for one o' his pals who was leaving for Canada, and asked him if he wanted to go. Cammie had said that he didn't, but Betty coaxed him to at least take her tae the same pub for a drink, and if he changed his mind then he could go up stairs and join them."

"So that's how ye kent Max would be there?" Alex, pursed his lips. "Ah saw ye here wi yer mobile, so that must have been Betty letting ye ken Duffy had arrived."

Jean acknowledged what had been said. "Ah got masel ready as planned. Ah had bought a dark tracksuit and a balaclava, as well as a pair o' trainers two sizes too big for me and stuffed the toes with newspaper, so if I left any footprints the police would believe it was somebody taller than me. I had left my car in the car park behind the pub and waited for Betty's call to tell me when Max Duffy had left to walk home. I was hoping he widnae ask his brother for a lift, and I would lose the chance, for to be honest I don't think that I could go through yon again. As it turned oot however, he didnae.

As luck would have it, Max left by himself and I saw him frae where I waited in yon wee vennel. He crossed the road, and I saw him spew up ower where the bridge was broken, so I took a chance and ran across the road. There was naebody aboot and the boy had just turned round when ah made to hit him with ma wee club. He fell backwards, right ower the broken bit. I didnae wait tae look ower just in case somebody came oot the pub. I got back to the car and drove up the Elphinstone Road to the place Betty and II had already dug a hole to bury the tracksuit and everything else I had worn. Then I changed into ma own clothes and came home."

Alex sat silent, his eyes on his distraught daughter. Eventually he said, his voice gentle and sympathetic.

"Revenge is no whit it's cracked up tae be is it Jean?"

His daughter looked up from wiping her eyes with a handkerchief she had taken from her pocket. She shook her head. "No it's no. I kent that as soon as I took yon bit club to him. Whatever Max Duffy had done, he was still somebody's son."

"So you believe you have killed the boy? Is it this that's worrying ye Jean?"

"Aye. I don't think I will ever forget that last look on the laddie's face." Jean's eyes filled with tears.

"So this is why you want tae go tae the polis, and tell them what ye have just telt me? The papers say that Duffy had been drinking and must have lost his balance and fell ower the parapet." Alex quoted from memory from the newspaper that had carried the story.

"Aye, but I ken different."

"There were nae marks on his body except for where he had fallen. So ye couldnae have hit him, or the polis would be saying that there were marks on his body that were inconsistent wi the fall or words tae that effect."

"Maybe no, except ye cannae get away frae the fact ah set oot tae murder the laddie," Jean said desperately.

"But ye didn't, did ye? So leave it there, Jean. Your goin tae jile is no goin tae stop ye frae thinkin what ye are thinkin, at least no for awhile. Ye'll get ower it, the same as ye are daen wi Colin. If ye were tae get a sentence, what guid wid it dae? It would not only be you that would suffer, but yer man- Jenny, Peter, Glen and the wee yin, with, Max Duffy having caused mair grief than he has done already."

Jean looked up at her father, and for the first time her face lit up fractionally, as if by telling her father it had lifted a great weight off her mind.

Alex saw the change and gave her a smile, the same smile he had given her when she had been naughty and he had forgiven her. "Had Duffy lived he would maist likely have a thing or two tae answer for, anyway."

Jean looked puzzled, failing to understand what her father meant.

" When the polis found Duffy he was wearing a Rolex watch, which the polis have traced to having legitimately belonged to a certain Gil Robertson. Makes ye wonder does it no?"

"Is that supposed tae make me feel better? Whatever the boy has done, it has nothing tae do with me."

"Am only sayin Jean, the laddie was nae use. Ye didnae kill him. But if he had lived, am sure that in time, somebody else would have. So away and take yer coat off before Peter and yer man come back frae Jenny's, and I'll put on the kettle for a cuppa."

It was true, Max Duffy had not been the nicest of people, but there was always some good in everyone. And as she began to feel better at what her father had said, she was reminded of how the boy had helped her own Peter. Now, she thought, it was up to the good Lord to decide.

Jean rose, she so much wanted to thank her father, not only for what he had said, but also in the way he had said it. Instead, she took off her coat, and as she did so Alex turned at the kitchen door. "Ye ken Jean, Tranent is a guid place tae live. Maist folk are honest, it's only the Maxs' that waste it. And in this day and age, ye can find a Max in any street, in any town."

Cammie walked to the chimney through grass and rotting nettles, white in the morning frost. At the base of the chimney he took out the small metal box he had found in his drawer. He had not recognised it at first until he had opened it and saw the family photo taken so long ago, beneath which lay a small piece of writing paper, in his brothers handwriting telling him that there was much more than this box to find 'up the lum'. Cammie had smiled at this. Now he was here. He bent down and put a hand up the chimney, recalling at having done so many years before. He felt what appeared to be a plank of wood and pulled it down, and a sack dropped at his feet. Cammie stood up. There was no one around. He untied the rough string that bound it and peeked inside not knowing what to expect.

Cammie returned from the car where he had counted the money from the sack. This amount of money he knew could not in any way have been saved by Max. How honest or dishonest it was, he had no way of knowing, only that his brother wanted him to have it.

The man made his way back to the chimney through the knee high grass, frost brushing against his jeans. Carefully pushing the sack back up the chimney, he replaced the plank of wood wedging it against the flue. This done he walked back to his car.

Cammie had taken a little of the money, it would help him save for his marriage to Betty, if she would have him, although he was confident of her saying yes. And when he had thought it over more carefully he would return for the remainder of the money, and take a little at a time so no one would question his sudden change of fortune.

Cammie took in a deep breath and started the car, driving on to the main road, and on towards Longniddry, his mind still on Max. Whatever he may have been, or what he had got up to, he had still been his brother. Perhaps, Max had he lived long enough, might have seen the error of his ways, then again, knowing the man, perhaps not. This he would never know.

It was because of these thoughts that he had been unaware of the car passing him in the opposite direction and turning onto the small country road that he had just left, where, outside of the derelict building, the estate agent helped the young couple from his car.

"It may not look much to you at this time," he was saying, "there is only really the chimney, and what is left, will be quickly cleared away, but when it is finished, what a view you will have over the Forth. We have purchased the land from the farmer, and can now start building at any time…and should you agree to purchase we can have it ready for you by….."

**The End**